LEVI STRAUSS

LEVI STRAUSS

The Man Who Gave Blue Jeans
to the World

LYNN DOWNEY

UNIVERSITY OF MASSACHUSETTS PRESS
Amherst and Boston

Copyright © 2016 by Levi Strauss & Co.
All rights reserved
Printed in the United States of America

ISBN 978–1-62534–229–4 (cloth)

Designed by Sally Nichols
Set in Arno Pro
Printed and bound by Sheridan Books, Inc.

Jacket design by Kathleen Swaizola
Jacket photo: Last known portrait of Levi Strauss, c. 1890.
Courtesy Levi Strauss & Co., Inc.

.

Library of Congress Cataloging-in-Publication Data
A catalog record for this book is available from the Library of Congress.

British Library Cataloguing-in-Publication Data
A catalog record for this book is available from the British Library.

All photographs courtesy Levi Strauss & Co. Archives, San Francisco.

For Bob Haas

CONTENTS

Photographs follow page 164

PREFACE

At 5:12 a.m. on April 18, 2006, I stood on my tiptoes at the intersection of Kearny and Market Streets in San Francisco, trying to see above a crowd of fellow early risers. This morning marked the centennial of the city's great earthquake and fire, and I stood a few paces from Lotta's Fountain, the annual commemoration spot.

The ceremonies began at the same hour and minute as the great quake of 1906, and as they progressed, I chuckled as suave mayor Gavin Newsom stammered like a schoolboy when a ninety-nine-year-old woman flirted with him on stage. As I stamped my feet to keep warm in the early chill, my mind began to wander, and it landed on Levi Strauss, the founder of Levi Strauss & Co., where I worked as company Historian.

Levi died four years before the quake, so he didn't have to watch his company burn to the ground on the first day of the three-day firestorm that followed. The devouring flames had marched toward Nob Hill at one block per half hour, destroying the house where Levi spent the last quarter-century of his life. His four nephews, who now ran the business—Jacob, Sigmund, Abraham, and Louis Stern—rebuilt the family firm, but they couldn't resurrect the fifty years of history that had been wiped clean by the flames.

And because they were busy, and didn't think it was important, they did not write down what they knew about their Uncle Levi: how he came to San Francisco during the Gold Rush and started his wholesale dry goods firm, how he took out a patent with a Reno, Nevada, tailor to create the world's first blue jeans, why he didn't get married, how he faced down an angry customer who threatened to kill him, or how his generosity made life better for San Francisco's citizens. Because they kept their memories to themselves, Levi's life became as insubstantial as the ashes that blanketed his stricken city.

Standing on Market Street, looking around a sea of people so that I could catch a glimpse of history, I realized that this book really began with the first tremors of an April morning one hundred years before.

I was hired by Levi Strauss & Co. as the first corporate Historian in 1989. During the 1980s many American corporations realized that heritage could help them stand apart from their competition, and they started up in-house archives. Levi Strauss & Co. began to think about this idea, too. And when a few managers from the international division told CEO Bob Haas how vintage clothing and advertising would be great for marketing the products overseas, he took notice. By the summer of 1989 a new position had been created, and I was the lucky girl who got the Historian job.

My first task was to create the official company Archives, starting with boxes of historical materials that had been collected or saved over the years. My mission was to make the Archives a living, working part of the business. I spent months getting acquainted with the contents of these boxes: clothing, documents, advertising, photographs, films, record albums, posters, and other artifacts, all dating from about the 1910s to the present. I knew that the company's headquarters and factory had been destroyed in 1906, and was not surprised that there were few corporate records. Some courageous employees had thrown important ledgers in vaults as the fire made its way up Battery Street, but that was all that survived. I was saddened to realize that Levi's personal records were also missing.

I tallied up the loss: price lists, handbills, catalogs, dry goods, examples of early jeans, jackets and shirts, photos, Levi's naturalization papers, his letters, any diaries he might have kept, even his own clothes. It was a blow, like waking up one day with partial amnesia. But I didn't yet realize how much the absence of those materials would affect my work.

In addition to organizing the Archives, I also got up to speed on the company's history. I worked my way through the existing documents and followed this up by visiting local libraries and archives. I read company histories that had been written over the years and old newspaper articles about the activities of the firm and the founder. I also talked to employees and retirees.

During this corporate immersion I was puzzled by the wildly conflicting "facts" about Levi Strauss and the creation of blue jeans I kept reading and hearing about. For example:

Well-meaning people told me that Levi was either a tailor, a tent maker, a shopkeeper, or an aspiring Kentucky rancher.

I watched actor Red Buttons portray Levi Strauss as a lovesick, frustrated miner on a 1960 episode of the television show *Death Valley Days*.

The London Sunday *Times* published an article stating that the company had been founded by Claude Lévi-Strauss. The French anthropologist.

A man called me one day in the early 1990s to say that he wanted to write a corporate history of Levi Strauss & Co. "After all," he said, "everyone knows the name Dolly Levi." When I asked him what he meant, he said, "Well, it's the same name as one of your founders." "Founders?" I asked. "Well, yes," he replied with some smugness. "Mr. Levi and Mr. Strauss, right?" Wrong.

Stories about the invention of blue jeans were even more fallacious. The most common one went like this: Levi was born in Bavaria and moved to New York with his family around 1847. In 1850 he sailed around Cape Horn and landed in San Francisco. There, desperate miners, wandering around in ripped trousers, convinced him to make sturdy pants out of tent canvas, a material he had brought with him from New York and that he later dyed blue. In other versions Levi imported blue denim from France. Rivets— the metal fasteners added to jeans for extra strength—came along in the 1870s after a Nevada miner named Alkali Ike kept losing his ore specimens from his pockets, and a tailor named Jacob Davis made him a pair of riveted pants.

It was all very confusing.

After many months of reading, sifting, and investigating, I came to a depressing conclusion: all of these stories were fiction. Even worse, Levi Strauss & Co.'s own advertising department was the source for most of them. I discovered that someone came up with these tall tales some-time around World War II. They were then presented as gospel to reporters and authors. By the time I was hired, this "history"—and quite a few embellishments—had been published in dozens of books, newspapers, and magazines. Once the Internet came along, the tales found their way online, which meant that these stories not only lived in the impermanence that is print but in the permanence that is cyberspace.

So how could I dispel the myths and find the true story when all the primary sources, and Levi's own voice, no longer existed? As my daily duties permitted, I hit the road and became a very mobile Historian.

I viewed dozens of microfilm reels at the California State Library. I sat in my pajamas in front of my computer for weekends on end searching for Levi in digital newspaper collections. I squatted in the aisles of the genealogy section of the New York Public Library. I interviewed Jewish scholars on both coasts and mined the business collections of the Baker Library at Harvard. I hired a guide and went to Panama to re-create Levi's trek across the isthmus when he journeyed from New York to San Francisco. I made a pilgrimage to his home village of Buttenheim in Germany, where I walked the wooden floors of the house where he was born and saw his family's name on documents in the Bavarian State Archives.

It took years, but I finally pieced together Levi's story. It's a simple, and very American, tale.

Bavarian-born Levi Strauss emigrated with his mother and sisters to New York in 1848, and worked in his brothers' dry goods business on the Lower East Side. In 1853 he moved again, this time to San Francisco, taking the route across the Isthmus of Panama. There he opened a West Coast branch of the family firm on the San Francisco waterfront. He was a distributor, a wholesaler of fine dry goods—clothing, bedding, purses, combs, handkerchiefs—and his customers were the small stores of the American West.

In 1871 a Russian immigrant and tailor named Jacob Davis, living in Reno, Nevada, started making work pants out of a canvas-like material called "duck," reinforced with metal rivets at the points of strain for extra strength. He wanted to patent and manufacture his new pants, so he contacted Levi

Strauss, his fabric supplier. The two men applied for a patent on the process of making riveted work trousers and were granted Patent Number 139,121, on May 20, 1873. Soon thereafter they started making riveted denim pants for western working men: the first blue jeans.

I wondered why the company veered so far from the truth when it told the story of the founder and the jeans, and I eventually came up with three reasons:

The colorful origin myth about using tent canvas to make the first jeans was a reaction to competition in the clothing market, where it was important for Levi Strauss & Co. to establish itself as the company that invented the blue jean.

During the nineteenth century the company also made riveted pants from brown cotton duck, and someone had donated a few pairs of these trousers after the earthquake and fire. Duck fabric looks a lot like canvas, and these trousers might have been the inspiration for the "tent canvas pants" part of the story.

And, finally, there weren't any historical records to work with. Not only had the company's papers and artifacts gone up in flames in 1906, but there were also no records from the New York end of the business, J. Strauss Brother & Co. business records from family firms were generally discarded over the years either because they took up valuable space or because subsequent generations didn't understand their historical value. The one bright spot in this black hole was the rich collection of government records about the family in German archives.

Once I figured all this out, I began to write and lecture about Levi and the history of blue jeans. But I discovered that people don't like to let go of their cherished myths. They act as if you've taken away their favorite old, ratty sweater and given it to Goodwill. Not only that, well-known historians (who should know better) have perpetuated the mythology in books published long after I made the correct information available on the company's website, in interviews, and in my own writings.

These tall tales do Levi Strauss a disservice. They cloud his accomplishments and his flaws, reduce him to a smiling, cardboard cutout, and obscure the true origin of blue jeans. But the correction of historical errors is not the only reason to write a biography of this man. Levi's life, stripped of mythology, is an important story, one of the founding narratives of American culture: immigrant makes good. Not only makes good, but makes something everyone loves and, in the American tradition, gets it named after him.

There's yet another reason. Once he moved to San Francisco, Levi built his business and his life around nearly every touchstone of the history of the American West: mining, railroads, real estate, commerce. He was also committed to philanthropy, education, and the welfare of children. Add the tough, riveted denim pants to this list, and it is easy to see how much Levi Strauss helped to make the modern West.

Because of who he was, Levi was exactly the right man at the right time to help birth the blue jean. He arrived as an unremarkable immigrant, one of millions, a speck in the swarm of humanity that washed up on American shores. What was it about the trajectory of his life that made Jacob Davis choose him as his partner? And what was it about Levi's business savvy that made him realize Jacob's idea was good enough to risk a hefty financial investment on?

It probably helped that he was also in the right place. San Francisco has always encouraged individual initiative, and as the economic hub of the Pacific Rim in the nineteenth century, it encouraged commercial initiative above all. Levi and his city grew up together. They both had a heart that beat for business. In fact, Levi Strauss & Co. is one of the few Gold Rush businesses to still survive in San Francisco. Others include Wells Fargo Bank, Boudin Bakery, and Ghirardelli Chocolate. What other city could give you the essentials of life, all in one place, so early in its history: jeans, sourdough, chocolate, and a place to keep your grubstake.

It's surprising today to learn that during Levi's lifetime, and even at his death, the jeans were secondary to his identity. He was known as a merchant, a philanthropist, and a beloved uncle. He was the kind of man that fathers went to for advice about prospective sons-in-law. He could also be ruthless in business, whether collecting debts from fellow merchants, refusing to hire Chinese workers, or covering up unpleasant facts that would hurt San Francisco commerce.

In 1960 a writer for the Levi Strauss & Co. employee newsletter interviewed a woman who had worked as a sewing machine operator when Levi
was still running the firm. She summed up his character in a way that best
captures this complicated man:

"He was tough, but a fine fellow."

Many fine fellows (of both genders) made writing this book not only easier
but a tremendous joy.

Without Tanja Roppelt, the director of the Levi Strauss Museum in Buttenheim, Germany, I would never have known how Levi grew up, the size
and makeup of his family, or the hoops they all had to jump through to come
to America. She showed me Levi's home, made his early life real for me, and
shared my glee while we looked at documents about the family in Bavarian
archives. This story starts in Germany, and Tanja made that possible.

Dr. Robert J. Chandler, who knows everything about San Francisco history, was practically on speed dial as I read and began to write about Levi's
life in that city. Bob's knowledge of business and finance was a huge help
to this numbers-challenged historian, and his friendship made the road
smoother.

Stacia Fink, my good right hand during my years as company Historian,
took on many additional duties when I was on the trail of Levi's life in Germany, Panama, and points closer to home. She was also a sounding board
for some of my wilder theories.

Dr. John Michael, a direct descendant of Jonas Strauss, generously
shared his research and his photographs to help me tell his family's part of
the story.

Explorer and guide Hernán Araúz literally put my feet on the paths that
Levi traveled when he crossed the Isthmus of Panama in 1853. On a train
ride, a couple of jungle treks, and in a boat on the Chagres, Hernán showed
me a historical Panama like no one else could. His enthusiasm and knowledge helped me understand the Panama route, and he gave me an unparal-
leled personal experience.

Researcher extraordinaire Sydney Dixon Cruice found information at
the National Archives in Philadelphia that I would not have been able to

find on my own. In doing so, she helped answer questions that had been unanswerable since 1906.

Sara Gilbert's research into the history of Emory City, British Columbia, provided me with a delightful historical tidbit.

So many Levi Strauss & Co. employees cheered me on as I researched their founder during my years at the firm that I can't name them all. I think you know who you are.

Scholars, archivists, and colleagues all over the country were a tremendous help when I needed historical context or documents. Chief among these are Alison Moore, Jill Hunting, Hasia Diner, Ava Kahn, Paula Freedman, Joanie Gearin, Barbara Berglund, Melissa Leventon, Inez Brooks-Myers, Gabriele Carey, Jim Hofer, Guy Rocha, Pat Keats, Susan Goldstein, Tracey Panek, Frank Davis, Marshall Trimble, and Stan Benjamin.

Institutions, as much as people, give of themselves to historians, their collections as alive as their caretakers. I owe the greatest debt to the following: California Historical Society, Bancroft Library, California State Archives, California State Library, Society of California Pioneers, California State Railroad Museum, Calaveras County Archives, San Francisco Public Library, Nevada State Archives, New York Public Library, Baker Library at Harvard University, Manchester Historical Society, U.S. National Archives, Bavarian State Archives, National Library of Panama. And, of course, the Levi Strauss & Co. Archives.

Matt Becker, my editor at the University of Massachusetts Press, has been a delightful collaborator since 2008, when we first talked about a Levi Strauss biography. His faith in me and my topic kept me going.

Mark Yateman's cowboy good sense and sharp editor's eye helped make my prose sparkle.

Patti Elkin was an early and most welcome listener while I read the manuscript to her as it came off the printer.

Jeanne Hangauer and Taina Kissinger of Visual Presentation know how to make historical images shine.

I owe the biggest debt of gratitude to Kay McDonough, who had my back from the very first moment I told her I wanted to write this book. She is my most fierce and attentive reader/editor, and my oldest friend.

The gracious family owners and shareholders of Levi Strauss & Co. folded me into their history from the day I began work as company Historian and always lent a willing ear when I wanted to share stories about their collective past. For more than anyone, this book is for all of you, and for your extended families: Bob Haas, Wally Haas, Betsy Eisenhardt, Peter Haas, Jr., Mimi Haas, Doug Goldman, and Alice Russell Shapiro. I also cherish the memory of having met and worked with Walter A. Haas, Jr., Peter E. Haas, and Evelyn D. Haas.

And, finally, this book would not exist if not for Bob Haas. He hired me as the company's Historian, supported my research, and believed in the story I wanted to tell. Thank you, Bob. It has been a privilege to spend these last twenty-five years with your great-great-grand Uncle Levi.

LEVI STRAUSS

CHAPTER 1

ENLIGHTENED NATIONALITIES

In mid-December 1894, two men stepped off a Southern Pacific train in Benson, Arizona, and walked across Main Street through a drizzling rain toward the Grand Central Hotel. With its self-proclaimed reasonable rates, first-class rooms, and the best of meals, it was the logical choice for the men who wrote their names in the hotel's register: Adolph Sutro and Levi Strauss.

Benson was an important hub for the Southern Pacific Railroad, and millions of dollars in silver from nearby Tombstone passed along its rails. Anyone wanting to visit Benson from San Francisco could get there on a direct SP train in just a little over two days. Men from all walks of life and business found themselves in town, and the names Sutro and Strauss were familiar throughout the West.

Sutro, for example, had made millions with the "Sutro Tunnel," which drained off the excess water from the silver mines of Nevada's famed Comstock Lode, making the ore easier to extract. He held property all over San Francisco, opened a public bath for his fellow residents, and had just been elected mayor of the city.

Strauss was a prominent San Francisco merchant, philanthropist, and the man behind a new kind of denim work pants, reinforced with metal rivets for strength. Ads for his famous trousers appeared regularly in the *Tombstone Epitaph* newspaper, which published the two names within a list of the Grand Central's recent arrivals in its December 16 issue.

The appearance of these names on page three of the *Epitaph*, next to the story about a stage robbery, most likely didn't cause a stir. It should have, though.

Because the men were impostors.

Both Sutro and Strauss were in San Francisco when their doppelgangers got off the train. Levi Strauss was in court telling Judge Hebbard why he was unable to serve on the Grand Jury. Adolph Sutro was talking with his staff about the upcoming visit of General Booth, founder of the Salvation Army, who would arrive in San Francisco on the 17th.

In the days before mandatory identification and wide use of photography, it was fairly easy to pretend to be a prominent figure from another state. All you had to do was wear a broadcloth suit and, considering the snow that threatened at wintertime in Benson, a fine, heavy overcoat. No one would ever know who they really were, and the two fraudsters doubtless received excellent service during their stay at the Grand Central.

This wasn't the only time someone used the power of the Levi Strauss name to gain an advantage. In 1898 a well-known California bunco artist named George Bowers showed up in Los Angeles. There he bought some expensive clothes, equally expensive champagne, and booked a room at the Van Nuys Hotel. He then skipped out on his bills and fled to Sacramento. Before leaving, he shipped himself six valises of ill-gotten goods using the name Levi Strauss. He was arrested when he arrived in Sacramento and hauled back to Los Angeles, along with his luggage. He was unable to prove his "Levi Strauss" identity, so the police kept the bags and their contents.

What kind of man inspires such bizarre imitation? Getting your name in the newspaper isn't enough. That name has to be associated with integrity, wealth, business, or culture. And it doesn't really matter how you got there.

Humble origins were no deterrent to anyone wanting to get ahead in the city spawned by the Gold Rush. Immigrant Jews, like Strauss and Sutro, after escaping the European laws that so restricted their lives, found a refreshing lack of anti-Semitism in San Francisco and throughout the Golden State. As early as 1857, a reporter for the *Daily Alta California* newspaper wrote an article praising Jews, calling them one of the "enlightened nationalities."

But that was far in Levi's future. His early life, like that of his fellow Jewish newcomers, began as humbly as what nineteenth-century Bavaria had on offer.

Hirsch Strauss knew every tree, path, house, and village in his territory. A peddler who lived life on his feet, he carried household goods, news, and gossip to the customers on his turf, which ringed the region around his home in Buttenheim. He shared this life with hundreds of other Jewish peddlers, who walked or rode across the Bavarian hills, a place familiar to so many tourists today thanks to years of Oktoberfest advertising. But to Hirsch and everyone in his family, home was really called Franconia.

Named for the sixth-century Germanic tribe called the Franks, Franconia was one of the five duchies of medieval Germany. Later folded into the Holy Roman Empire, it had its own identity in the northern portion of today's Bavaria. Even today, people who live in the area will be the first to tell you that they are Franconians, not Bavarians. They are proud to claim Buttenheim as one of their own, whose fame extends beyond its reputation for fine beers. The village is part of Upper Franconia, and in the Middle Ages it was a market town and a stop on an important trade road that linked Hungary, southern Russia, and northeastern Germany together, both commercially and culturally.

Buttenheim's main street is the Marktstrasse, or Market Street, and on November 16, 1780, Hirsch Strauss, son of Jacob and Meila, was born at Marktstrasse 134. He had an older brother, Lippmann, born in 1774, but no one knows how many more siblings there might have been. Jacob was a cattle trader, one of only a few acceptable occupations for rural Jews in Franconia; the others included leather, horse, and oil traders. Another was peddling, the work that young Hirsch chose when it was time to take up a trade.

Another Buttenheim resident, Madel Baumann, was born in 1787, and she and Hirsch were married sometime around the summer of 1811. Their children soon began to arrive. Jacob was born in 1812, when the family was living at Marktstrasse 33. He was followed by Rösla in 1813, who was born at Marktstrasse 83, a few doors away, where Hirsch and Madel had recently moved. Jonathan was next in 1815, followed by Lippmann in 1817, and Maila in 1821.

Less than nine months after Maila's birth, Madel Strauss died, at age thirty-five. Widower Hirsch, who spent days at a time away from home, needed to find another wife to help take care of his five children. Female relatives or neighbors would have helped him for a while, but that couldn't last. The children ranged in age from nine months to eleven years, and given the demands of his wandering life, he could never have raised them alone. No one expected him to, either.

On November 14, 1822, Hirsh, now forty-three, married Rebekka Haas, another Buttenheim resident. Born on July 6, 1800, at Marktstrasse 76, Rebekka's parents, Seligmann and Henela, were, like Hirsch's father, local cattle traders. Rebekka and Hirsch lived in his home just up the street at number 83, and on December 24, 1823, their daughter Vögele was born. Then, on February 26, 1829, they welcomed their last child and only son together. The boy whom America would transform into the man called Levi Strauss began life with the first name Löb.

Young Löb was born into a society that believed it had "emancipated" its Jews and given them the rights of full citizens. In reality, Jews had only those rights that made the Bavarian government and Christian society comfortable.

A dip into books about Bavaria will rarely mention its Jewish history. To be fair, the region's Jewish population was never a majority. Jews first show up in the historical record in the tenth century, as traders in gold, silver, metals, and even slaves, and they were also money lenders. But over the next seven hundred years Jews were repeatedly expelled or exterminated, allowed to return, and then forced to leave their homes again. At the end of the seventeenth century they began to trickle back in, and by the early nineteenth century nearly all Bavarian Jews lived in the Franconian region of northern Bavaria.

When Bavaria became a kingdom in 1806 under the new King Maximilian I, the government had to figure out a way to incorporate its newly acquired lands and diverse peoples into a cohesive state. Jews had slowly made some civil gains during the Napoleonic era: the right to attend schools in 1804 and the right to bear arms in 1805, for example. But these advances revived medieval fears that a socially integrated and prosperous Jewish population would be harmful to Christian life and business. In 1809, a new law declared that Jews were a religious society only, a *Privat-Kirchengesellschaft*. This meant that they were citizens of Bavaria in terms of their duty to the state but were restricted when it came to their actual rights.

Then, on June 10, 1813, Bavaria codified this law even further into the *Judenedikt*, known also as the Jew Law, the Jew Decree, or the Emancipation Law. Its thirty-four articles turned the region's Jews into secular, German citizens, and removed their standing as a purely religious group. Cunningly written to appear as though Jews were on the receiving end of greater priv-ileges, in reality the new law placed an iron grip on every aspect of Jew-ish life, from the political to the most personal. Jews could now engage in occupations that had been closed to them in the past, but the government did not want this success to translate into greater numbers of actual Jews. The law severely restricted immigration into Bavaria, and each village had to maintain a *Matrikel*, or register of all Jewish residents. Only those who were listed on the Matrikel could marry or change their residence within the boundaries of the kingdom.

In addition, the right to marry was limited to the eldest son in the family. A younger son could marry only if a childless couple gave up a spot on the register for him, if he married a widow represented on the Matrikel, if he left his village and married in another, or if a place on the list opened up. And, of course, these conditions had an equally profound effect on young women, whose opportunities for marriage were tied to their village's eligi-ble men. Unsanctioned unions and illegitimate births were sometimes the result.

In their status as a Privat-Kirchengesellschaft, Jews had complete auton-omy over the organization of their communities, from maintaining a trea-sury and collecting taxes, to the operation of schools and synagogues, see-ing to the creation and maintenance of cemeteries, choosing rabbis, and imposing justice. Each community had a lay leader or chairman, called the *Parnaß*, chosen by the heads of each local family.

Religious life was very traditional, though there was a dearth of rabbis, because the one Yeshiva or seminary where they could be trained was in faraway Fürth, near Nuremberg, and it was closed by 1830. Where there was no rabbi, the Parnaß was the religious leader. Synagogues were small and rarely looked any different from the buildings that surrounded them. There were no "ghettoes" in Bavaria, though most Jewish families lived conveniently near the synagogue and ritual bath. Under the Judenedikt, however, the government was in charge of how Jews practiced their faith. And now that Jews were citizens of Bavaria they were expected to live as secular people. They were allowed complete freedom of worship, but rabbis had to have command of the German language, be registered on the Matrikel, and be free of the "blemish" of usury. Only villages overseen by a local police force could have a rabbi. Congregations without a synagogue could worship in private homes, but Jews could not have secret private gatherings for any other reason.

Cattle trading was a traditional and important occupation for rural Jews such as Jacob Strauss and Seligman Haas, Löb Strauss's grandfathers. But its value to the Jewish community went deeper than livestock management. It was part of a village-to-village market economy that dealt in both cash and credit. By law Jews couldn't buy land to feed the cattle that they bought to resell for food and hides. So they made contracts with Christian peasants; they would pasture a cow or two and maintain them in exchange for a portion of the animals when they were eventually sold. Jewish dealers also bought day-to-day necessities from local craftsmen for cash and sold what they needed for credit. They were a vital link in Franconia's economic life.

Peddling was an older and even stronger tradition. The word for peddler in German is *Hausierer,* or house-to-house trader. This word, and this profession, could mean everything from hauling a wealth of goods in a substantial wagon drawn by healthy animals, to the pack of small household items that the poorer men carried on foot and that they displayed on a tray held by a strap looped around their necks.

However they conducted their trade, peddlers were Bavaria's local and international mercantile connection. They also served as creditors to free-holding landed peasantry and small craftsmen. With no railroads to link small towns and major cities, peddlers were essential to Bavarian commerce. They were also a conduit for communication. Walking or riding from village to town to city, peddlers carried news of the region and messages from family and friends to those separated by geography and economics. Distance receded and life was made more convenient when the familiar face of the peddler came into view.

Peddlers worked within a system called *medina,* the Hebrew word for territory. Each peddler had his own medina; it could be a village, a medium-sized town, an individual client, or a combination of these. However, a peddler's own home village was considered neutral and open to anyone. Those who could not afford a horse and wagon sometimes became small shopkeepers. But the majority filled a pack with needles, scissors, fabrics, and other household items and walked their medina, usually returning home for the Sabbath each week. In some areas the shortcuts they took through forests or open fields were called *Judenwege* or *Judenpfade* by Christians: "Jews' paths."

Once in effect, the Judenedikt decreed these traditional occupations off limits, and Jews were forced to take up farming and crafts. There were some exceptions, though. Men who were already engaged in peddling before 1813 and could not learn any other trade were allowed to continue. Others learned a new trade on paper but practiced the old one in reality.

The government didn't just consider the economy in its attempts to modernize Jews. It also inserted itself into the deepest and most personal parts of everyday Jewish life.

Children of both sexes were required to attend public schools along with Christian children, though Jews could open their own schools if the teachers they hired were appropriately educated and were subjects of King Maximilian. Jewish children could receive religious education but not until they proved they had received a certificate from a secular, preparatory school.

Language also fell under the Judenedikt. By the 1820s, Bavarian and Franconian Jews were required to speak Judeo-German, a dialect of German with Hebrew characters. It became the language used for daily life. Men and most women had a rudimentary knowledge of Hebrew, but it was mostly for ritual use.

Business records, in addition to birth, marriage, and death registers, and the minutes of community meetings, now had to be kept in German. This put a strain on women more than men who, in their mercantile contacts with Christians, had more opportunity and need to learn written and spoken German. But even so, it was a difficult cultural change that extended even into identity.

Jews now had to adopt German family names, if they did not have them already, though the government did not make any pronouncement about first names, as long as they weren't used as surnames. This threw over the traditional practice of using a father's first name as his children's surname. A man named Isaac whose father's name was Abraham would be called Isaac Abraham, for example. It took nearly twenty years after the adoption of the Judenedikt for this change to take effect, and by that time most children were being given German rather than Hebrew names, though the practice was not universal.

The Judenedikt left its mark everywhere, from individuals to entire villages. Buttenheim, and the Strauss family, were among them.

The Buttenheim of Löb's childhood had a small but thriving Jewish community, and he was surrounded by all the cultural symbols of his family's faith: a synagogue, ritual bath, school, and cemetery. Jews had lived in Buttenheim off and on since around 1450, and by 1668 four households of sixteen people made up the entirety of its Jewish settlement.

Since the Middle Ages local laws had prevented Jews from buying houses in Franconia unless they were abandoned or uninhabitable. Around 1525 a few Jewish families began to settle in the ruins of what was called the Upper Castle, finding both building materials and a legal loophole in order to settle permanently in Buttenheim. The castle was the former property of local Christian barons, and it was destroyed and rebuilt a few times until its final abandonment during the upheaval of the Thirty Years' War in the 1640s. Soon after settlement, Buttenheim's Jews established their first, simple synagogue at the Upper Castle location.

In 1740 construction began on the second, and permanent, synagogue. Under its low roof were a prayer hall, schoolroom, and a number of apartments. It had the traditional separate halls for men and women, and the Torah shrine was placed against the east wall. The ritual bath was added later to the northern side of the building, with the nearby Deichselbach River supplying the water.

According to contemporary accounts, the inside of the Buttenheim synagogue was not only appropriately designed for worship but was also beautiful. The inner walls were stenciled with designs featuring grapes, leaves, and laurel wreaths. Columns topped with Corinthian capitals flanked the Ark, and other parts of the building bore carved inscriptions in the Rococo style. Candles provided illumination, of course (and in fact were the only lights used until the 1930s), and the building was lined with windows. The community must have been especially happy when the first rabbi was appointed in 1767, after twenty years without one.

Following many years of local wrangling, Buttenheim's citizens founded a Jewish cemetery, and the first burials took place there in 1819. Before that year, the dead were transported to the city of Zeckern, a journey of several days. This meant the additional heartache of laying the departed to rest much later than allowed by Jewish ritual.

The community was growing, and it was not unobserved. As the nineteenth century got under way, and agitation against Jews in Franconia increased, rules about how and where Jews could settle affected Buttenheim profoundly. Well before the Judenedikt of 1813 came into play, Jews who wanted to settle in Christian villages could only do so by permission of the local aristocracy. The Baron of Seefried and his family lived in Buttenheim and had jurisdiction over its Jews. This family had succeeded the previous baronial family of the Stiebars when the last male Stiebar died in 1762. But the names made little difference. When it came to building a home and expanding Jewish presence in the village, the yea or nay still came from a Christian aristocrat.

Even when a Jew was granted leave to build a new home, it had to take up as little land as possible. In general, property lines went no farther than the place where water dripping off the eaves hit the ground. A house so built was called a *Tropfhaus:* a drip house. These small homes lined the Marktstrasse, and were owned or rented by people who could not afford their own land. As this was the "market" street, the homes were also surrounded by the businesses that keep a small village alive: an inn, a tavern and brewery, bakery, forge, and even a large farm. The local Christian minister also had a home near the center of town, its prominent location an unspoken reinforcement of Bavaria's attitude toward its Jews.

In 1820, a regional count of Jews and their trades revealed that 176 of Buttenheim's 822 residents were Jewish. This 21 percent sounds like a healthy number, but when compared to the population count in 1763, something becomes very clear: in the space of two generations, and under the influence of the Judenedikt, Buttenheim had lost 25 of its Jewish citizens.

The house on Marktstrasse 83 was built around 1687. As its original and current residents were Jews, it was also that strange species called a Tropfhaus. First constructed as a simple one-story, half-timbered home, it was altered around 1723, when larger windows were added, and, ten years later, a second story was built.

Before the Strauss family moved in, a previous owner created a separate entrance for the upper floor so that two families could occupy the house. Hirsch, his first wife Madel, and their growing family moved to the ground floor at 83b sometime before Rösla was born in 1813. Widower Hirsch brought Rebekka to live there after they were married, and by this time a day laborer named David Schneider lived upstairs with his wife and children.

The Strausses shared three rooms. There was a large living room, which was the only part of the house heated with a fireplace. Next to this room was a sleeping chamber or possibly another living room, and the house also had a small kitchen. The children slept two or three to a bed, on mattresses made of straw covered with calico or other simple fabric. Dishes were plain earthenware, and tables and chairs were made of the least expensive wood. All told the two adults and seven children shared about 645 square feet of space.

Löb went to the Hebrew school in the synagogue, whose teacher, Hänla Lehrburger, was hired after the rabbi decided to leave Buttenheim in 1825. Löb worshipped there with his family, did chores around the house, and played with his youngest siblings and the other children in the village. He also had a lot of cousins. By the time Löb was born his uncle Lippmann had been widowed and remarried, and was the father of ten children.

Above all, life revolved around Hirsch's itinerant trade. He continued to work as a peddler, even though the Judenedikt forbade its practice. Nearly fifty years old when Löb was born, he could not pick up a new profession. His sons, however, were not so lucky. They could not follow in the family business or choose any other traditional Jewish trade.

Since Jews could not engage in their traditional occupations, brothers Jacob, Jonathan, Lippmann, and Löb were expected to become farmers, tanners, weavers, cobblers, soapmakers, or other small craftsmen. And even though they might find training or work, they would have to do it alone. The new rules regarding marriage made most men ineligible as husbands, and the available women were snatched up by those who were.

By 1837, eighteen members of Buttenheim's first generation of Jews to grow up under the shadow of the Judenedikt made a collective decision: to leave their home and never return.

Jacob and Rösla Strauss, Löb's half-brother and half-sister, were among the eighteen. Sometime after March 1837 Hirsch gave Rösla enough money to emigrate to New York. At twenty-four, she traveled there in the company of other Buttenheim residents. Even mature women rarely made transatlantic journeys by themselves. Where and with whom she lived once she got to New York is unknown, but she had enough money with her for a dowry. Twenty-five-year-old Jacob moved instead to London, where there was also a substantial Jewish population.

Obviously Hirsch was doing well as a peddler, because he had the means to give both children the funds they needed to make their respective voyages. There are no records of a stable at 83 Marktstrasse, indicating that Hirsch probably did not have a pack animal, which were expensive to take care of. Perhaps he also had a small legacy from his father, or from Rebekka's. However he managed it, Hirsch was able to provide for his family beyond mere subsistence.

After Jacob and Rösla left home, there were still five children in the house: Jonathan was 22, Lippmann was 20, and Maila 16, the children of Hirsch's first marriage. Vögele was 14 and Löb just 8. Rebekka was not yet

40, and she would have no more children. No one knows if Jonathan and Lippmann tried to learn one of the new craft trades. At their age, they were expected to be well into their professions, but how they contributed to the family economy is unknown. One thing is certain, though: they did not marry, and the bleak outlook for their work and domestic lives must have weighed on them as much as it had on their older brother and sister.

The Judenedikt was designed to make proper citizens of Bavaria's Jews, and it did.

For the United States.

As the government gave with one hand and took away with another, thousands of Jews left Bavaria and Franconia to find religious and social tolerance across the ocean. By the early 1840s two more Strausses were among them.

Their departure began slowly. On March 20, 1840, Jonathan, who had already changed his name to Jonas, signed a document relinquishing any claims to his father's estate. In other words, rather than waiting for an inheritance from his father after he died, he took his share early. He then journeyed to the port of Bremen for passage to New York, possibly taking the ship *Susan,* which left port on June 5 and arrived in New York on August 15. A year later, on March 24, 1841, Lippmann signed a similar statement and, presumably, went off to join his brother soon afterward. Between April and December of that year, there were nineteen sailings from Bremen for him to choose from, though his name has not yet been found on any 1841 passenger lists.

New York City drew many Europe-weary emigrants, even in the 1840s. This was well before the huge mass of humanity made its way across the ocean in the 1880s to fill up the Lower East Side. The earlier, less well-known wave tossed thousands like the Strauss siblings into Manhattan, thanks to restrictive laws, famines, and revolutions. By this time New York was already a buzzing hub of commerce and offered the enterprising foreigner a vast array of ways to make a living, and perhaps even a fortune.

From its beginnings, New York was a place for merchants. Men like John Jacob Astor built up businesses that then got the attention of investors and partners in Great Britain and Europe. Astor and others also brought in family members from outside the city to work for their firms. Visitors and kin alike ended up staying in the city, and many foreigners became citizens. After the War of 1812, New England–based ship builders, commission merchants, and shipping firms dominated the waterfront. The opening of the Erie Canal in 1825 linked New York to the Midwest, creating conduits for the movement of goods and people into and out of the mid-Atlantic region. This allowed manufacturing, from ships to musical instruments to clothing, to take hold in New York, as the opening of more transportation networks drew workers from the countryside and additional foreign countries.

Immigrant Jews left their homeland for many reasons, but they wanted just one thing at the end of their journey: work. New York wasn't the only place where they could find and sustain a job; some men worked the peddler's roads in New England. But New York was the most populous destination, and it had the most potential. In the late 1840s Jews were spread out all over Lower Manhattan, and in community there was comfort, the opportunity for worship, and good prospects for sustainable and satisfying labor.

Rösla would have written to Jonas and Lippmann and told them about life in New York. She married peddler Isaac Lebermuth around 1838, and he may have influenced, or paved the way, for his brothers-in-law to emigrate.

Meanwhile, back in Buttenheim, Hirsch continued to wander his territory. But he was showing signs of tuberculosis as his children left home, and he died on June 10, 1846, at the age of sixty-five. He was buried in Buttenheim's Jewish cemetery, at the edge of the village. Rebekka had to then face a lot of paperwork and some big decisions.

Settling her husband's affairs meant getting financial statements from the older children. Rösla sent her stepmother a document proving that she was married and that she had received her inheritance before she left Buttenheim. Her brother Jonas witnessed her signature. In his affidavit, Jacob stated that his father had given him 250 Gulden to pay for training as a tailor and that he expected no further money from the estate. He lived at No. 2 Lemon Street, Goodman's Fields, Whitechapel, one of the traditional neighborhoods for Jewish immigrants in London.

Löb, at age seventeen, was still a minor. Fatherless, he required a male guardian to make decisions for him, and Rebekka asked her brother Isaak Haas to take on this responsibility.

Always thinking about her family's future, Rebekka took a surprising step in the summer of 1846: she married Hirsch's brother Lippmann, now a widower for the second time. She, Maila, Vögele, and Löb moved to his home at 134 Markstrasse, though she still owned the lower floor at 83b. Then, on September 15, just a few weeks later, Lippmann died. In his will, he left his house to Rebekka.

Now a double widow in possession of two homes, but with no husband or grown male children to protect or support her, Rebekka made the only logical choice she could. It was time to move to America.

CHAPTER 2

THE FATE THAT HAS BEEN ASSIGNED TO ME

B efore 1837, the year when so many young people left Buttenheim, the state of Bavaria had not cared much about emigration. But the hemorrhaging of residents due to famine and crop failures in previous decades, as well as the Judenedikt, made officials start to worry, not so much about the departure of tax-paying citizens but about their possible return as paupers. So, after 1837, no one could leave the country without the government's permission. Obtaining this permission meant following complicated procedures that made desperate emigrants think twice about abandoning their country for another. And the rules applied to everyone, Jew or Christian.

Within a few months after Lippmann's death, Rebekka got started. First, she had to collect birth certificates for herself and the children. At some point she had to provide documentation showing that everyone had a clean criminal record and that she had enough money to cover the cost of the passage to America. She also had to prove she had enough money to pay for the family's upkeep in the United States. And in case she didn't, and came back to Bavaria with empty pockets, Rebekka had to make a donation to the "poor box."

On March 17, 1847, she filed a petition with the *Regierung,* or Royal Regional Court of Bavaria. The court required petitioners to give the reasons they wanted to emigrate. Rebekka, her brother Isaak, and son Löb all gave statements to the court.

Rebekka did not mince words:

> After the death of my husband I lost the support of my maintenance. My older sons, who could come to my aid, have emigrated, thus I am in embarrassment as to how I may progress or support my son Löw [*sic*], who has not learned the business of trade and has no desire to learn it. My sons who are located in America have landed on their feet for, according to their letters, they are successfully engaged in business. I have therefore decided to emigrate with my remaining children and to seek my goal in that other part of the world. My son Löw is now at the point where he can support himself and, if necessary, support me.[1]

Although Isaak would not be joining his sister in America, he agreed with her decision. He said as much in his statement, and also brought up the risks of an ocean voyage, but he understood that it was impossible for Rebekka to live as a widow in Buttenheim. And he knew that Jonas and Lippmann—now called Louis—would receive her happily in America.

As Löb's guardian, Isaak could have kept the youngest Strauss boy with him in Buttenheim, but he would have still faced the specter of the Judenedikt and its stranglehold on life and work. Isaak knew this and was willing to let him go. As he wrote in his statement, "[Löb] and his mother are very fond of each other and a parting would have a negative influence on his state of mind."[2]

Löb echoed his mother's reasons and feelings about emigration:

> The favorable news that I have received from my stepbrothers in America has [convinced] me to follow them, even though I do not have at this time a specific occupation, but my brothers will take care of that. No members of my family will stay behind. I will share the fate that has been assigned to me with them in foreign lands. I thus join my mother in her plea.[3]

In their documents, both Rebekka and her youngest son refer to one of the most important factors in the decision to emigrate. Löb shows no inclination to take up any sort of work in Buttenheim, despite being eighteen years old. There is a sense of weary fatalism in his statement, as well. On the surface, this makes him sound like a typical petulant teenager, but there was more going on.

As Jacob, Jonathan, and Lippmann all knew, the young Jewish men of Buttenheim faced a bleak future. The newly minted Jonas and Louis were proof that prosperity awaited hard workers in New York. The two brothers were obviously sending letters back about their success and the opportunities for work.

Rebekka's feelings are clear. She not only worried about her son's ability to make a living but about his capacity to support her in her old age. Although she raised her three stepsons from the time they were children, Löb was her only biological son. She depended on him most of all. And though she does not say this explicitly, she was no doubt worried about finding husbands for Maila and Vögela.

She may also have known about the most deeply troubling consequence of the Judenedikt. The rate of suicide among Jews in the mid-nineteenth century was higher in villages like Buttenheim than in nearly all other Jewish communities in Germany. The reason for such an appalling figure was, in a word, despair. Fear for her children's survival may have been as powerful a motivation to emigrate as concern over their financial future.

There is also another way to look at these statements. Rebekka wanted to get her family out of Bavaria. Surely there was not much of a future there for either her or her son. Her daughters might never find husbands in Buttenheim, either. The official in charge of reading her documents would understand this. But she had to make this clear without overtly criticizing the government. The statements are wreathed in the language of proper citizenship; without work, they would become dependent on the state. The better gamble for Bavaria was to let the family try their luck in America.

Rebekka's next step was to publicize the family's intentions in a major newspaper, to alert any potential debtors that they were about to leave the country. Her notice appeared in the May 1, 1847, issue of the *Königlich Bayerisches Intelligenzblatt für Oberfanken* in Bayreuth.

On June 4 Rebekka then applied to the *Landkreis* in Bamberg, the local administrative district, for permission to travel to Bremen to catch a ship for New York. She had to prove to the Landkreis that she had no outstanding debts and that her son had either done his military service or paid its financial equivalent. Jews were not exempt from military obligation to the state, and it's very likely that Löb's service was paid for, either out of Rebekka's inheritance or by her brother, Isaak.

Two weeks later, on June 18, Rebekka sold 83b Marktstrasse to Anna Maria Newmann for 260 Gulden, as she and the children were still living in the house she had shared for those few weeks with Lippmann. And then, on June 26, 1847, the Regierung approved the family's application.

In choosing to leave Bavaria, Rebekka and her family were experiencing a process that historians refer to as "push" and "pull." They were being pushed out of their native land by the effects of the Judenedikt, a powerful motive to emigrate. But they were also being pulled toward America by the family members who were already there.

It was rare for an entire family to emigrate all at once. Financing was an issue, of course, but in the case of the Strauss family, Hirsch's health had prevented him from making the trip, and Rebekka and the younger children would not have left without him. The departure of the older children to America and England was not just to give them greater opportunities for work and marriage. It was also a way to test the waters for the rest of the family.

This is the "pull" factor. When the oldest son or sons were sent to America, they almost always wrote glowing reports about their lives and encouraged their siblings and parents to join them. We don't know if Jacob, living in London, made any attempt to convince his family to head to England instead of America. Rösla went to New York, not London; perhaps she knew there were better marriage prospects across the ocean, or she might have had acquaintances there.

However, it was almost a year before the Strausses actually left Buttenheim. Rebekka had to write letters to Jonas and Louis to let them know they were coming, of course. Once in New York the entire family would need to live together, and she needed to confirm there was room for everyone in the home that Jonas and Louis shared.

Finding a New York–bound vessel also took some time. Ships left from Bremen or, more accurately, Bremerhaven, the actual port for the city of

Bremen. Not all of them went to New York, and weeks could go by before the next sailing. But once she and her family were ready, Rebekka would have contacted one of the authorized ticketing agents to book her passage.

She needed to buy four tickets, and at a cost of about 65 Gulden apiece, the 260 Gulden she received when she sold her house easily covered these fees.

There was also some more bureaucracy to navigate. Rebekka did not sign the final emigration papers until April 1848. Tax records filed in October of that year show that she still owned the house at number 134 but that she was in America by that time and being "represented" by her son. As the oldest son living in New York, Jonas was the likely candidate for this role.

Researchers on both sides of the Atlantic (including this author) have spent many hours looking for the Strauss family in the passenger lists of America-bound German ships. Between May 1 and October 31 more than fifty ships left Bremen for New York. Unfortunately, no one has found a record of the actual ship that the Strauss family took. This is not unusual. Lists get lost, names don't get recorded, or spellings get so mangled that there are no traces of the real names.

Nonetheless, sometime between late spring and early fall of 1848, Rebekka, Maila, Vögele, and Löb gathered themselves together, said their goodbyes, and began the long trip to Bremen.

Today, the distance between Buttenheim and Bremen is 335 miles of modern highways. In 1848, the distance was about the same, but getting there involved bumpy rides in wagons drawn by horses or donkeys, a more comfortable ride in a type of stagecoach (if you had the money), or miles of walking. Since she already had used the profits from the sale of her house to pay for the ship passage, Rebekka may not have had a lot left over to pay for a coach. Perhaps the delay in sailing allowed her to pull together more money for the additional travel expenses. Had they had waited another year, however, they could have traveled far more comfortably, nearly the entire way, via the new King Ludwig rail line.

Bremen was not the only port in Germany where emigrants could catch a ship for New York. Hamburg was another, but Bremen had many advantages. The port of Bremerhaven was built in 1830 when the mouth of the

Weser River, leading to the North Sea, had become too choked with sand to be navigated. The city of Bremen regulated transportation, and local laws mandated that ship owners taking passengers to America had to provide food and water, instead of making them bring their own. In addition, the size of the living space on ships leaving Bremerhaven conformed to U.S. laws. And even more important, the death rate on ships from Bremerhaven was lower than that from Hamburg.

Once in Bremen, voyagers had to wait for a few days to get seats on a steamboat to take them up the Weser to Bremerhaven. This took about five hours, depending on the weather. Staying in the city could be expensive, so passengers hoped for a quick trip to their vessel. And once on the Weser, as Bremerhaven came into view, people like the Strausses, accustomed to village life, could only have been astounded at what they saw. Passenger and merchant ships bobbed and bumped against one another at the dock, sails flapping. Sailors and dockhands loaded and unloaded both goods and people, accompanied by the sounds of creaking ropes, thumping crates, wheels on stone and wood, and startling profanity. The smells were equally surprising.

The ships that took emigrants to the States often doubled as freighters, carrying American goods like cotton and tobacco to Europe, and returning to the United States filled with passengers. The Strauss family probably traveled in steerage, and not in one of the above-deck cabins, which were much more expensive. Called the "between decks" because they were located below the main deck and above the hold where freight was stored, even the best designed, most spacious steerage accommodations were a rolling, tumbling, dark, watery, waste-filled hell that emigrants remembered for the rest of their lives.

Each passenger had about fourteen square feet of space to inhabit, with only about six feet of ceiling height. Crammed within this narrow space was a bolted-down type of bunk bed, along with provision boxes, designed to protect either food or precious personal items, sold by the hundreds in departure cities like Bremen, from rats or other vermin. If they could, passengers also squeezed in things like cutlery, and perhaps a chamber pot. Nails were driven into the wall for hanging clothing, meats, cheeses, and other preserved foods. Everything beyond what the travelers had on their backs took up precious space, making the journey, which could last from four to twelve weeks, even more claustrophobic. And if there weren't enough people to fill the steerage area, the empty spaces were often stuffed with cargo.

When seas were calm, steerage passengers could sit on their beds, mingle with one another, and even go up on deck. But during storms or periods of high wind, they had to stay below and just hold on: to themselves, their families, their belongings. Anything not stowed or otherwise secured would slide with great velocity along the floor. And not even the largest chamber pot could hold the volume of vomit that accompanied the seasickness of the first few weeks on the water.

Although Löb was the youngest member of the family group, he was the only man. At age nineteen he might have either felt or was made to feel responsible for the safety of his mother and two sisters. Families stayed together in steerage, and although beds for single men were separate from those for single women, the potential for sexual assault was very real (and often a reality). Members of the crew were sometimes the culprits.

So fear could be, and often was, the prevailing emotion on a transatlantic voyage. Boredom was another, and it features in many of the diaries kept by travelers. Abraham Kohn, for example, left Bavaria in 1842 and documented his trip from Bremerhaven to the New World. He endured a long sailing of about seventy-two days thanks to a storm that shattered one of the ship's masts, more wild weather, and disappearing winds.

"Life on board ship is extremely tedious," Kohn wrote on July 30, 1842, eighteen days after leaving port. "The indifferent food and uncomfortable beds are depressing, and only hope and the constant companionship of our fellow men keep up our spirits." Sightings of whales and icebergs alleviated some of the tedium, but when there was no wind, "the boredom is hardly to be tolerated."[4]

Reminders of mortality included shipboard deaths or even, on Kohn's voyage, the remains of a shipwreck he watched floating past their vessel. "How many, O Lord, have found their lonely grave in the waves?" Kohn wrote. "And yet, seen from land or considered in some inland port, the idea of a wrecked ship seems to arouse even more horror than does the actual sight at sea." In the next paragraph, Kohn changes direction and describes a glorious sunset, which was "an inspiring sight for all of us!"[5]

No doubt Rebekka, Maila, Vögele, and Löb experienced at least some of the ghastly conditions of steerage passage. If they were lucky, they also had moments of wonder and awe, as well as favorable breezes. Then, finally, they staggered up on deck to wait for their first view of New York.

Before they made landfall, ships were halted outside of the main channel. A doctor would go on board to inspect the crew and passengers to make sure they were not suffering from smallpox, yellow fever, typhus, cholera, or any of the raft of infections that people brought with them or developed in the bacteria-laden soup that was steerage. These examinations were not comprehensive, but doctors could quickly spot the telltale symptoms of contagion and act accordingly.

Sick passengers were whisked off incoming ships and sent to the Marine Hospital on Staten Island, also called Quarantine. Sometimes an entire ship was redirected to Quarantine on the evidence of a few ill arrivals. Healthy passengers were kept under observation separately from the infected ones and were released once doctors were certain they would not develop symptoms.

The hospital had a surprisingly good reputation. One newspaper reporter in 1847 observed that sick immigrants "would be better off on the green at Staten Island than they would be in our already overcrowded Hospitals in the City."[6] To keep Quarantine in business and to prevent immigrants from straining municipal resources, each person on board had to pay a hospital tax. After 1845 this was usually around fifty cents per passenger.

After they were cleared of the specter of disease, passengers gathered their baggage and prepared to make a customs declaration. This concluded, the ship finally docked on an East or Hudson River wharf. The Strauss family was fortunate in one respect: when they eventually landed at one of the wooden piers, they stepped onto a relatively modern structure built out into the river. Twenty years earlier, ships had maneuvered into "slips," which were simply stagnant basins of water that oozed off of the main river frontage.

Once they put their feet on solid ground, travelers met family or friends who helped them negotiate their way into the city and into their new life. Kohn gave voice in his diary to what many of them experienced: "I enjoyed my first sight of the city immensely, but, as I proceeded through the crowded streets on my way to see my brother, I felt somewhat uncomfortable. The frantic hurry of the people, the hundreds of cabs, wagons, and carts—the noise is indescribable. Even one who has seen Germany's largest cities can hardly believe his eyes and ears."[7]

The Strauss family probably felt the same. And in addition to the crush of people and vehicles, the port itself was astonishing, for there could be as many as 900 vessels tied up at one time along the East River piers, each of which stretched 200 to 300 feet into the water.

Unfortunately, some men on the wharf had sinister intentions. New York had a serious problem with crooks who preyed on wide-eyed, overwhelmed ship arrivals who spoke no English, whom they could detect with a glance. "Runners" worked for nearby boardinghouses, and once they spotted their prey, they made offers of fine lodging, while picking up luggage with an assertiveness that few could resist. Passengers watched their bags being taken away and could only follow behind, finding themselves booked against their will into shabby establishments where they were charged outrageous prices. If they couldn't pay, their possessions were forfeit. Officials generally referred to these "swindlers of strangers" as harpies, or other similar epithets.

Destitute, sick, or simply frightened new arrivals could get help from the Hebrew Benevolent Society or from the Female Hebrew Benevolent Society, both founded in the 1820s. These groups helped emigrants find lodging, food, and family members. Rebekka and her children did not have to deal with the runners, however, and they had no need to apply for assistance. For Jonas and Louis, no doubt, were waiting in the dockside crowds, ready to take the family to their new home.

After arriving in America in 1840 and 1841, the brothers had moved into a part of the city that was becoming known as *Kleindeutschland,* or Little Germany (and occasionally also called Dutchtown, from *Deutsch*). The name, however, referred mostly to the Christian arrivals from German regions such as Prussia. German Jews shared parts of the neighborhood with their Gentile countrymen in the 1840s, but there were many barriers between the two groups, such as language, culture, and, of course, religion. The enclaves where German Jews gravitated, within and on the margins of

Kleindeutschland, became the more well-known Jewish Lower East Side by the late nineteenth century. And while the area did not resemble scenes from the squalor-filled photographs typical of the later Gilded Age, living conditions were on the outer edge of acceptable.

When less well-off European immigrants moved into this part of Lower Manhattan in the 1840s, the wealthy homeowners who had claimed the area in previous decades began to move uptown. Homes that once had held a single family were then converted into multifamily structures, soon called tenements.

The tenements were such a financial gold mine that landlords threw together even more of these human beehives. Cheaply constructed, the buildings could take up an entire lot, extend back 50 or 60 feet, and were sometimes 5 to 6 stories tall. Built of brick, stone, or wood, they were situated near dank alleyways. And if there were any open spaces behind existing tenements, enterprising speculators put up another house.

The most unfortunate residents lived in cellar apartments, which were so awful that they were eventually outlawed. Others lived one floor up when a workshop or small store took up the street-level space. Newcomers, whether single men or whole families, sometimes moved into boardinghouses, managed by everyone from widows to out-of-work sailors. They rented out rooms and provided meals for an extra fee. If emigrants managed to evade the gauntlet of runners at the dock, they could find a boardinghouse in the Jewish sector for a fairly reasonable price, though damp interiors, lack of air, and vermin were always present. Boardinghouses were just a stopgap, a temporary solution to the permanent problem of finding a place to live.

In other words, the concept of "home" in this part of New York bore no resemblance to what it meant in the blossoming Upper East and West sides of Manhattan. The Strauss family, and thousands of their fellow Jews, lived in housing, not a house.

The city was divided into "wards," corresponding to neighborhoods that also served as political and administrative districts. For the most part ethnic and cultural groups lived near one another in specific wards. Prussians, for example, dominated the Tenth Ward, at the southwest corner of Kleindeutschland. German Jews were scattered throughout the Seventh, Eleventh, and Thirteenth Wards. While random, and in no particular geographical order, ward numbers were more about identifying potential political allies and ethnic groups than about location. For Jews, especially, clustering in different wards meant greater opportunities for commerce and cohesiveness. They would sometimes share in the German-national organizations founded by their Christian neighbors, but they generally created their own societies for culture, education, medical care, recreation, and charity.

They also built synagogues. The earliest Jews in New York were Sephardic, descendants of the men and women who were thrown out of Spain and Portugal beginning in 1492. They arrived in New Amsterdam as early as 1654, and started Congregation Shearith Israel in 1730. In 1825 the first Ashkenazi congregation, B'nai Jeshrun, was founded by discontented English and Dutch members of Shearith Israel. Ashkenazim were Jews from Western Europe, and this synagogue was soon one of many founded by the vast waves of German Jews who ended up in New York during the 1830s and 1840s.

Existing records suggest that Jonas (and later his wife and children) belonged to congregation Shaary Shomaim, founded in 1839 by German Jews who broke away from congregation Anshe Chesed, and which was located at 122 Attorney Street. The family had a few synagogues in the neighborhood to choose from; the 1848–49 city directory listed ten of them. Unfortunately, there is no way to know how early Jonas, or any other members of his family, may have joined the congregation, whether they chose one that was taking up the new practices of the American Jewish reform movement, or whether they were purely traditional. Shaary Shomaim was a well-attended congregation, and by 1898 was called Shaar Hashomayim, the year it merged with today's Central Synagogue.

Certainly the synagogue was a different kind of place in America than in Europe. True to the new life in the New World, synagogues that had been centers of both religious and social life in the old country were now simply places of worship. Religion had not been separate from community life in Europe, where there was no barrier between faith and communal fellowship, or between social and religious gatherings.

But in America, Jewish fraternal orders such as B'nai B'rith, founded in 1845 and similar in organization and goals to the Masons or Odd Fellows, took over an important cultural role that had been the synagogue's alone. By joining these orders, young men could share ideas, make business contacts, listen to lectures from prominent rabbis, and find ways to serve their community.

Masonic lodges functioned as a comforting meetinghouse for New York's merchants and a place to cement business ties. Although Masonic and other organizations became extremely anti-Semitic later in the century, Jews joined them in great numbers without controversy in this earlier period. These lodges have been called "secular synagogues" by some historians, and members obviously took to heart the American concept of the separation of church and state.

As new residents and new citizens (many if not most Jews applied for naturalization almost as soon as they got off the boat), Jewish immigrants were energized by the lack of social restrictions that had so bound them in Europe. Emotional and intellectual restrictions also fell away. Yet they did not reject the traditional structures of their previous lives; they simply re-imagined them.

Work, however, took on a much more familiar form. Jews embraced the new but did not want to throw out the old, and when it came to making a living, what had worked in Bavaria had proved to also work well in America. Well before Jonas and Louis emigrated, Jews took up a tradition that their ancestors knew well: peddling.

Although their father was a peddler, Jonas and Louis didn't learn that trade when they lived in Buttenheim. The Judenedikt made sure of that. But once they were settled in New York, they had to find some means of making a living, and they likely turned to peddling, something that was culturally familiar, if only by association. It was the type of job that needed little capital to get started and little instruction before the aspiring peddler headed out to find customers.

Luckily, the brothers knew someone in New York who could help them.

Jonas and Louis Strauss lived and worked without leaving many footprints in the historical record after their arrival in the United States. However, both men, likely in 1841, put their names on some government documents as soon as they could: petitions for naturalization.

In 1846 they show up again, on certificates granting them citizenship, after they fulfilled the five-year residence requirement. Jonas was naturalized on February 21, and Louis on October 3. To complete the process they each needed a witness to confirm they were who they said they were and to vouch for their character. As his older brother, and a new citizen, Jonas took on this duty for Louis. Jonas's own witness was Isaac Lebermuth, their sister Rösla's husband.

When he arrived in New York in 1840, Jonas presumably moved in with Isaac and Rösla, who probably lived somewhere in or at the border of Kleindeutschland. Jonas could have taken rooms in one of the many neighborhood boardinghouses, but history and tradition suggest that he lived with family members, even if their home didn't have a lot of space to spare. The Lebermuths already had one child by this time, and when Louis arrived the following year, there were two babies in the house. By 1847, the first year that Jonas and Louis show up in city directories with their own address, there were five children on hand. Crowding aside, it is hard to believe that the brothers would have been shuffled off to a place where they had to pay money to live with strangers.

Isaac was a "pedlar" (as the word was sometimes spelled). He could easily have helped the brothers pick up the necessary skills and grubstake their inventory: ribbons, needle and thread, clothing, and so forth. But their territory did not wind through verdant hills and into bucolic villages. The Strauss brothers were urban peddlers. Their customers lived and worked in the crowded tenements and small shops of the Jewish quarter, the residential areas of newly made suburbs, and in dormitory-type housing on the waterfront.

It was not an easy life, no matter how much help you got from relatives. Abraham Kohn took to peddling the roads in New England when he could not get work in a store, and he was very clear about its hardships. "Thousands of peddlers wander about America; young, strong men, they waste their strength by carrying heavy loads in the summer's heat; they lose their health in the icy cold of winter."[8] Kohn had the disadvantage of working in rural America, where there was both competition and some suspicion of Jews. Urban peddling could be just as hard, but unlike Kohn, the Strauss brothers and their fellows did not have to sleep outdoors along country roads.

However, it's possible that the brothers did head outside of New York City. By the early 1840s, Cincinnati, Pittsburgh, and Louisville had become centers for Jewish trade and, especially, trade with New York, the source for the goods that folks in the hinterlands wanted. Although these cities had their own residents and their own peddlers, newly arrived New Yorkers sometimes made the trek down the Ohio and practiced their trade in the towns that lined the river.

No matter where you did it, peddling had not only discomforts but dangers. On May 13, 1841, a jewelry peddler named Manasseh Goldberg went to New York's waterfront and took his wares into the many boardinghouses for sailors there. Along the way he entered one place owned by a man named Hugh Burns. When Goldberg came in, Burns grabbed him by the whiskers, called him a "damned Jew," and proceeded to rough him up, with help from another man named Daniel Boyle. The two men went through his pockets and took all of his money, and when Goldberg demanded it back, they beat him even harder. He went to the police, covered in blood and bruises, and filed a complaint. Burns and Boyle were tried for robbery and assault, and though they supplied witnesses who said that Goldberg started the fight, Burns was found guilty (Boyle was let off).[9]

Stories like this meant that peddling was rarely a lifetime career. It was always a means to a better end, and once a peddler had amassed enough capital he usually put down his pack and opened a small store. Isaac Mayer Wise, one of the most revered Jewish scholars of the nineteenth century and the founder of Hebrew Union College in Cincinnati, wrote about America's Jewish peddlers and the misery of carrying goods on one's back. The lucky ones, whom he called the "aristocracy," became "store-princes." This was better, though not always ideal. After a peddler was "a slave to the basket or the pack" he would still end up "the servant of the shop."[10] Servant or no, a storefront was better than trudging. And by 1847, Jonas and Louis Strauss had become store-princes themselves.

CHAPTER 3

STORE-PRINCES

John Doggett, Jr., was one of a number of publishers who printed and distributed directories of New York's residents, a tradition that began in 1786. Like the telephone book of later years, these volumes listed business and home addresses, and also featured pages of advertising, helping to boost commerce for the enterprises listed inside.

Doggett's directory of June 1847 included the following listing: "Strous, Jonas & Brother, fancygoods, 393½ Grand, h. 393½ Grand." There was also a listing for "Strous, Lipman, fancygoods, 393½ Grand." In other words, Jonas and Louis worked and lived at this Grand Street address. The following year, in June 1848, Doggett's showed the brothers working and living at 203½ Division Street. Their appearances in these city directories show that they had managed to scrape together enough money to open a store and keep their own home. And since both were at the same address, their business would have been at street level, with the brothers living on the floor or floors above.

The directory's misspelled names are intriguing, although given that Americans often had trouble deciphering foreigners' handwriting, the errors are not unusual. In the 1848 directory the "Strous" listing is still there, but there is also a "Jonas Straus, drygoods," as well as "Straus & Brother." The name is still inaccurate, but it's at least closer to the correct spelling. Perhaps the original incorrect name was kept there for continuity, or it may have just been a clerical error. By 1850, only the "Straus" spelling appears, and it is not until 1851 that the additional "s" is finally placed at the end of the brothers' last name. "Lipman" becomes "Louis" in the 1850 directory, though he had already used that name when he was naturalized in 1846.

The brothers' company name also followed an American tradition. "Straus & Brother" meant that the firm was headed by an older brother in business with one or more younger siblings serving under him. As the oldest brother and, presumably, founder of the company, only Jonas's name was good enough to be spelled out, such as it was.

The brothers obtained their store inventory right there in New York. By the late 1840s, the city was crammed with factories of every size, small artisan workshops, and immigrants "sweating" at home doing hand-sewing, flower-making, or embroidery. Jonas and Louis would have made contacts with small manufacturers in New York when they worked their peddling territory in previous years. When it was time to open a store, they had their suppliers already lined up. They could have contracted directly with a factory, or worked with a middleman, or "jobber," who organized a crew of small workshop or home workers to make items specifically for them. It's also possible they managed a wholesale business and that their "store" was one-stop-shopping for peddlers and small storekeepers, who then sold the goods to their own customers.

The men and women making these goods were also Jews. Once in America, Jews generally did not live in rural areas or turn to farming, since agriculture was not something they brought with them from Europe. Even when vast swaths of land opened up for settlement, Jews stayed in cities like New York, and at a time when their skills were most needed. America was rapidly filling up its urban spaces, and by contributing to this economy, Jews found a way to ensure their success. They labored in businesses as varied as cigar-making, engraving, bookbinding, and needlework. Records about their working life are scarce, though. Did they experience what some contemporary writers called "poverty, misery, beggary, starvation, crime, and licentiousness"?[1] Certainly non-Jewish laborers were already working in the squalid conditions that prevailed in the Lower East Side later in the century.

If they did experience hardship, they knew it wasn't forever. It was just something that had to be endured on the way to the ultimate goal: self-employment. And that was achieved with hard work, good connections, and help from family. Peddling was usually the first rung on this ladder, and the storefront came next. Becoming a manufacturer, managing factories and middlemen, and employing relatives and fellow Jews was the pinnacle, and one that many men reached. There were also the few "merchant princes," who commanded glorious department stores, or fabulously successful wholesale businesses, and who lived in upper-class splendor outside of Kleindeutschland. Wherever a man fell on this scale of mobility, you can be sure he was always looking upward.

The Strauss brothers, who now had a stationary place of business, started out dealing in "fancygoods." These were such items as embroidered collars, fabric trims, and paper flowers, among other fripperies. That is, products that were more ornamental than functional. By 1849, however, the directory listing for Straus & Brother stated they were dealers in "dry goods," which covers a lot more territory.

Lazarus Isaacs, another Jewish retailer, had a store at 5 Division Street, in Kleindeutschland, and his stock of dry goods included the following:

> Hats
> Trims (flowers, leaves)
> Buttons
> Braid
> Bolts of red cotton velvet
> Boys "Leghorn" hats (simple straw hats)
> Plaid dusters
> Fringe[2]

"Dry goods" also included coats, pants, vests, and other clothing, as well as shoes and boots, needles and thread, scarves and hats. It was an all-purpose phrase to describe products that were distinct from foodstuffs and hardware, which were purchased from other merchants.

Some Jewish men came to New York and bought goods for the stores they ran outside of the city. Samuel Auerheim had a store in Bradford,

Pennsylvania, and bought his stock from S. L. Rosenheim & Co. on the Bowery, and from J. Ulmann & Sons, at Cedar Street, nearby. When he came to town, Auerheim picked up laces, hosiery, hair pins, and children's mitts, among other articles. Dry goods, then, meant everything from basic clothing, to underwear, to hair ornaments, to bolts of cloth.

The brothers' home and store at 393½ Grand Street was about halfway between the Bowery and the East River in 1847. There was a Mechanics and Traders Bank in one direction, and a coal yard in the other. A chemist's shop, Merkle and Dung, was next door, run by the Reverend Philip Merkle and his partner, Albert Dung. All were surrounded by buildings labeled "first class" construction on the New York real estate maps, also called fire insurance maps, which were published by William Perris. These buildings typically housed bakers, hat manufacturers, brewers, coppersmiths, wheelwrights, and private stables. The class designation on the map referred to the quality of the building required for housing particular types of businesses.

The Grand Street home and business was a first-class dwelling, made either of brick or stone, with a store underneath, and a slate or metal roof. However, the building next door was in the "third class" category, though it was also made of brick. This designation included cabinet, candle, and musical instrument makers, woolen mills, chair manufacturers, and other small factories. The 400 block up the street consisted primarily of wood-frame homes with stores underneath.

By June 1848 the brothers had moved to 203½ Division Street, a more substantial thoroughfare. Ann Gilbert had a corset business next door, and the Rutgers Female Institute was just two blocks away. This was a day school for girls and young women who wanted either a basic "English" education or courses to prepare them for college. It might have been a good place to sell some fancy goods. Across the street was shoemaker J. H. Windeler, umbrella maker John Wilkinson, and L. Meyer & Co., a grocery store.

Like Grand Street, this block of Division had a lot of first-class buildings with ground floor storefronts, though there were second-class structures in nearby blocks, as well. Jonas and Louis lived in a first-class brick or stone structure again, with a store underneath. And in both locations there was a police station within walking (or running) distance. Wherever the brothers went, they seem to have found themselves in neighborhoods with diverse businesses.

Life in New York wasn't just about economic survival. The men who left Europe for America expected to find wives, as well as work, at the end of their long voyage. Sometime between 1842 and 1844 Jonas married Sophia Metzger. By the time the brothers opened their storefront, Jonas and Sophia had two children, with eight more to come. Louis, still unmarried, lived with his business partner and brother, and not with sister Rösla.

Jewish women not only took care of the children but were also part of the family economy. The wives of some store owners, as well as their daughters, often sewed the clothing sold in the family business, and even worked the front counters. A small store, which likely describes the Strauss brothers' business, depended on female participation for its very survival.

In the early part of the nineteenth century, when Jews were firmly in place in New York, but not in great numbers, they experienced little discrimination. In the city, and in the hinterlands before the Erie Canal made urban visits more manageable, Jews were, for the most part, simply a cultural oddity. Once they arrived in America, they were relieved to find no government-mandated exclusion, downtrodden peasants, or state-sanctioned violence. Familiar to Christians from the Bible, they were welcomed as representatives of a religious past.

As the century progressed, they also became a potential source for conversion. Organizations such as the Society for Meliorating the Conditions of the Jews were well organized and well attended. This particular society was founded because the "remarkable agitation of the Jewish mind furnished strong motives for more enlarged efforts for their salvation."[3] It was a gentle rebuke of Judaism, not the all-out hatred that men like Manasseh Goldberg experienced on the waterfront. The fact that Goldberg's assailant was convicted of assault and robbery meant that the rights of some immigrant Jews, at least, were being respected. At the same time, unfortunate cultural perceptions about Jews did float around the city, sometimes aided by Gentile writers, especially as midcentury approached and there were more Jews in more places in New York. They were conspicuous by their accents, their clothing, and the type of work they chose.

George G. Foster, a writer and self-ordained observer of New York, from its nabobs to its nether regions, wrote about some of the city's Jewish residents in *New York by Gas-Light: With Here and There a Streak of Sunshine*, published in 1850. The chapter on the notorious Five Points neighborhood, just a few blocks from Kleindeutschland, takes a legitimate Jewish business—the selling of used and cheap ready-made clothing in stores sometimes called "slop shops"—and turns its proprietors into fences of stolen property. These "Israelites," in his view, are a type of human kite, or raptor, "formed to be feared, hated and despised, yet to prey upon mankind."[4]

For the most part, however, life and work for New York's Jews was a road with few obstacles. The idea of the self-made man (and sometimes woman) was not a goal only the native-born could achieve. Making a good living, and enjoying true personal agency, was denied them in Europe but encouraged and celebrated in the United States. The Strauss brothers and their fellow Jews linked the comforts of their culture to the excitement of a major metropolis, and made themselves into a new kind of American.

Rebekka, Maila, Vögele, and Löb arrived in New York between the spring and fall of 1848. For at least a year, Rebekka had worked to organize her affairs and prepare her children for emigrating to America, which means that her stepsons in the States must have been aware of her plans. Depending on when they arrived, they either moved in with Jonas and Louis at their original home on Grand Street or their new home on Division Street. The brothers probably moved to Division Street in anticipation of the need for more rooms for the new family members.

It is easy to imagine the emotions the two branches of the Strauss family felt when they finally saw each other on the dock. Jonas, Louis, and, if she was there, Rösla, had not seen their stepmother and siblings for between seven and eleven years. Löb, now nineteen, would have the most hazy memories, certainly of his older half-sister, who left Buttenheim when he was only eight. In some respects everyone had to get reacquainted, but it surely did not take long. Besides, there were things to do, and most of them involved the youngest brother. It was time for Löb to learn a trade.

Once he, his mother, and his sisters got to know the neighborhood,

went to temple, and met Jonas and Louis's friends and business acquaintances, Löb would have been taken aside and told how he was going to help
the family firm. This would not have been a surprise. How he managed, and
what he did over the next two years, is a mystery, but there are some clues,
thanks to the 1850 census. On July 17 of that year, the census taker knocked
on the door of the house on Division Street. He recorded who lived there
and what kind of work the men did.

Jonas and Sophia were listed first on the government form, as the elder
brother was considered the head of the household. Next to Jonas's name,
under the column for "Profession, Occupation, or Trade of each Male
Person over 15 years of age," was the phrase "Dry Goods." The children
(Matilda, Nathan, and Henry) were then listed underneath Sophia's name.
Rebekka—now spelled Rebecca—came next. "Lewis" followed her, with
his profession given as "Pedlar D.G." (Dry Goods). Finally came "Levy,"
also a "Pedlar D.G." The last name on the list, indicating just how successful
the family business had become, was Caroline Murabean, a servant.

Two names were missing from the census record: Vögele, who changed
her name to Fanny, and Maila, eventually known as Mary. Both women
were married by mid-1850: Fanny to David Stern, and Mary to William
Sahlein, both immigrants from Germany. Marriage was one of the main
reasons young Jewish women wanted to emigrate to America, with or without their mothers. Rösla had set the example by marrying Isaac Lebermuth
within a year or so after her arrival, and Fanny and Mary weren't far behind.
They also didn't have time to waste; Mary was twenty-nine in 1850, and
Fanny was twenty-seven. Since American women, whether first-generation
or more recent immigrants, were usually married by about age twenty-two,
they had some catching up to do.

Information about David Stern's emigration, work, and marriage is elusive, if only because his name is so common in the existing records. (To
find a specific David Stern in mid-nineteenth-century New York is to invite
despair.) Thanks to California voter registration documents, we do know
that, like all the other men in his extended family, David did become a naturalized citizen. In 1852, David, Fanny, and their son Jacob, who was born in
April 1851, lived on Delancey Street, near the Bowery. David was probably

in the clothing or dry goods business, as well, though whether he was a tailor, shopkeeper, or peddler is unknown.

William Sahlein is easier to track down. He was naturalized in New York on March 16, 1849, and in 1850 he was working as a tailor, while he and Mary lived in the Thirteenth Ward, and their son Henry was about nine months old. In 1852, William was still a tailor, and was living with Mary and their son Henry on Grand Street. Another son, Moses, would come along in 1854 or 1855, with daughter Rosa following in 1857.

Choosing American names was important to newly arrived Jews. We know that Löb later chose the name "Levi," certainly after he got to California. But it was spelled with a "y" instead of an "i" in the 1850 census. Perhaps the clerk wrote it down incorrectly because he was not as familiar with his Bible as he could have been.

Levy, or Levi (as he spelled it for the last fifty years of his life), was the name Löb would have used in his new profession, which was, apparently, peddler. But he wasn't an itinerant wanderer among the tenements or in the countryside. His brother Louis was also a "pedlar." Given his long residence in the United States, and his partnership with Jonas, Louis didn't drag a pack around. As representatives of Straus & Brother, Levi and Louis were more like traveling salesmen, visiting the family firm's regular customers and drumming up new business. The use of the word "pedlar" on the census again indicates the clerk's own preconceptions about Jews, rather than reality.

As part of the training for his new working life, young Levi had to learn English, and quickly. Jewish emigrants whose businesses depended on interaction with Americans picked up as much English as possible. They learned the language from friends and family who preceded them, from neighbors, and from sympathetic customers. Their children learned English in Jewish schools, and the less fortunate were taught the language in orphanages. While using English for temple service was sometimes controversial, there was no question that the up-and-coming generation of Jewish Americans would speak English as their native tongue. They could also help out at home if language was a barrier to daily life for other family members.

In the two years since his arrival, young Löb had become Levi, both to himself and to the outside world. Like his brothers, Löb took a name that was more familiar to his new, Christian countrymen. It was certainly easier to pronounce. However, he used his birth name again less than a year after the census was taken, when he applied for citizenship.

Becoming a citizen allowed for a level of participation in society and politics that was unheard of in Europe, and also smoothed business relations. All the Strauss men and their brothers-in-law were naturalized. Under the law, Fanny, Mary, and Rösla, as well as Jonas's wife, Sophia, automatically became citizens when they married their new-citizen husbands. So it was logical for Levi to begin the process, too. On January 25, 1851, "Loeb" Strauss (spelled for Americans who did not understand the umlout over the "o" in the middle of his name) applied for naturalization in the New-York Superior Court.

By mid-1851 the family had moved again, to 165 Houston Street, which was, as usual, the home and business address. But before then, Doggett's directory showed two other people at the Division Street house: James and George Straus, in the business of "drygoods." There is no record of anyone in the immediate Strauss family with these names, and they only appear in the directory for 1850–51, though a separate publication only has George, and not James. Their appearance is a bit of a mystery.

Jacob, the oldest Strauss brother, could have relocated to New York from London to be with the rest of the family, and changing his name to James would have made him more "American." Naming a son "George" would have accomplished the same purpose. Since these names only appear in 1850–51, the men might have lived with the siblings for just a short time and then moved out. There are other James and George Strauses in subsequent directories, but there is no way to know if they are the same ones. There is a much simpler explanation as well: James and George Straus were no relation at all and were listed with the wrong address.

The Houston Street home was on a major thoroughfare between Avenues C and D. Unlike the brothers' previous locales, this was a second-class brick or stone building, with a store underneath. This doesn't mean it was of shoddier construction but that it was a commercial structure. In general such buildings housed heavier industry, like paper mills or coach making. The Strausses' neighbors here included Samuel Rossman, also in dry goods, laborer Ambrose Buk, and peddlers Isaac Hamburg, Abram Hyman, and Leopold Schlasinger. Close by was a Methodist Church, an iron foundry, and a school. Store expansion, or starting up manufacturing, would necessitate larger quarters for both the business and the family.

Whatever the reason, the family now lived near Union Market, one of the main shopping areas in New York. Governed by the city, with a clerk on site to manage its daily workings, Union, like other markets, opened very early but was closed by noon each day so that the stalls could be cleaned out. On Saturdays, however, it stayed open until midnight. The station house of the police department's Eleventh Patrol district was also at the market, as well as a fire bell housed in a distinctive cupola.

The Strauss family probably kept kosher, although many Jews had a tenuous relationship with traditional foodways once they got used to life in America. Back in Europe, they would have eaten dark breads like rye and buckwheat, and these would be easy to find in the many local bakeries in Kleindeutschland. There were at least six bakers in business within a three-block stretch around the Houston Street home in 1852. Given their evident success, and the proximity to Union Market, the Strausses ate well. Fish and other meats, potatoes, turnips, and additional staples were always available, and matzo meal was also on grocers' shelves throughout the neighborhood.

Midcentury New York offered more than just drudgery. It could also be a lot of fun. P. T. Barnum's American Museum on Broadway opened in 1841 and was popular across all social and economic groups. "General" Tom Thumb, the two-foot-, three-inch-tall young man who was one of Barnum's greatest attractions, performed regularly at the museum impersonating Napoleon and doing song and dance numbers. In 1850 a new exhibition about China at the American Museum was also drawing crowds and getting rave reviews from people like famed Swedish singer Jenny Lind, whom Barnum also introduced to America.

Public gardens, like Castle Garden on the Battery, and Vauxhall on the Bowery, were good places for picnics, and easy to get to via the many available omnibuses. These were large, fifteen-seat coaches pulled by a single horse along a specific route throughout the city. Short boat rides to Long Island for walks and picnics were also popular. Immigrant Jews rarely if ever took part in the German cultural customs of Kleindeutschland, however. They barely shared a language with their Christian countrymen, much less anything else, and the rowdy beer halls that were strewn all over the district held no interest.

Other activities were more educational than entertaining. Jonas, as the head of both the family and the business, might have been a member of a Masonic or other fraternal organization. Whether he felt his brothers needed to participate is unknown, but it's likely that the benefits of lodge membership trickled down to their working lives.

Family members also read newspapers. There were plenty of English-language papers around, including the *New-York Daily Times* and the *New-York Herald.* There had been German-language papers published in New York since the 1840s, but they were geared toward the Protestant immigrants, not the Jewish ones, and were not written in the hybrid of German and Hebrew that families like the Strausses brought with them from Bavaria. And besides, reading a paper in English was a good way to improve language comprehension.

The first Jewish-interest newspaper published in New York was *Israel's Herold,* which appeared in March 1849 and only lasted three months. Other cities with sizeable Jewish populations had papers such as Philadelphia's *Occident,* which debuted in 1843 and, like the others, was printed in English. But it would be difficult to get an out-of-town paper on a regular basis.

Then, on October 26, 1849, Robert Lyon came out with the first issue of *The Asmonean.* An English Jew who had emigrated to the United States in 1844, Lyon published his paper with the support of the city's most important synagogues: Shearith Israel, Rodolph Sholom, Shaary Shomaim, and Anshe Chesed. This weekly paper was an appealing mix of local and foreign news, which was not limited to Jewish topics. There were also editorials, stories, book reviews, and, of greatest interest to the merchants of Houston Street and beyond, articles about trade, shipping, and general commerce. The motto on the paper's masthead was "Knowledge is Power," and though

Lyon was new to journalism, he was politically savvy and knew when to punch up and promote a news item that came across his desk.

From the day he arrived in America, young Levi's life was a round of family, worship, and nose-to-the-grindstone application to learning English and every detail of the dry goods business. He and his family were helping to create the new New York: one that bustled with both people and industry, and with commercial links to settlements springing up along America's rivers, lakes, and into its rich westward farming country.

They didn't know it yet, but they were about to help create something else new a few thousand miles away. On November 23, 1849, just a month after the first issue came off the press, Lyon's *Asmonean* featured a boldface advertisement placed by "M. Solomon, refiner and assayer," a member of Henry Solomon's refining company at No. 45 Ann Street:

CALIFORNIA GOLD DUST! CALIFORNIA GOLD DUST!

Jonas and Louis may have heard of a place called California after they got settled in New York. By January 1848, as plans for the family's move to New York were coming together, Jonas and Louis continued to prosper, and they were looking at moving from Grand Street to Division. They had no reason to think about California, out there on the other side of the continent. However, something extraordinary was about to happen.

The story is well known. On January 24, Midwest native and amateur geologist James Marshall was working on the tailrace of a sawmill he was building for Swiss entrepreneur John Sutter on the American River near Sacramento. He used the millrace as a giant sluice, and after flushing the millrace down to bedrock, he looked into a small, still pool, put his hand into its freezing depths, and brought out the nuggets that would ignite one of the greatest mass migrations in history: the California Gold Rush.

When the news trickled back east, it was generally met with yawns. There had actually been a few gold strikes around the South during the nineteenth century. When substantial amounts of gold were discovered in northern Georgia in 1829, white men scurried into what were the lands of the Cherokee Nation in order to find it, leading a few years later to the relocation of the tribe via the infamous Trail of Tears. There was even a promising gold discovery in Virginia in 1848, which did not amount to much. But on December 5 of that year, President James Polk, after receiving reliable reports and a sample of the metal, announced to Congress that a significant strike had been made. The presidential imprimatur gave the news authenticity and immediacy.

On December 8, the text of the California military commander's report to the president was printed in full in New York newspapers. On December 11, the *New-York Tribune* carried a letter written from Monterey, California, in August, in which the writer compared the thousands of men tearing around the goldfields to hogs let loose in a forest.

By early 1850, the *Asmonean* began to report on the numbers of Jews leaving New York for California. These articles spoke of both mercantile success and the ease with which the "Israelites" were able to replicate the community ties they enjoyed in the East.

If New York was a haven for Jews escaping economic and spiritual persecution, giving immigrants an infrastructure within which to get on their feet and make new lives, California shone as a blank slate. There, Jews saw that they could make their own infrastructure, and, in the process, provide themselves and their families with the comfort and security that narrow Kleindeutschland sometimes denied them.

Jews were aware of California's opportunities. From the very beginning of the rush, they hopped on boats for the gold region, to be among its first, and most prosperous, merchants. And San Francisco was the fulcrum around which their businesses were built.

CHAPTER 4

A LIMITLESS OPENING FOR INDUSTRY AND TALENT

Considering how important San Francisco and its bay would become, it's interesting to note how much early explorers either ignored or completely overlooked the site. The expeditions of Cabrillo, Cermeño, Vizcaíno, and even the feared Drake sailed right by the entrance to San Francisco Bay between 1543 and 1602, making landfall in present-day Marin or Monterey instead. Spain had claimed the coast for itself but did not think it had to do much to keep it. However, English and Russian encroachment by the mid-eighteenth century made King Charles III realize he needed to take steps to keep the Spanish flag flying along the Pacific.

The best and fastest solution was to get a military presence into Alta (upper) California as soon as possible. And that meant going both overland and by sea. In early 1769, a group of soldiers and citizens left Mexico and headed north. They were divided into four groups: two went by land, and two shipboard. Don Gaspar de Portolá, a Spanish army captain, was made governor of Alta and Baja California and named head of the entire expedition. Spain's future in this corner of the New World was now in his hands. By June all four groups had made it to present-day San Diego, where Franciscan missionary Junípero Serra established Mission San Diego de Alcalá, the first of the twenty-one missions to be sprinkled along California's western edge over the next fifty-odd years.

Portolá didn't stay long, because his goal was the bay at Monterey, well known to the early explorers. His overland group headed out again, and when they found their coastal route blocked by mountains, they turned inland. By doing so, they actually trekked past Monterey Bay without seeing it. At the end of October they found themselves on the coastline looking at the Farallon Islands, which Portolá knew were well north of Monterey.

Disappointed at his navigational error, Portolá decided to just keep going north. He sent one of his scouts, José Ortega, to ride out and find the best route. As he and his company rode along the cliff edges, they crested a ridge and saw an immense and sheltered expanse of water with fingers stretching forever north, east, and south. It was, of course, San Francisco Bay, and they were the first white men to see it. Coincidentally, other members of the party had wandered around the southern area and saw how far into that region the water traveled, as well. But rather than being elated at the naval potential of such a large bay, the expedition's leaders saw it only as an obstacle. They returned to Monterey and then to San Diego, arriving there in January 1770.

By the spring of 1776 further exploration and the establishment of a mission and a presidio (fort) near the bay of San Francisco gave Spain the foothold it wanted. The devastating encroachment of horse soldiers, settlers, and missionaries on local Indian lands and the tribes that inhabited them—Coast Miwok, Wintun, Yokut, and Costanoan—cannot be overstated, and these Native peoples were swept aside as the little outpost expanded.

The new citizens of the area named both a sheltered cove and the village beyond Yerba Buena, for a local perennial that sprawled over the hillsides (*Clinopodium douglasii*). Yerba Buena's growth was followed by a long period of stagnation, as it was ignored by Spanish bureaucrats who were happy enough that they had set up their standard presidio and mission, institutions that generally ran themselves. But when Mexico won its independence from Spain in 1821, now taking Alta California as its own, it kept fewer troops at the garrison. By the 1830s rumors about the splendid bay became fact as shiploads of men from New England and beyond dropped anchor there.

Mexico wasn't happy about all the visitors but was powerless to stop them, except with regulations that were often ignored. Americans began to settle and build businesses linking the village to ranchos in the interior and trading hides and other local products with the men who helmed visiting mercantile vessels. Yerba Buena was becoming a very English-speaking town, and its political organization was looking less like Mexico and more like Boston.

The eyes of a number of countries were turning toward California by this time, and authorities in Washington were getting nervous. Congress was determined that if Mexico lost its hold on California, the United States should pick it up. Men who had made their home there were also determined to keep it, and in June 1846 a homegrown insurrection called the Bear Flag Revolt took the town of Sonoma, a key military outpost north of San Francisco. What the rebels didn't know was that the United States was already at war with Mexico. Captain John B. Montgomery, master of the USS *Portsmouth,* was ordered to occupy Yerba Buena. Soldiers and marines landed in the cove and marched to today's Portsmouth Square, raising the American flag and announcing that the United States had annexed California and war had commenced.

California was folded into the United States with the signing of the treaty of Guadalupe Hidalgo in February 1848, and with the conclusion of the Mexican War. Two years later, California became a U.S. state without being named a territory first. Although territorial status was the usual path to statehood, the region's gold, and the need for the U.S. government to control it, made this leapfrogging imperative.

Something else had taken place during the war years. On January 30, 1847, the local *alcalde* or mayor, Washington A. Bartlett, announced that the town of Yerba Buena would henceforth be known as San Francisco.

A reporter writing in the February 19, 1852, issue of the *New York Times* stated that the "febrile symptoms" of the California Gold Rush were not a passing fad. "Here, then, is a limitless opening for industry and talent," he wrote. If anything describes the Jewish approach to the challenges of the Gold Rush, it is the words "industry and talent." With foresight gained from years of hard work, and good news from those who were already in California, Jewish merchants realized that the best way to make money in mining was not to squat in a snow-fed river but to have dry clothes ready for those who did.

Having perfected the peddling and then wholesale and retail merchandising of American goods while in New York and in Ohio River towns, Jewish merchants who went to California went there well prepared. Few of them ended up as peddlers, mostly because California had enacted an onerous tax on peddlers in 1851. But these merchants knew that opening stores in the small towns that blossomed throughout the gold region was the best hope for success. And they knew there were men they could trust who were running the wholesale houses in San Francisco, and who would be their suppliers, because they were also Jews. Some stayed in New York and supplied California retailers exclusively. As the port city nearest the goldfields, San Francisco was perfectly suited to be the waystation for goods and men.

Immigrants like the Strauss brothers came to New York just as a demand for men's ready-to-wear clothing arose and then exploded. As more young men joined the middle class, they enjoyed a growing prosperity, but this didn't always mean that they could afford tailor-made, and personally fitted, trousers, shirts, and vests. What had been considered "slop" clothes, such as those worn in the dark shops of Five Points, became both respectable and a new source of revenue for small manufacturers. Greater textile production in New England, and expansion of slave labor in the South, also fueled this output.

And as they had moved from peddling to opening a store, Jews and others who entered the clothing business relied on tiers of producers and manufacturers. Workers in their homes or in small shops produced for jobbers, who then sold the goods to wholesalers and distributors. These men, in turn, had retail customers who got the items into the hands of the final purchaser, or consumer. By 1853 this interconnected system made the ready-to-wear clothing business one of the biggest industries in the country, with New York as its hub. This category included the garments prized by the new white-collar class, but also covered the rougher shirts and trousers worn by farmers, laborers, and, soon, California gold miners.

With these links firmly in place, Jews who headed for California did not go there empty-handed, or with empty pockets. All they had to do was decide whether they would work the wholesale end of the business, or the retail. The choice was personal, and based on whom they knew in New York who could be their best partner. The retailers set up shops and homes in California's gold regions, in towns like Nevada City, Sonora, Placerville, Spanish Hill, Jackson, Marysville, and myriad others. The wholesalers, on the other hand, landed in San Francisco and stayed there. They were the ones with the strongest ties to the producers in New York, and on advice from their customers in the hinterlands, they knew exactly what to buy.

Back in New York, jobbers loaded clipper ships with clothing, dry goods, hardware, and other essentials. Gold country merchants arranged for shipments of goods to a San Francisco commission merchant on the waterfront, and then for transportation to their store. They could also send orders to one of those reputable San Francisco wholesalers.

By 1852, the Strauss family was surely hearing many stories about the travels of their fellow Jews and their successes in California. Friends and neighbors shared letters from relatives out west, and commercial ties were made and strengthened as it became obvious that the "rush" was not a fluke. Although some Jews went to California for a while, made a handsome profit, and then came back to New York, the majority decided to make California their permanent home. Because so many remained, others did too, and then all these newcomers encouraged family members in the East to join them. Jewish merchants helped little gold rush towns prosper, helped build small cities into major ones, and provided everyone from miners to comfortable families with what they needed.

In fact, by the early 1850s, it was obvious that more than sturdy work clothes and boots were required. Fine clothing and dry goods items such as lace mantillas, ladies white stockings and collars, and French silk mitts were showing up on store shelves by this time. The former rough-and-ready gold region of song, story, exaggeration, and paintings, was slowly becoming the settled state of California.

The frenzy, the "rush," the need to get out west and grab some gold, held many meanings for the seekers. Men—and some women, too, of course— wrote and talked about the gold itself, the soft metal shining in their pans or dust sparkling as it poured out of buckskin bags. Gold meant wealth, but wealth was relative. It wasn't just about buying the most expensive house, furnished with French imports. There were other dreams beyond material goods. To a laborer, enough gold could mean no more calloused hands, or a back no longer bent under a hod filled with bricks. Middle-class, white-collar clerks longed for escape from the stifling regimentation of the office. Women benefited from the gold coming to them in exchange for everything from laundry to pies, at prices unheard of back east, or enjoyed the relief from household labor once their husbands struck it rich. At the conscious level the rushers thought only of holding the gold in their hands, but at the deeper level of true desire, gold meant freedom.

America's Jews had it very clear in their minds that gold was a means to an end, and not an end in itself. It was another avenue to achieving the goals that consumed them from the minute they hit American soil: economic autonomy, support for their families, participation in a shared community, and freedom from fear. California, and its queen city San Francisco, promised all of this, and more.

No one knows when the Strauss family decided to send one of their own to San Francisco. There were a lot of factors to consider before taking this step, but it's likely they first had to choose who was going to make the trip. It is easy to imagine the dinner table or shop counter conversations that went on before the family came to their decision.

Jonas was probably not considered at all. He was the patriarch, the oldest of the sons living in New York, the head of the business, and the father of a growing family. Louis was unmarried, and he knew the business inside and out after working so long with his brother. But he was thirty-five years old in 1852, not exactly a young man in those days. The brothers-in-law, William Sahlein and David Stern, were younger, but also had growing families and were just that: in-laws. They had their own businesses and no stake in the future of J. Strauss & Brother, except as it affected their wives. Isaac Lebermuth was also out of the running for the same reasons, and he was also much older.

That left Levi.

He was twenty-three, had five years of New York dry goods experience under his belt, and was unmarried. The family eventually chose him to take on the responsibility of building the family's business in California, for most if not all of these reasons. But there may have been others, too.

For one thing, California's Jews had set up religious and social institutions as soon as they could. The *Asmonean* reported regularly about Jewish efforts in the state to create the cultural connections they needed in their new home: "Our correspondent in San Francisco . . . speaks in glowing terms of the brotherhood, and unanimity existing amongst our people, and after lamenting that their wavering intentions of permanently settling in California have as yet, prevented the erection of a suitable edifice for a synagogue, gives details of the purchase of a plot of land for a burial ground, and the institution of a benevolent society (there are poor in the land of Gold!) both before reported in our columns."[1] In other words, Levi would find familiar comforts in San Francisco, and safety nets for a young man on his own.

If Levi had shown no talent for commerce, if he had succumbed to New York's temptations and spent his nights in dissipation, or if he had decided to take up a different line of work, he wouldn't have been right for the job. Had that been the case, Louis probably would have made the trip. Failing his ability to go, the family would have turned to William or David, or might not even have taken the chance on California at all The fact that they did send the youngest brother on what was known to be a dangerous journey and risky commercial undertaking meant that his much older brothers had complete confidence in his abilities.

We don't know how Levi felt about this opportunity, or if he even saw it as an opportunity. It's intriguing to speculate about whether it was his idea or whether he was simply informed of the family's decision and had no say in the matter. In other words, did he jump or was he pushed?

The next thing for the family to decide on was what end of the business they would be in. In essence, Levi would be going to California to start the western branch of the firm. It could have been a storefront in the Sierra, but the brothers decided to set up shop as wholesalers on the San Francisco waterfront. This is a clue as to what the New York business looked like, as well.

Now came the "when." Levi was due to take his oath of citizenship in

January 1853, and this important step could not be missed. The family could take advantage of the time to amass the funds and the goods to get the new business started, as well as save for his ticket, which they could buy from a number of agencies along Broadway and near the waterfront. By 1852 there were regular clipper ship sailings out of New York for California, their holds filled with groceries, dry goods, farm tools, seeds, clothing, and wines.

In December 1852, the *Winged Racer,* described in the *Asmonean* as a "magnificent new clipper," was berthed at Pier 27 on the East River.[2] Its hold could handle a few tons of light freight, and newspapers throughout the city ran ads advising merchants and shippers to get in their bills of lading soon, in order to get their goods to San Francisco right away. The ship left port around December 13, expected to reach the West Coast in about one hundred days by taking the route around Cape Horn. Among the boxes, crates, bundles, and barrels in its hold was a shipment destined for San Francisco and consigned to "L. Strauss."

On January 31, 1853, Levi and Louis went to the Superior Court of the City of New-York in City Hall. There, "Loeb Strauss" swore to support the U.S. Constitution and to renounce his allegiance and fidelity to the King of Bavaria. Louis, as witness, stated that Loeb had resided in the United States for five years and that he was a man of good moral character, attached to the principles of the Constitution. With the signature of Mr. Campbell, the court clerk, and his own, Levi became an American citizen, writing "Loeb" on a piece of paper for the last time.

Five days later, on February 5, Levi made his way to a pier at the foot of Warren Street, on the North River, the old name for the Hudson near Battery Place at the tip of Manhattan. Nearby were a number of bonded warehouses, coal and iron yards, and seedy hotels. He was most likely not alone. Huddled together for comfort against cold and anxiety, members of the extended Strauss family said tearful goodbyes to their son, their brother, their brother-in-law, or their uncle.

After they finally let him go, Levi boarded the U.S. Mail ship *Georgia,* under the command of Captain David Dixon Porter, on leave of absence from the U.S. Navy. They took off at 2:00 p.m. precisely. Levi would easily make it to San Francisco before the *Winged Racer* and its consignment of dry goods. The *Georgia* was a steamship. And it wasn't going around the tip of South America like its cousin the clipper.

It was going to Panama.

If you wanted to make a relief map of Panama out of flour, salt, and water, the isthmus would be where you'd squeeze the dough to make the skinniest part. This fifty-mile-wide strip fascinated and frustrated conquistadors, pirates, and the U.S. Congress during the 350 years after Rodrigo de Bastidas had the first European sighting of Panama's shores. Columbus and Balboa also made their mark on the isthmus, and it was Balboa, after crossing the barrier to the Pacific, who first realized its commercial potential: as a shortcut from the mines of South America to the treasure ships of the Caribbean.

The Spanish carved roads through vine-clotted ravines to create trails for the mule trains that carried silver and gold from Peru and Bolivia to the town of Portobelo. There, ships were filled with the spoils of Potosí and pointed toward Spain, unless detained by privateers like El Draque: England's Sir Francis Drake, who died of dysentery in 1596 while in Panama and whose coffin, dropped in waters off Portobelo, has never been found. For more than a century, from 1713 until 1819, Panama was part of the viceroyalty of Nueva Granada in Bogotá and was briefly independent after that period. It then joined Simón Bolívar's Gran Colombia until its demise in 1830, when it became part of the new republic of Colombia. Then, in the early nineteenth century, the United States began to look toward the isthmus.

The U.S. government wanted to put steamships into operation as both naval warships and mail carriers. In March 1847 Congress approved a bill calling for the construction of warships and the establishment of mail contracts between the Secretary of the Navy and individuals or companies ready to operate the lines. To cut the time needed to transport the mail and, eventually, allow for passengers to use this route for travel from East to West, it was decided to make part of the passage overland via the narrow Ithmus of Panama. By spring 1848 the United States Steamship Company, the New York and San Francisco Steamship Company, and the Pacific Mail

Steamship Company had ships in operation, and their owners looked forward to the benefits that their government contracts would bring them.

Their timing could not have been better.

When news of the gold discovery in California made its way east at the end of 1848, frenzied men bought out the pick-and-shovel inventories of hardware stores and said goodbye to worried families. Knowing that there were steamers leaving for Panama, they headed by the hundreds for New York to catch the next available boat, clogging docks and the boats themselves.

The reason to choose Panama can be summed up in one word: speed.

There were three ways to get to California from the East and Midwest at the end of the 1840s. One was in a clipper ship going around Cape Horn at the tip of South America, then up the coast to San Francisco, like the *Winged Racer.* Residents of New York and other mid-Atlantic states usually chose this route, because to head overland, you would have to get to a jumping-off place like St. Joseph or Independence, Missouri, a hard trek on its own. Once chosen, both of these routes could take from three to six months (or longer), and each had its own unique dangers.

Trails across the country were unmarked, with scarce or bad water. Indian attacks were rare but always on emigrants' minds, and diseases like cholera claimed more lives than historians will ever know. A clipper ship journey meant frigid cold and searing heat, and the rounding or "doubling" of the Horn was such a horror it inspired dozens of seafaring songs. A typical refrain was "I wish to God I'd never been born / To drag my carcass around Cape Horn."

If speed wasn't the object, either of these routes would get a traveler to California eventually. But if it was gold, speed was essential. Getting to the American River as soon as possible meant choosing one of two Central American routes. One, created by "Commodore" Cornelius Vanderbilt in Nicaragua, took travelers on a very wet journey on the San Juan River and Lake Nicaragua, and then on a road the rest of the way to meet San Francisco–bound steamers on the Pacific. The Panama route was more popular, and conditions improved as the 1850s progressed.

The first leg of this trip was steamship passage from New York. While trips around the tip of South America continued to rely on sail, shorter trips like those taking gold-seekers to Panama used the now-perfected steamship, which first appeared in the early 1800s for transporting commercial goods and crops on the nation's rivers.

The ships puffed from New York through the Caribbean to the mouth of the Chagres River on Panama's eastern coastline. There, passengers loaded themselves and their baggage into "bungoes." These flat-bottomed boats, piloted by indigenous people, took an average of two days and nights to reach one of two trailheads (either Cruces or Gorgona, depending on the season). Travelers then either rented a mule or walked the final eighteen miles to Panama City, sometimes waiting days or weeks for another steamer to take them to San Francisco. By the time Levi Strauss landed in Panama around Valentine's Day of 1853, the crossing was a more organized and modernized operation. The Panama Railroad was partially completed across the isthmus by this time. In addition, the steamship companies put more ships into service, so the men and woman who made it to Panama City rarely had to wait more than a day or two for a boat to take them to San Francisco.

The family knew about the Panama route the same way they knew about the opportunities in California: letters from those who had made the trek west. These would have been full of information about the logistics of the Panama route, its advantages, and its perils.

Levi probably traveled on a second-class ticket. The U.S. Mail steamers connected to those of the Pacific Mail Steamship Company once they reached Panama. A second cabin ticket on the *Georgia* was $45, equivalent to $1,250 today. If Levi purchased a through ticket, to cover the costs of going across the isthmus, the total was about $200, a rather staggering $5,500 in today's currency.

This is another clue about the Strauss family's financial situation. Traveling via the isthmus was not the cheapest way to go; had money been a factor Levi would have gone via clipper around the Horn. But choosing the speedier route shows a determination to get the San Francisco business started soon and the financial wherewithal to make it happen. Even second class was luxurious compared to steerage, as he knew all too well. His ticket entitled him to spend his days in one of the saloons that doubled as dining and reading or writing rooms. He slept in a large cabin with multiple and separate, curtained berths, and the first- and second-class passengers ate at the same table, though not at the same time.

On the day before he landed in Panama, Levi descended to the hold to look for his stowed baggage. He had it weighed, and paid between 10 and 15 cents a pound to have it transferred to another part of the ship in preparation for landing in Aspinwall (now called Colón), the city on the Caribbean side of the isthmus.

As the steamer came close to its moorage in Navy Bay, Levi could see a rim of white beach fronted by colorful homes and commercial buildings made of brick and adobe. Just beyond, looming like a jaguar about to strike, were the mangroves and sinewy vines of Panama's mountain interior, the passengers' next destination.

Levi and his fellow travelers had a few free hours to wander through the bustling city, filled with unique people, birds, animals, and smells. Hubert Howe Bancroft, the historian and writer whose book collection formed the nucleus of the Bancroft Library at the University of California, Berkeley, crossed Panama in 1852. He didn't think much of his first glimpse of Aspinwall, saying that it boasted "the finest vultures on the planet."[3]

Eventually, everyone boarded the Panama Railroad for the next leg of their journey. Built in 1851, the railroad's investors originally conceived it as a way to speed the U.S. Mail across the isthmus, and then realized its appeal to the gold rushers. When Levi arrived in February 1853, the train only went about twenty-three miles across. It terminated in the village of Barbacoas, on the Chagres River, a trip of about two hours (shortening the crossing by at least a day). Once on the train the passengers could sit with a pitcher of ice water and gaze out the windows at the emerald blur of passing foliage or at the astonishing primary colors of the macaws that flew just above their sight line.

At Barbacoas the bustle began again. People grabbed their luggage, firearms, life preservers, kettles, and umbrellas, and converged together to board one of the waiting canoes for the trip up river. This was a shorter trip than in previous years as well, especially if, like Levi, you made the crossing in the dry months. During the rainy season between May and December the heat and humidity were nearly unbearable.

About four hours after setting off, the canoes landed in the village of Gorgona, where one of two rough trails led from there to Panama City. The other track was at Venta de Cruces, created by the Spanish centuries earlier as their treasure trail. In the dry months, Gorgona was the preferred route, as it was a bit shorter. Levi spent a night or two in Gorgona, a jumbled collection of one hundred–odd buildings nestled together above the river. It had everything a traveler could want: hotels, saloons, gambling houses, and restaurants. Some buildings were nothing more than small, thatched bamboo structures, but even those were welcoming.

When it was time to take the final, eighteen-mile leg of the trip to Panama City, everyone either started walking or rented a mule. By 1853 most people bought a through ticket for the Panama transit, which gave them passage on the steamer from New York, a ticket for the train, boat passage, and mule rental, and another steamer ticket up the Pacific Coast to San Francisco. If you didn't pay for the mule ahead of time, you could still add on the price at Gorgona. A mule ride saved you a full day or two of travel, but it cost $18, equivalent to nearly $500 today. I like to think that Levi's family sprang for a mule, and if so, he would have rented the animal from either Hurtado & Hermanos, who also acted as the Wells Fargo agents on the isthmus, or from Woolsey's Express and Transportation Line.

Although the river transit had its dangers (alligators, drowning, yellow fever), the trails were the most worrisome part of the journey. Travelers were at their most vulnerable, because both roads went through narrow canyons or dense jungle, which gave highwaymen plenty of places to hide. Robberies and murders happened on the trails at all times of the year, though they mostly targeted those going home from the goldfields, their packs full of the plunder of the American River.

The train, boat, and mule trip was a sensory revelation exceeded only by the explosion of colors and noises that was Panama City. After getting off their mules, or struggling into town on foot, the last locale before the last boat trip presented visitors with a combination of Central American gaiety and American enterprise. As Bancroft observed, "There were avenues of fruit and vegetable stalls; while through the open doors of the veranda the more aristocratic traffickers displayed their dry goods, groceries, and liquors. The main streets in the central part of the city were lined with hotels, shops, and gambling saloons, newly-whitewashed and adorned with flaming signboards in English vocables, while on nearly every other house waved the stars and stripes."[4]

Whatever the lures and delights of Panama City, Levi was probably more than ready to catch the next boat for the final stretch of the trip to San Francisco. A number of steamers bobbed together in the Bahía de Panamá (Panama Bay), including a few belonging to the Pacific Mail Steamship Company. They were unloading passengers, luggage, and mail for those making the trip back to New York, and preparing to take on the next batch of passengers for San Francisco. If Levi had purchased a through ticket, he would be entitled to board any available Pacific Mail steamship. He ended up on the *Isthmus,* Captain Harris at the wheel, along with 274 other passengers. At 3:00 a.m. on Monday, February 21, the ship steamed away from the Bahía on its way north.

These past few weeks must have a revelation for Levi. Beyond the novelty of all he encountered, managing these new experiences can only have given him confidence. And even though he had no family members with him, there were other Jews on board that he could share language or worship with. He must have taken a yarmulke or hat with him, as well as a prayer book and possibly a *tallis* or prayer shawl. These items would be with him in his cabin, not packed down in the hold, and would have brought him comfort, even if he was excited and anxious to get going, jumping into his new life with the exuberance of youth.

He had a lot of time to think about these questions, if they occurred to him. Some evidence suggests he traveled with another young man who was also headed to San Francisco or the Jewish stores of California's gold region. Their families may have known each other in New York and elected to send their relatives on the voyage together.

Five days after leaving Panama, on Saturday, February 26, while still at sea, Levi celebrated his twenty-fourth birthday. On Wednesday, March 2, the *Isthmus* pulled into Acapulco, Mexico, at 4:40 a.m. The passengers were allowed to disembark and wander around for a few hours, then the steamer sailed again at 1:00 p.m. On Friday, March 11, it docked in San Diego at 6:30 a.m., but left again at 8:45 a.m., probably only having taken on fuel. On Sunday, it landed in Monterey at 5:00 p.m., dropped off and picked up the mail, and headed back out again an hour later.

There was just one day to go.

CHAPTER 5

HARD LABOR AND WILD DELIGHTS

When gold was discovered in January 1848, San Francisco's population was about 850. By 1850 it was over 20,000. When the first census was taken in 1852, the count was up to 35,000.[1] Like a sluice box on the American River, San Francisco was now the place through which thousands of people swirled, and millions of dollars in gold made their way into banks from Montgomery Street to Wall Street.

During the first few years of the rush, San Francisco's appearance was not very impressive. Buildings were generally made of wood, calico, canvas, spit, and hope, and this made them vulnerable to the disastrous fires that tore through the city; there were six major fires between 1848 and 1851 alone. In 1850 some residents and merchants began to rebuild in brick or stone, adding iron shutters both for protection and theft deterrence. After the worst fire of all, on May 4, 1851, nearly everyone who rebuilt used more fire-resistant materials, and while they were at it, created a more beautiful and imposing San Francisco, one that looked like the commercial center it was becoming.

San Francisco had also started building and maintaining its wharves, critical for a city that relied on taking in supplies and men, and shipping out gold. Fueling the mining region meant getting merchandise via steamboat to Sacramento and points east, such as Marysville and Stockton. Clipper ships, which brought massive amounts of dry goods, foodstuffs, rope, iron, and other items from New York, could not navigate on the inland waterways that led to Sacramento. Transshipping merchandise required a developed seaport with warehouses, piers, and access to horse-drawn transportation. Yerba Buena Cove was the perfect place, and it was around the cove that most of the wharfage clustered and where warehouses were quickly erected.

The first pier constructed was Long Wharf, extending out from Commercial Street, between Sacramento and Clay. By the end of 1849 it was 800 feet long, was expanded several hundred feet further over the next few years, and was later renamed Central Wharf. But once the Panama steamers started dumping shiploads of hopeful miners into the city, Long Wharf was joined by other piers in a two-mile stretch along the cove and around Telegraph Hill to Black Point, the site of Fort Mason Center today. The new structures were imposing: Clay Street Wharf was 40 feet wide and 1,800 feet long, while Cunningham's Wharf, at the foot of Battery Street, was a T-shape, and six enormous clipper ships could tie up alongside it at one time. The sight was always astonishing to visitors, including a writer for the *Daily Alta California,* who said that the bay possessed "sufficient room for anchorage of the vessels connected with the commerce of the whole world."[2]

Shops, restaurants, and offices clustered together on the wharves for the convenience of the merchants, commission agents, and shipping-related businesses that depended on the waterfront. Finding enough space for merchandise storage was a big problem, but there were some big thinkers in town. When these clever opportunists looked out onto the bay, they saw empty ships, bobbing silently with no one at the wheel or on deck. Hundreds of gold-fevered sailors abandoned their vessels as soon as they made landfall in San Francisco, staying only long enough to outfit themselves for the trip inland. Wily entrepreneurs hauled the ships right up to the shoreline, made them secure, and turned them into warehouses and lodgings.

Even before the Gold Rush, locals had started filling in the low-lying portions of Yerba Buena Cove so that wharves could be thrust out into the water. This made it easier to offload incoming cargo; no longer would lighters or similar small craft have to go out into the bay to take merchandise off the clippers and row back to shore. At first the fill was made of dirt, garbage, and the flea-ridden sand that abounded along the water's edge as landfill. Pretty soon workers had to go farther west to find more sand, and then rock, which was hauled in horse-drawn carts or "steam paddies," small trains that scooted along temporary track lines through the city and toward the ever-growing shoreline. Eventually the landfill also included carcasses of the former sailing ships turned storage structures, which had finally rotted and became unusable.

By 1852 the graceful crescent shape of Yerba Buena Cove displayed barely a curve, and gridded streets appeared where once there was water. The city also started to improve the condition of the streets. There was no reason to have state-of-the-art wharves if wagons full of merchandise had to roll along substandard thoroughfares. For years the city's roads were either dirt or layers of wooden planking, neither of which held up well in wet winter seasons. Planks had to be constantly replaced and mud was simply treacherous. As the 1850s progressed, some streets were regularly graded and re-planked, while a few of the more important byways such as Montgomery and Washington were laid with cobblestones.

The city was the life support system for the mining regions, but it couldn't just be a place where people bought what they needed and then took off. The men (and eventually their families) who ran the mercantile businesses wanted to have lives of their own. Most of them came from other cities and were used to a certain degree of economic and cultural amenities that they were not willing to live without. They also had to have faith that enough gold would be found, and over a long enough period of time, to sustain and grow local commerce. Even so, for the first few years of the rush, life in San Francisco was as much of a gamble as the games of poker and faro being dealt in its gaming halls.

Well before 1853 it was obvious the gold was going to keep flowing, and by that year the city had nearly everything that any new resident would need: 160 hotels, 66 restaurants and coffee saloons, 63 bakeries, 5 public markets, 43 private markets, 20 bathing houses, 15 flour and saw mills, 18 public stables, 19 banks, 10 public schools, 18 churches, 14 fire companies, 8 benevolent associations, and 200 lawyers.[3]

Historians have a term for the kind of meteoric urban growth that San

Francisco experienced: "instant city." But that term is misleading without its context. It implies expansion on the order of a mushroom springing up indiscriminately in an overwatered lawn. Powerful internal and external forces must be in place to mold a small space like San Francisco into the buzzing hub of the continent's western half. The Gold Rush got that started, but its concrete foundation was commerce.

At six o'clock in the morning on March 14, 1853, the *Isthmus* steamed through the Golden Gate into San Francisco Bay and landed on Central Wharf. Passengers collected their luggage and gave their names to the customs agent. And here is where the mystery of Levi's traveling companion enters the picture.

On the passenger list for the *Isthmus* are the words "Levi Strauss & svt." Levi was not likely to have traveled with a servant, which is what "svt" meant. But it's possible that his co-voyager had to travel in steerage, rather than in second class with Levi. Steerage passengers were rarely if ever listed by name on official documents. The two men probably stood together in front of the customs agent who, noting companions who did not travel in the same class, assumed that the disheveled man from steerage was Levi's servant. In any case, no one will ever know who that "svt" was, or whether he and Levi stayed in touch after arrival, or where this other man eventually ended up.

Once passengers were discharged, probably fairly soon despite the early hour, Levi wobbled off with his luggage and tried to get his land legs while taking in the sights. As he made his way down the pier he saw a major seaport, the third one of his life. In some respects, San Francisco's waterfront was no different from Bremerhaven or New York.

If he then looked west, he would have seen what was unique to his new city: graceful hills, slowly being covered with buildings, but some still in their natural form, seemingly painted against the bright blue sky. The city was enjoying unusually sunny and pleasant weather this first week in March, such a contrast to the icy winter Levi left behind in New York—and pleasanter still than the air of Panama, which even in the dry season could be sticky.

He was also surrounded by throngs of people who, early as it was, were gathering where the *Isthmus* was berthed. Some were waiting for the long-anticipated arrival of friends and family. Others were merchants, anxious for word from eastern business partners, or for the bales and boxes of goods they had ordered for their western customers. And others awaited mail from loved ones or newspapers from their home towns. With the ship tied up and ready for unloading, the crowds were also increased by the arrival of dock workers, shipping clerks, rackety, horse-drawn wagons, and porters, intent on their jobs. A steamer arrival was a time of great activity and emotion. In the words of contemporary observers,

> The expresses hurry off their packages, mails are landed, decks are cleared, and the passengers have all found a temporary lodging. The post-office establishment is meanwhile as busy as possible, arranging the letters for delivery. Merchants open their private boxes and find the all-important missives they looked for. Anxious crowds gather at the windows and with beating hearts ask for the longed-for, half-expected letters. The reader may readily imagine their mingled hopes and fears as the clerk answers their inquiries. He who is blessed with news from home tremblingly unfolds the precious epistle in the street, and devours, as it were, with gloating eyes, the substantial words. The disappointed seeker turns ruefully away, to hope for success next mail.[4]

As Levi walked down Central Wharf and looked around, he saw a mind-boggling variety of people and businesses. Within eyeball distance were the offices of ship brokers Scrutton & Hale, wharf manager William Ledley, commission merchant and importer William H. Mitchell, machinist P. Orman, and liquor importer John Roberts, to name a few.

After taking all this in, Levi needed to do a few things to get both his life and his business started. Given how the city's Jewish merchants kept in close contact with their friends and family back in New York, Levi probably had someone waiting for him to arrive. Letters could have been sent ahead of his sailing, to alert a merchant, a member of the local synagogue, or any number of Jewish citizens that a young man was on his way and needed assistance with housing and setting up his new firm.

Like the merchants who preceded him, Levi must have arrived with letters of introduction to these same locals. These letters would be addressed to someone in town, and on arrival, Levi would call on the recipient and hand him the letter. It would give Levi's name, the name of the mutual acquaintances in New York, and ask that he be given assistance in his new venture. A typical letter said something like this: "I shall deem it a personal favor if you would give him all the information and advice he may need, and introduce him to such persons as he may desire to know."[5]

Finding a place to live was at the top of Levi's list, and he could either have stayed with a local family—once he was introduced to them—or he could have stayed at a reasonably priced hotel, such as Isaac Hillman's Temperance Hotel on Davis Street. There were also many boardinghouses scattered near the waterfront. City directories don't give a home address for Levi until 1856 (and there was no directory printed in 1855), but that doesn't mean he wasn't comfortably housed somewhere close to the wharf.

He could also have been living at his wholesale warehouse. Some new arrivals slept in their stores "on a mattress and blanket where the fleas don't let me sleep."[6] Levi would have rented warehouse space right away, which was probably arranged for before he left New York. At first he just needed a place to hold the dry goods that Jonas and Louis were sending him via the *Winged Racer* (and future clippers), and perhaps some office room for managing his paperwork. But the main purpose for the space was to store and display the items his future customers would soon order.

Levi's first warehouse was possibly on California Street, between Sansome and Battery, surrounded by other commercial buildings catering to the needs of the waterfront. Sometime before the end of the year his new firm was located at 90 Sacramento Street, also between Sansome and Battery. This shows how well connected he and the brothers already were to local merchants and business practices. Battery Street was the only avenue connecting the main commercial district (roughly equivalent to the city's financial district today) with warehouses arranged all the way down to the waterfront. As a central location, it was nearly perfect. This was essential, because Levi's business was tied like a sailor's lanyard to the life of Yerba Buena Cove.

On March 30, the *Winged Racer* arrived at Central Wharf, after 106 days at sea. The cargo and its paperwork were handled by a local commission merchant, a task he performed for everyone who had goods on board consigned specifically to them. The *Winged Racer*'s goods were managed by Hussey, Bond & Hale, whose office was at 73 Sacramento Street, near Battery, just a block away from where Levi had set up shop. The next day Levi went to Hussey's offices to get the paperwork, pay the freight charges, and arrange to have the goods transported to his warehouse. He had to organize all this before 5:00 p.m., because at that exact hour Hussey's would close their doors for the day, and any unclaimed goods would be stored at the owner's risk and expense.

Hussey, Bond & Hale were not the only commission merchants in town, but they all served the same function. Hussey's competitors included F. C. Sanford, Alsop & Co., D. L. Ross & Co., F. Argenti & Co., and Crosby & Dibblee. These merchants also ran dockside auctions. Some eastern manufacturers sent holds full of goods to the city on spec; that is, they were not consigned to someone like Levi Strauss or other local wholesalers. They would bet on these merchants snapping up their goods on arrival at one of the many auctions held wharfside, but they wouldn't always win. For one thing, cargo sometimes landed in poor condition; long voyages in the hold of clipper ships led to mold growth, and even speedier shipments across Panama had the same problem.

Levi did have to be concerned about the condition of the dry goods that Jonas and Louis sent him, but he did not have to worry about outbidding other merchants for them. With his brothers as his partners, he could, once he got to know his market, ask them to send specific articles, which he would take possession of once they were dumped off the incoming boats. He may have attended the occasional auction though, especially once he had regular customers in place. There might have been an unusual item for sale now and then that he hadn't thought of or that was, for a short time, in great demand.

He knew what was coming for him on the *Winged Racer*, of course. He also knew that two more shipments were on their way to him from New York and what they contained. On January 8, a few months prior to Levi's own arrival, the ship *Celestial* had set sail with cargo consigned to "Levi & Strauss." As far as records show, there was no firm with this name in the city, so this was just a typo and was actually meant for Levi.

A few days before January 27, Levi and his brothers had collected another shipment of dry goods, which was loaded onto the clipper *Oriental,* leaving that day for San Francisco. Since the *Winged Racer* took about one hundred days to get to the city, Levi knew that the next two ships would show up sometime in early May.

With this information in hand, knowing that three shiploads of dry goods would start arriving at the end of March, he hit the pavement to find his first customers. The easiest and most efficient way to get started was simply to call on the retailers already established in San Francisco. Basic dry goods and clothing could have gone to F. Henderson on Sacramento, between Battery and Front, or to A. Bartol, on Montgomery between Washington and Merchant. Hotels and restaurants could also have been on his list, especially if white goods such as linens and towels were in his inventory. And if he managed also to bring in some fine frock coats and other elegant items, Keyes' Original Clothing Emporium, at 178 Clay Street, was another potential customer.

He had some stiff competition within the wholesale world, and even from among his fellow Jews. Some of them also had goods on the *Winged Racer:* Schloss Brothers, William Steinhardt, and Seligman & Co., among others. But the city, and the web that connected it to the hinterlands, was still growing, and there was plenty of business to go around.

Whether by accident or design, Levi arrived at the right time to make business connections. In 1850s San Francisco commerce ran on a seasonal schedule, very much tied to what was happening in the mining regions. Spring and fall were the busiest and most productive times for merchants, whether wholesale or retail. Ore production fell in the summer, as it rarely rained from July to September, and water levels fell. Water was essential to many mining operations, and the heat also affected miners' health. Things got busy again in the fall but only until the rains began in November or December. Roads between the city and the gold regions were still rudimentary and nearly impassible in the winter, whether because of mud or snow. These harsh conditions led to increased freight charges, and some merchants just stocked up for their local customers before the rainy season, which then began a new season of gold production. Nothing stopped the gold flowing into San Francisco, though.

Steamers to and from Panama were in port regularly, and mail from New York usually made it to San Francisco within three to four weeks. Levi had no doubt written to Jonas that he had arrived safely and that his shipments were also in hand. He also would have received a letter in mid-June or so, telling him that another consignment of dry goods would arrive in early September on the *Invincible,* which sailed at the end of May. Or, a later missive would have told Levi not only about the *Invincible*'s expected arrival but also about the *Young America,* which left New York in mid-June laden with more of the brothers' goods.

With the summer ahead of him and no more ships coming until September, Levi wrapped up his introductions to the local retailers and, if he followed the pattern of his predecessors, headed to the gold country. His first stop was most likely Sacramento, the gateway to the northern mining regions and a busy potential source of additional retail customers (it would become California's capital in 1854, further enhancing its importance). Getting there was no pleasure trip, though. Steamboats left from the Pacific Wharf at 4:00 p.m. for an overnight trip, arriving at the dock in Sacramento early the next morning. If they were on time, that is. The boats were frequently late, packed in more passengers than they should have, served questionable food and drink served by snarling waiters, and were not cheap. The trip across Panama was probably more pleasant.

Following arrival at the dock in Sacramento, the next ordeal was a stagecoach ride to one of dozens of gold country towns. This time of year the roads were dry and manageable, but the temperature was not. After the cool fogs of a San Francisco summer, Sacramento's searing heat was a shock. When ready, the coaches took off "with a whiz and a roar and a rattle," full of as many people as the proprietors could stuff inside.[7] Once his business was finished, Levi reversed the trip back to San Francisco.

Clothing retailers abounded in the towns of the northern mining region, and records from later years show that Levi had customers in Auburn,

Folsom, Downieville, and Sacramento proper, among others. Letters of introduction must have served him well here, too. But San Francisco was his base, and with more ships coming in September, and the fall buying season upon him, he would have stayed put for the rest of the year. Four more ships with dry goods consignments from Jonas and Louis came into the city between November 9 and December 13.

At some point Levi ordered the design and printing of billheads, which he used to invoice his growing list of retailers. And although he was in San Francisco representing J. Strauss & Brother, the name on those invoices was *Levi Strauss*.

In 1855 journalist and occasional politician Frank Soulé, along with John H. Gihon and James Nisbet, compiled and published a remarkable book called *The Annals of San Francisco*. This enormous tome recounted the history of the city from the early exploration period to the current day. It covered everything from the history of the post office, to benevolent institutions, to the great fires, to a month-by-month accounting of the events from 1853 to 1855, with copies of the California Constitution and the city's charter thrown in. It is a clear-headed look at San Francisco's personality, as well as history. In describing the city's life during 1853, the authors wrote that San Francisco was still, as in its early rowdy years, a place of "hard labor and wild delights."[8]

Levi was certainly experiencing the hard labor part of life in San Francisco. But what about its wild delights?

As Levi made his way through San Francisco's streets, he brushed past a diversity of humanity that he would never have encountered in the narrow cultural borders of Kleindeutschland. Men and women representing a vast scope of global geography strolled the avenues, shopped, ate in restaurants, rode public conveyances, and met visiting friends in hotels and boardinghouses: Chilean, Australian, Chinese, French, German, Hawaiian, English, and African American. This list was constantly being amended by new arrivals. Some of them gave up their professions in their home countries or home states, and took any kind of job in the city just to be near the gold fields or near that source of potential wealth in the city itself. Dentists turned to barbering, laborers tried their hand at running stores, clerks and lawyers became waiters.

And like New York, San Francisco wasn't just about work, and visitors frequently remarked on how much time residents spent in pleasurable pursuits. Theaters, public gardens, and traveling circuses were among the most popular entertainments across all ages and cultures.

But with all this jumbled humanity and jumbled priorities came desires left unfulfilled from previous lives. And they weren't always the most socially acceptable desires. San Francisco was not unique among cities in having a seedy side, of course. But there was a sense among those who spent time gambling, drinking, whoring, and taking opium that they could enjoy themselves more openly in this far western city than they could in New York, London, Santiago, or wherever else they were from.

The vortex of vice in San Francisco was the Barbary Coast, so named prior to the 1860s because its atmosphere and residents resembled the notorious pirate lair of the Barbary Coast of North Africa. The Barbary Coast was also the place where men were unwillingly "shanghaied" to work on outgoing ships heading, mostly, to China. The neighborhood was situated roughly where Pacific, Broadway, Washington, Montgomery, and Stockton Streets are today. Pacific was the place to go if you wanted to drink, watch half-naked women dance, or grab a cheap meal in a grimy restaurant.

The Barbary Coast was just about five blocks from Levi's warehouse. Would he have strolled over there to see the underside of his new home? Would he have partaken in any of its alluring activities? This will always be an open question, but history and a look at some of his activities make this unlikely. Another deterrent to vice was his faith.

A young Jewish man like Levi could go to a strange city like San Francisco and know that if he needed help starting his business, if he got into trouble, or if he got sick, there were safety nets in place to keep him from going under. His fellow Jews, having been in San Francisco since 1849, had started up organizations that provided both real and emotional support to new arrivals. The first Jewish services were held in September 1849, and about the same time the First Hebrew Benevolent Society was organized by Poles from Prussia to provide care and comfort for sick or needy Jews.

Less than a year later, a group of Bavarian Jews created the Eureka Benevolent Society, which had the same aims. Founder and guiding spirit August Helbing was a dry goods dealer, and he understood first hand that the only activities available to young men in the early years were gambling, or theatricals, or worse. Unwilling, for the most part, to engage in socially deviant behavior, Jewish men spent their evenings in their stores or warehouses, thinking about their families, and wondering why they were there. Participating in benevolent societies, helping their fellows, gave young Jews a sense of social accomplishment and personal fulfillment, even as they knew they might need charitable services themselves someday.

By 1851 Jews also had two synagogues to choose from. Both Temple Emanu-El and Sherith Israel were opened in April of that year and were attended by locals along cultural lines. Sherith Israel's congregation was made up mostly of Prussian, Polish, and Russian Jews, while Emanu-El saw its ranks filled for the most part with Bavarians. Both synagogues began their lives in rented storefronts on Kearny Street. Levi was a member of congregation Emanu-El and attended his first Passover in San Francisco the third week of April, 1853. In late summer 1854 a new Temple Emanu-El was dedicated on Broadway between Mason and Powell Streets (where the Broadway Tunnel is today). This was near a fashionable residential district where many Jewish merchants lived and was a short walk to their stores or warehouses.

Worshippers in San Francisco experienced less anti-Semitism in their new city than any other place they had lived, but it still simmered. On the one hand, newspapers and city leaders praised the Jews for their hard work and good citizenship, noting that they were rarely drunk or disruptive. However, some visitors were surprised at how well respected the city's Jews were. Many had come from cities where Jews were still seen as the "other" and were not used to the relative equality they enjoyed in San Francisco. While they were not fully integrated into the social structure of Gentile San Francisco, no barrier of prejudice was in their way, and Jews were able to achieve astonishing and rapid commercial success.

In her book *920 O'Farrell Street: A Jewish Girlhood in Old San Francisco,* author Harriet Lane Levy, who was born in 1867, described the Jewish merchants her father and their neighbors knew and did business with: "As soon as they accumulated a little money they came to the city, became wholesale merchants, jobbers, or manufacturers, acquiring prestige and complacency as they rose . . . Each had a paying business, a family, a house and lot, and some money in the bank. Each stood firm on his feet, looked the world straight in the eye, and knew that he measured up well by the standard of God and man."[9]

This is not to say that Jews didn't know how to have a good time. In June 1853 the *demimonde,* the marketplace, and San Francisco's elite joined forces to raise money for charity and provide entertainment both titillating and tame.

Lola Montez had come to town.

Irish-born Marie Gilbert began a career as a dancer when she left Ireland to seek instruction in Spain. She performed in London, throughout Europe, and all the way to Russia. She deserted the army officer she married before her career took off and collected lovers wherever she danced, including the composer Franz Lizst. Her most famous paramour was King Ludwig I of Bavaria, who named her Baroness Rosenthal and Countess of Landsfeld, and installed her in a palace, where she encouraged him to institute liberal reforms in his kingdom. When he was sent into exile because of these ideas, she left both him and Bavaria. She then went through a marriage ceremony with a rich Englishman, and in 1851 fetched up in New York. There she turned to dancing again and, calling herself Lola Montez, became famous for her erotic (for the time) "Spider Dance."

Despite her salacious reputation, Montez was also known for giving benefit performances. In January 1851 she danced to aid the New York Firemen's Welfare Fund, and a few weeks later did the same to help injured fire fighters in Philadelphia. Then, in May 1853, she crossed the Isthmus of Panama with her future husband, Patrick Hull (though it's not clear she had actually divorced her first), whom she met on the boat, and arrived in San Francisco on May 21.

Soon after she landed, Montez was approached about doing a benefit for the First Hebrew Benevolent Society. She was already booked to perform with some local actors and a traveling Bohemian violinist named Miska

Hauser and, of course, to do the Spider Dance. She agreed, and one of the society's directors, M. Barnett, a local clothing dealer, wrote an open letter to Montez in the *Daily Alta California* newspaper to thank her. The date was fixed for June 9 at the American Theatre, on Sansome Street between California and Sacramento. Highly convenient for nearby merchants, it had just been renovated and could now accommodate nearly three thousand people.

Although all who attended enjoyed the entire evening of theater performances and music, they were there to see Lola Montez do her Spider Dance. And it is easy to imagine that Levi Strauss, along with other young, unmarried Jewish men, was also in the audience that night, which was described as crowded to excess. The benefit raised $3,456 for the Society, equivalent to nearly $90,000 today.[10]

Over the next two years, Levi continued to build his business, and fell into a comfortable commercial routine of taking in shipments from his brothers and finding new customers.

Only two ships (that we know of) brought goods for the business during 1854. The following year was busier. Between April and December of 1855, seven ships came into port with goods for Levi Strauss. And in July, Levi made the first shipment of gold back to New York to fill the coffers of J. Strauss & Brother and to pay for future shipments of dry goods. That month he sent $10,041 to Jonas on the steamer *Cortes,* equivalent to nearly $250,000 today.

What's remarkable about this activity is that in February 1855, a financial panic brought much of San Francisco's business to its knees, though the problems had started in the fall of the previous year. Property owner and builder of a wharf he named for himself, Henry Meiggs, had a lot of loans that he could not repay. In October 1854 he skipped town for South America, leaving enormous debts behind him and causing city bankers to become very nervous.

At the same time, a dry winter meant less water in the gold regions, which meant less gold to mine and deposit into San Francisco banks. The banks could therefore not make loans, or they made them with exorbitant interest rates. When a railroad supported by investments of the bank of

Page, Bacon & Company went under, the bank—one of California's two largest—did too. This was followed by the failure of Adams and Company, California's other largest bank. A run on San Francisco's banks caused nearly two hundred bankruptcies. Though the city had financial ties to New York and other urban centers, the Panic of 1855 was, for the most part, a local phenomenon, thanks to the city's economic anarchy in the first years of the Gold Rush.

Despite the panic, Levi sent five more boatloads of gold to New York between August and December, making a grand total for the year of a little over $80,000 ($2 million in today's currency). This pile of money was worthy of the word used to describe it: treasure.

CHAPTER 6

STEAMER DAY

In the nineteenth century, "treasure" was the all-inclusive word for gold, gold dust, gold bars, gold and silver coins, or anything you could use to buy goods or services. During the California Gold Rush, it was also used to describe the gold coming out of rivers and mines. This makes sense, because the word conjures up the excitement of sudden and surprising wealth, something sparkling and magical.

To merchants, though, treasure was a commodity that could literally slip through their fingers. Until a branch of the U.S. Mint opened in San Francisco in 1854, and began supplying California's coinage needs two years later, the only medium of exchange was gold dust or privately minted coins. By the middle of that decade, after the government authorized an Assay Office for the city, gold bars became the best way to ship treasure to eastern bank vaults.

Gold—as dust or unrefined metal—was always an important medium of exchange, though. Customers who shopped the retail stores in the mountain towns, which sold dry goods, cigars, liquors, clothing, fancy goods, farm equipment, and hardware, paid for their purchases in gold dust. The store owners would use the dust to pay their own suppliers, employing a method unique to the Gold Rush: they gathered up enough dust to pay a small collection of invoices from their own suppliers and sent both the paperwork and the gold to one of their main San Francisco purveyors, such as Levi Strauss.

Levi had a scale in his office to weigh the dust and figure out its value according to purity and the current rates. Generally gold dust circulated at $17.50 an ounce in the early years of Levi's business. After weighing and measuring the dust, he would then use it to pay off all of his customer's miscellaneous bills, depositing the remainder to his account as credit against that customer's future business. In essence, Levi and other merchants acted as bankers for their own customers.

Gold dust wasn't the only form of currency in town. There were plenty of coins in circulation in California, as private mints produced enough gold to meet all commercial and personal needs. Until 1859, foreign coins were legal tender throughout the United States. However, U.S. Customs duties had to be paid in U.S. gold coin.

Although the extravagant prices of the early Gold Rush years had fallen, the cost of living in San Francisco was still on the high side. Meats cost about 38 cents a pound ($10 today), butter was $1 a pound ($27), a dozen eggs fetched $1.25 ($34), and monthly rent for basic housing could be as high as $20 ($500 dollars).[1]

Running a business could be just as expensive. There was so much to pay for: insurance against the loss of goods while they were being shipped, water damage from the voyage, and the sad but inevitable problem of theft. Freight rates from New York to San Francisco could be anywhere from 10 to 50 percent of the value of one's consigned cargo. But that wasn't the end of it. After the steamer arrived in port, merchants had to pay fees to pilots, the harbormaster, and the wharf owners. Then, men like Levi had to hand over custom duties, pay for the cost of transporting the shipment from the boat to the warehouse, rent on the warehouse itself, and finally, an annual city license, which fluctuated according to a merchant's monthly receipts. To make things more complicated, federal law prohibited payment of import duties with gold dust until 1854. So merchants had to import U.S. gold and silver coins from the East just to pay the local custom house.

All of this made one or two days during the month the most important ones in the calendar. They were known as "Steamer Day." Twice per month, when the Panama and Nicaragua steamers left port, merchants scurried to call in all outstanding debts, pay off their own, and send treasure, letters, and orders to eastern partners or suppliers. San Francisco merchants gave generous credit to their customers in the mining regions, but cash was due by Steamer Day, the day the boats left the dock, heading south.

At the same time, the boats brought in business and personal correspondence, information on eastern markets, and the necessary coinage. Very little actual business was transacted on Steamer Day, as merchants were too busy running around to collect as much money, and as many orders, as possible. Which wasn't always easy. As one merchant lamented, "What should have been paid before last steamer-day not yet forthcoming!—what was a *cash* transaction two days ago not yet settled for! Why, it was shameful, unbusiness-like, atrocious conduct! Where did such people expect to go to when they died?"[2]

In September 1858, Steamer Day fell on Yom Kippur, the Day of Atonement. In order to allow Jewish merchants to observe the holiday, it was postponed by city officials. This gesture was a testament to how important Jewish businesses were to the city's overall economy. The *Daily Alta California,* the newspaper most sympathetic to commerce, approved the move, saying that Jews were respected and esteemed by all.[3]

Henry J. Labatt, a San Francisco lawyer and journalist, agreed with this assessment of his cultural countrymen, attributing it to a number of factors. In an article he wrote for the newspaper *Voice of Israel* in 1856, he observed, "This position they have not acquired without great attention, honesty, industry and personal sacrifice, and by unremitting prudence and civility; and they seem determined to add to it dignity and wealth." He also pointed out how practical Jewish merchants were: "They seldom pay unwarrantable rents, being willing to submit to many inconveniences rather than indulge in extravagance." And he hailed California as a place of unheard-of freedom for Jews. "Nowhere in America is the Jew so well understood and so readily appreciated as in this State."[4]

Although Henry Labatt appreciated the lessening of the bonds of prejudice in the West, this attitude wasn't universal. It was a good description of the more successful of the city's Jewish merchants, but that doesn't mean continued success was easy. Getting a good credit rating, for example, was not a given.

The ratings firm R. G. Dun & Company, the forerunner of Dun & Bradstreet, nearly always mentioned whether a merchant was a Jew or an "Israelite" when it wrote up its credit reports. It and other similar firms automatically assumed that Jews were a poor credit risk. A typical report said something like this: "They are Hebrews. May be good [for credit] *if well watched;* they are *tricky.*"[5] Unless the descriptor was modified into something like "White Jew" or "Israelite of the better classes," anyone reading the Dun report might think twice about extending credit to a Jewish-run business. This could be a problem, for a good credit rating was crucial to extending a customer base beyond one's fellow Jews. Levi Strauss and his brothers probably had less of a problem than some in obtaining a good rating, because partnerships were looked upon more favorably than single proprietors, since they generated a larger amount of business.

By 1856, the Strauss family partnership in New York had changed its name, reflecting Levi's success in starting up and keeping the West Coast branch of the business afloat in the face of very difficult circumstances. By the end of that year, the firm was no longer called Jonas Strauss or J. Strauss & Brother. It was now J. Strauss Brother & Co.

This change in company name coincided with another big change in Levi's life. Sometime during the previous year, his sister Fanny, her husband David, and their two children joined him in San Francisco.

There were many reasons for the Sterns to make this move. Fanny was Levi's only full sibling. Jonas and Louis had always been a part of her life, but they were just half-brothers. As her family grew, she might have wanted her children to know their uncle. Also, if Levi's business was expanding, he would need help, and bringing a brother-in-law into the firm was not only traditional but also practical: he wouldn't have to hire a clerk with unknown abilities. Having his sister and her family with him would be both professionally and personally rewarding.

David and Fanny Stern's first child, Jacob, was born in New York in 1851, and their second, Caroline, in 1853. However, in between these years, it's possible that David was not spending a lot of time in the city.

In 1852, William Sahlein, the husband of Fanny and Levi's half-sister Mary, had an account in the New York Emigrant Savings Bank that was held in trust for Fanny Stern. This was a safety net for Fanny in case something happened to David. He may have been away from New York peddling or looking for work in another city. Accident or disease could make Fanny a widow rather quickly, so it makes sense that she would have funds available and that a male relative would manage them for her. The money itself either came from her husband or possibly even her brothers.

Sometime around May 1855 Fanny was pregnant again. Her third child, Henry, was born in San Francisco in February 1856, meaning that the family had relocated to the city the previous year. With the completion of the Panama Railroad across the entire isthmus in January 1855, the trip from east to west was materially easier. Travelers still had to take two steamer voyages, but those were more manageable now, even with two children under the age of four. Crossing from one ocean to another via Panama on a railroad, in a boat, and on a mule, as Levi did, however, was untenable for a young family. In advertisements, the Panama Railroad crowed that it was "The Only Safe and Reliable Route."

Rebecca likely came to San Francisco with the Sterns. With Fanny gone, there could be little to keep her in New York, despite the good relationship with her stepsons. Having her along would also be helpful in managing the children.

After their arrival, the Sterns, and probably Rebecca, moved in with Levi at his place on Minna Street, in today's South of Market area, between Mission and Howard, the first separate home address on record for him. The business was now at 62 or 63 Sacramento Street, still near the waterfront, about two miles from home, and an easy ride on a city omnibus. And by the following year brother Louis was also in San Francisco, living with the family. The men were not just there just to keep Levi company; they were now part of the company. Yet the company was still called simply Levi Strauss in San Francisco records, even though the New York City directories referred to the business as J. Strauss Brother & Co.

The year 1856 proved an interesting one. Levi shipped over $200,000 in treasure to New York, worth an astonishing $5 million today. And that spring, he, David, and Louis were involved in the largest movement of its kind in American history: the 1856 Committee of Vigilance.

This was actually the second such committee to be formed in San Francisco. The first, organized in June 1851, was a response to a poorly staffed and largely toothless police force and an easily bought judiciary system. At least seven hundred men, half of them merchants and many of them Jews and founding members of Temple Emanu-El, had joined the hastily created committee that summer. One of their goals was to rid the city of the Sydney Ducks, thugs of mostly Irish descent who arrived in San Francisco via Australia, where many had been residents of that country's penal colony. But there was lawlessness in general throughout the city, and in the space of one month, the committee brought ninety men before its officers, handed some over to local authorities, banished a few more, had one man whipped and four publicly hanged. The committee then disbanded, feeling it had done what was right for San Francisco. Many citizens and public officials agreed with them.

Crime did go down for a while, and life went on. But within a few years amnesia took hold and citizens began to complain again about an increase in crime and how city government did not put any long-term measures in place to prevent it after 1851. In addition, the city leaders did not do a good job of keeping prices and taxes under control, which was a headache for San Francisco's merchants. Because of the way the state constitution was written, individual cities in California had something called "home rule," meaning they could make their own laws as long as they did not violate the U.S. Constitution. In San Francisco, that meant a doubling of both taxes and city expenses by 1856. Fires, bank failures, and the dumping of unwanted goods by merchants unable to sell them did not keep elected officials from raising taxes and imposing new license fees on all business owners.

Between 1850 and 1856, San Francisco politics were under the thumb of a Democratic Party machine headed by David Broderick, who had cut his teeth in New York's Tammany Hall. Merchants accused him of stuffing ballot boxes and pandering to both immigrants and political patrons. Those on the receiving end of city fees accused Broderick and his entire party of bankrupting San Francisco.

Merchants had not paid much attention to politics before this time, although they complained about rising crime and prices. Some men served on local councils, and others were encouraged to run for political office in order to get "good" men into place in City Hall. That was a slow process, and the merchants did not have enough influence to make what they saw were needed reforms or to challenge the seats of power. That changed suddenly in the spring of 1856, though the momentum began the previous year.

On the evening of November 16, 1855, U.S. Marshal William Richardson and his wife attended a performance at the American Theatre. They were aghast when they saw local gambler Charles Cora and his mistress Belle (a well-known prostitute) seated nearby. Richardson asked the management to remove them, but they were allowed to stay, and Richardson felt his wife had been insulted by having to sit near a woman who was getting leers from the other patrons.

The next night Richardson and Cora met on the street, and by some witness accounts they seemed at first to have resolved their simmering antipathy. But Cora suddenly pulled out a pistol and shot Richardson dead in front of a store on Clay Street near Montgomery, in the heart of the financial district.

Cora was quickly arrested, placed into the custody of the city marshal, and locked up in the county jail. There was some rumbling about lynching, but most citizens wanted Cora to be tried according to law. He stayed in jail for the next few months, and when he finally came to trial, his plea of self-defense had traction with some of the jurors. The case ended in a hung jury on January 17, 1856, and Cora went back to jail to await his second trial.

While this was going on, a failed banker turned crusading newspaper editor named James King "of William" was also getting noticed. King (the "of William" was added to differentiate himself from the other James Kings in town) started the *Daily Evening Bulletin* after the failure of Adams & Co., where he had been a banker. He understood how hard it was to make a living in San Francisco and published many stories (sometimes a bit exaggerated) about the corrupt Broderick political machine.

After the Cora trial, King began to write articles blasting Cora, blaming Broderick's party for the hung jury, and for the shooting of Richardson in the first place. He then learned that James P. Casey, editor of the rival *Sunday Times,* had been elected to the town council because he had stuffed the ballot box in his precinct. King exposed the fraud and then reported that Casey was also an ex-con who had served time in Sing Sing prison in New York.

Casey demanded a retraction, but King said he would print the evidence in an upcoming issue of the paper. Casey responded to this by threatening to shoot King the next time he saw him. Unfazed, King said he would be leaving his office at the *Bulletin* at the usual time the following day, May 14, 1856. True to his word he left his office on schedule. He had only walked a few steps down Montgomery Street when Casey appeared in front of him, ordered him to defend himself, then raised a pistol and fired directly at King's chest, where the bullet punctured and passed through a lung. Still upright, King stumbled and was then helped by horrified witnesses into the nearby Pacific Express office, where they called upon doctors for assistance. Casey's supporters took him to the only place he would be safe from a mob: the city jail. Less than an hour later, the streets around the jail were swarming with a furious crowd.

The sheriff came out to talk to the assembly and swore that Casey would receive a fair trial. This was met with incredulous hoots and threats of lynching. Many in the crowd had been part of the 1851 Committee of Vigilance, and knew that calm heads and quick organization were needed.

Circulars advertising a mass meeting were printed and distributed, and a few hundred men showed up at a vacant warehouse on Battery Street. No action was taken, but another meeting was held the next morning on the second floor of a building at Sacramento and Front Streets, just a block and a half from Levi's warehouse. A new committee was formed, and between six and eight thousand men became members. By far the largest group came from the merchant class, and they pledged an enormous amount of money for operating expenses.

Business stagnated as the members did military drills to prepare for the committee's work. The fact that merchants had left their offices indicates just how much they felt the Broderick machine needed to be stopped and the economic oppression halted. The Sacramento Street headquarters were then fortified with bags of sand and dubbed "Fort Gunnybags."

On May 16, California governor J. Neely Johnson arrived in San Francisco to plead with the committee members to allow Casey to be tried in a lawful court. The vigilantes pointed out that the courts were run by men like Casey and Broderick and justice would not be served. Then, on May 18, the committee ordered that Casey and, because he was also a Broderick crony, Charles Cora, be brought to Fort Gunnybags for trial. The next day, a mass of men took up positions in front of the jail, and the sheriff, without resistance, handed the men over.

On the night of May 20, Casey and Cora's cases went under deliberation, and during the proceedings, James King of William died of his gunshot wound. Both prisoners were found guilty of murder. The city put on a magnificent funeral for King on the 22nd, and the two killers were hanged at Fort Gunnybags on May 23.

Over the next few weeks the committee rounded up men they considered suspicious and reviewed their crimes. They hanged two more, deported twenty-five, and ordered the rest banished from the city. The committee held a "Grand Review" on August 18, and by the 21st the leaders felt that they had done sufficient work to warrant disbanding the Committee of Vigilance.

Merchants turned to vigilantism because they felt powerless over market and political conditions. After asserting themselves as a committee and seeing how much they could accomplish as a group, they moved further into the political arena, not because they were interested in politics but because political action was the only way to keep business in business. Merchants in general, and Jewish ones in particular, began nominating candidates for the new People's Party, in direct defiance of Broderick. After the November elections, party members were in the majority of the board of supervisors, the office of the sheriff, and the mayor.

Jewish merchants were front and center in the 1856 Committee of Vigilance, as they had been five years earlier. They showed their support for the aims of the committee in many ways. After James King of William died, the sanctuary at Temple Emanu-El was draped in black, and an extra service was held for him to say kaddish, the Jewish mourning ritual. And many of the officers of the committee, such as journalist and Emanu-El board member Seixas Solomons, were important and influential local Jews. Albert Dibblee, a respected merchant who had come to San Francisco the same year as Levi, was one of the biggest donors to the committee.

Presumably Levi, Louis, and David were at the very least supportive of the aims of the Vigilance Committee, and at the most served as officers or active members. Whatever their personal feelings about vigilante justice, they stood with the merchants, they stood with their fellow Jews, and, in doing so, helped make San Francisco into the kind of city where they could continue to prosper.

By the following year, there was more family news. In October 1857 Fanny gave birth to another son, Sigmund. And William Sahlein, though still living with his wife Mary and their children in New York, was now associated with J. Strauss Brother & Co.

The business was increasing, too. The California Board of Equalization published a list of the city's personal property assessments in the August 20 edition of the *San Francisco Evening Bulletin*. Levi (spelled "Levy" in the listing) Strauss was worth $20,000, equivalent to nearly $500,000 today. One reason for Levi's prosperity was his diligence in collecting outstanding debts. Two of his customers, J. C. Eddy & Co. and H. Witkowsky & Bro., went bankrupt in 1857 and owed Levi Strauss $326 and $3,000 respectively. When necessary, as it was with Witowsky, Levi had the firms served with an attachment by the local sheriff in order to recover the money owed him.

By August 1857 Levi had shipped $156,000 in treasure to Jonas in New York. On the twentieth of that month, his brother Louis arranged for $76,000 (nearly $2 million today) to be loaded onto the steamship *Sonora*, headed for Panama. This gold shipment, and those belonging to Levi's competitors, along with mail and passengers, crossed the isthmus on the railroad to the coastal town of Aspinwall. Everything and everyone was then loaded onto the steamer *Central America*, and on September 4 the ship headed into the Caribbean toward Havana, where it would spend one night. On September 8 the *Central America* was on its way again, steaming up the East Coast toward New York.

On October 22 the steamer *Panama* arrived in San Francisco bearing passengers, mail, clothing, dry goods, and terrible news. The *Central America* had gone down in a hurricane 130 miles off Cape Hatteras, along the North Carolina shore, on September 12, with the loss of over four hundred passengers, and all the cargo and treasure. This was a "great and sorrowful calamity" for San Francisco, as many people in the city had friends or relatives among the dead. For merchants, it was a financial catastrophe. More than thirty companies or individual business owners had sent a total of $1.5 million dollars in treasure on the ship, a value of nearly $40 million today.

As the *Central America* was making its way up the East Coast, rumblings of a financial debacle that would be named the Panic of 1857 had already started to surface. In August the New York branch of the Ohio Life Insurance and Trust Company had gone under when it was discovered that all of the company's capital had been embezzled. The firm had also speculated in railroads, which defaulted on their debts. City bankers immediately restricted loans and other basic transactions, and on the street this translated into inevitable collapse. Panicked investors began to sell stocks, and merchants struggled as manufactured goods sat unsold in warehouses. Hundreds of companies went out of business.

The loss of the *Central America* meant that over a million dollars in gold was now at the bottom of the Atlantic and not in New York bank vaults. Thanks to the new technology of the telegraph, news of the disaster sped from New York to New Orleans. Depositors began to withdraw their accounts at a frightening rate, and the entire American economy shriveled. It took nearly two years for a recovery to take hold.

The effects were felt in San Francisco too, of course. Wholesalers who lost money could not buy more goods if their credit was not top notch, with Jews somewhat at a disadvantage because of the prejudice that firms like R. & G. Dun held toward them. And it was difficult if not impossible to collect debts from local customers if they had also been affected by the disaster.

Overall, however, San Francisco weathered the panic well. The city was not dependent on or strongly linked to the kinds of businesses, such as railroads, that were failing in the East. San Francisco commerce was about the everyday: clothing, dry goods, cigars, liquors, books, groceries, and so forth. These commodities had less volatile foundations.

Levi Strauss survived and actually prospered. Because his suppliers were his own brothers, he did not have to worry about saving his credit rating with an eastern jobber. Jonas continued to send him consignments of dry goods, and between October and December of 1857, Levi shipped an additional $138,000 in treasure to New York. In fact, Levi was listed as one of the "heaviest shippers" on the manifest of the *John L. Stephens* steamship on November 21, 1857, along with Benjamin Davidson & Co., bankers and agents for the European Rothschilds; Parrott & Co. and Wells Fargo, both bankers; and James Patrick & Co., importers of wines, liquors, and cigars. As R. & G. Dun noted, partnerships, and specifically family partnerships, were a good credit risk, even if they were Jews.

A fair portion of San Francisco's merchant class was led by Jewish men who were respected by their peers both within their faith and outside of it. But they weren't all solid citizens. Levi, David, Louis, and the other Jewish families frequently saw one of the city's most colorful characters when they attended services at Temple Emanu-El. He was Joshua Abraham Norton, known to everyone in the city as Norton I, "Emperor of the United States and Protector of Mexico."

Born in England, Norton and his family lived for many years in South Africa, where his father had a business selling supplies for the shipping industry. After his father's death, Norton decided to try his luck in California and arrived in San Francisco in 1849. Like Levi, he became a merchant and invested in real estate as well. He had assets worth $5 million in today's currency. In 1852 he attempted to corner the rice market and ended up losing almost everything. He tried to keep afloat but filed for bankruptcy in 1856, eventually living in a workingman's boardinghouse, making a marginal living as a commission agent. No one noticed that he was also losing his mind.

In September 1859, Norton visited the editor of the *San Francisco Bulletin* and asked him to print a proclamation announcing his ascendancy to the throne as "Norton I." It was the first of many such documents, and it marked the beginning of the last twenty years of his life, during which time the restaurants, hotels, theaters, banks, and all public spaces and public officials in the city—including the police—allowed him to live within his sad delusion.

Norton took a keen interest in politics and issued decrees dissolving

Congress, dismissing the governor of Virginia for hanging John Brown, abolishing the Democratic and Republican parties and, presciently, ordering a survey to determine if a bridge could be built between Oakland and San Francisco. (It could: the San Francisco–Oakland Bay Bridge opened in 1936, and from that day to this, people throughout the Bay Area have lobbied to have it renamed the Emperor Norton Bridge.)

Although he was a member of Emanu-El, and many Jewish merchants helped support him with money or goods, Norton was too eccentric for the more conservative elements at the temple. When he died in 1880, officials denied him burial in a Jewish cemetery.

This aberration aside, participating in the tenets of his faith was as important to Levi and his fellow merchants as keeping up with gold prices. But there were obligations beyond attending services, and one that Levi took seriously was *tzedakah,* or the duty to help the less fortunate as a means of spreading righteousness and justice through the world. In addition to supporting the efforts of the Hebrew Benevolent Society in 1853, which assisted widows, orphans, and the destitute, Levi also subscribed five dollars ($125 today) to the San Francisco Orphan Asylum Society the following year. This Protestant charity was organized in 1851 to care for children who were orphaned because of cholera epidemics and other disasters. It is interesting that Levi chose to support a non-Jewish organization, and it also makes sense. With this donation, he both fulfilled the precepts of his faith and contributed to the future of his new city through support of its children, no matter their faith.

Jewish benevolent associations arose in response to the unique conditions Jews found in San Francisco. Although it was rapidly becoming a modern city, it was still remote. Many of its citizens seemed interested only in material wealth, and it was a hard place to make a living. Local Jews needed the strong bonds of faith and benevolence, not only for those in the city but for other Jews now moving further into the western states and territories. Without these ties, they would still be in a golden land, but they would be adrift.

CHAPTER 7

TREASONABLE COMBINATIONS

L evi ended the decade of the 1850s with a preview of his own future. In addition to enjoying continued commercial success and participating in the activities of his faith, he started to buy stock or become an officer in businesses outside of his own, served on juries, snatched up valuable real estate, expanded his philanthropy, and became interested in politics.

By the end of 1857, Levi not only had warehouse space in the important downtown district but also had a separate office a couple of blocks away. Shipments of goods coming in, and shipments of treasure going out, continued to remain steady, and Levi was still one of the top shippers in the city. By the end of the 1860s he was also receiving goods from the Pacific Northwest via the steamers that sailed regularly up and down the Pacific Coast. Rather than delivering New York–made dry goods, these shipments consisted of items such as raw wool, which Levi could sell to local manufacturers in exchange for a discount on the finished wool products or garments for his own wholesale stock.

But there were also losses, and as with the *Central America* in 1857, they were tied to disasters at sea. In August 1862, the cause was fire, not storm. The steamer *Golden Gate*, carrying passengers, mail, and treasure from Panama to New York, caught fire in its galley just over three miles from Aspinwall and burned to the hull. Over 175 people were drowned, and all of the papers and gold went to the bottom of the Caribbean. Levi Strauss lost $95,000 on the *Golden Gate*, one of the highest losses of anyone in San Francisco.

This was an even greater loss to the coffers of the United States. For nearly eighteen months the country had been at war, since the newly formed Confederacy had fired on Fort Sumter in April 1861, commencing the Civil War (also known then as the War Between the States or the War of Northern Aggression, depending on your viewpoint). The conflict would have less destructive but still profound effects on far-off California than on eastern states, and the merchants of San Francisco took a keen interest in the unfolding events.

On April 24, 1861, the Pony Express brought shattering news into San Francisco: Confederate forces had captured Fort Sumter, initiating, in the words of the *Daily Alta California,* "what may be a most disastrous war between the United States and the Cotton Confederacy."[1] The next day, a huge crowd gathered on Portsmouth Square, and brewing fears about slavery, secession, and imminent war were now discussed in broad daylight.

A number of Republican clubs had been formed during the 1860 election, when Abraham Lincoln was barely elected president. The split in San Francisco's politics was revealed in the city's election results: only 50 percent of voters went for Lincoln. And when the South seceded, these men put more energy into their clubs to fight what they saw as a threat from southern sympathizers. Many of them were veterans of one or both of the vigilance committees of the previous decade, and they used the organizational skills they had honed in that experience to wage a battle against what they saw was a threat to the Union.

The threat was real. Although slavery had been outlawed in California under the Compromise of 1850, southerners who had come to the state during the Gold Rush occasionally bemoaned their financial losses, believing they couldn't get ahead without their slaves. Few men openly defended slavery in San Francisco, but there were many who wished they could. They also wished they could hand over California to Jefferson Davis. Some of these men were state officials, and some were preachers who used their pulpit to further southern politics. There were many pro-Confederacy agitators outside of San Francisco as well, in remote areas where they could talk and agitate more openly.

Far from the fighting, the city was abuzz with war talk and war worries.

Most if not all of the city's municipal leaders were pro-Union, and even before the news arrived about Fort Sumter, they began to organize. They wrote to Washington to express their fears that the military officer in charge of the federal troops of the Department of the Pacific, General Albert Sidney Johnston, was too southern in his sympathies. Everyone knew the general thought the western states should secede before war was declared. He was dangerous, and San Francisco wanted him gone. Washington felt the same way; Johnston was recalled (his proactive resignation crossed in the mail with these orders), and General Edwin V. Sumner was sent in his place. Sumner arrived in San Francisco the very day the Pony Express first reached the city.

On Saturday, May 11, a massive pro-Union rally was held in San Francisco, dubbed "The Great Union Demonstration." A reviewing stand was built at the junction of Market, Post, and Montgomery Streets, facing the bay. Processions weaved through the downtown streets, ending at the corner meeting place: bands and military regiments such as the City Guards and the National Guard, as well as General Sumner and his staff in shiny carriages, paraded past the stand, followed by city officials, judges, members of the Society of California Pioneers (limited to those who came to California before 1850), the Fire Department, workingmen's associations, and a wagon, on the side of which was a cloth bearing the motto "Treason is but for a day / Our country is for all time / Sumter, the cradle of patriotism / Shall be the tomb of treason."[2] Individual citizens followed behind, and wherever the procession moved, they passed homes and businesses decorated with flags and spectators waving handkerchiefs. An estimated twenty-five thousand people came out to cheer for the Union.

Speech followed speech: politicians; the general himself; representatives of the pro-Democratic governor, John Downey; and religious leaders. Officials offered resolutions to further the cause of supporting and protecting the Union, one of which, approved unanimously by the cheering throngs, was the formation of a "Union Committee of Thirty-four":

> Resolved, That a Union Committee of Thirty-four for the city and county of San Francisco be appointed by this meeting; that said Committee have power to fill vacancies in their number; and that we

recommend to the other countries of the State the appointment of a similar Committee for each county, said Committees to be organized without reference to politics or any political object, but solely to aid the constituted authorities in the detection and suppression of any treasonable combinations or conspiracies against the Union and the public peace.[3]

The thirty-four men later named to serve on the committee included merchants, bankers, industrialists, and capitalists. And one of them was Levi Strauss.

This committee grew out of a worry that southern sympathizers could not be easily spotted. As historian Horace Davis wrote in 1861, "Your next door neighbor might be a Southern man. You traded together, met on the floor of the Exchange, belonged to the same church or lodge, your families were intimate, meeting constantly in social matters, and yet in public affairs he was an enemy, may be a spy. Extreme vigilance was necessary to meet the plotters in our very midst."[4]

Of the total number of men in the group three of them, including Levi, were Jewish merchants. They didn't represent a voting bloc, or even the same philosophical or political beliefs. Throughout the country Jews thought and voted as individuals, and some were neutral about the war and even about slavery. But in San Francisco as in other urban areas, most Jews believed that the expansion of slavery and the destruction of the Union would be not only bad for business but bad for them as new citizens.

One man, speaking for his fellow Jews in a letter to the *Daily Alta California*, explained, "As an American citizen, I feel it is my bounden duty to sustain with all my might that government which furnishes me protection at home and abroad, and I consider it the greatest calamity that could befall the human race, if traitors were suffered to break it up and destroy it."[5] The generally equal opportunity that Jews enjoyed could only happen in a United States which remained whole. And the word "protection" is telling. Memories of life in the Old World took long to fade.

Soon after the committee began its work, it organized a Home Guard. The city felt vulnerable after the regular army troops stationed at the Presidio, at the entrance to the Golden Gate, were dispatched to the fighting back east. With General Sumner's blessing, the group of men, about three thousand strong, performed military drills and lobbied to elect loyal politicians. When Leland Stanford, powerfully pro-Union, was elected governor, the Home Guard—which had spread out throughout the city to keep peace on Election Day—felt its work was done, and voluntarily disbanded. This was also the end of the Committee of Thirty-four.

All of San Francisco's merchants supported the Union cause, and they prospered, along with their city. By 1860 California's agricultural and livestock production ranked among the highest in the nation. When eastern ports were blocked or blockaded during the war, California's beef, wheat, and wool found their way to waiting markets in Great Britain, and all the products were funneled through San Francisco. The city's merchants were self-sufficient; their isolation from the East did not cripple them in their dealings with other markets. Dry goods, groceries, hardware, fancy goods: all were still needed, and all found their way into and out of the city.

Even as the war raged, David Stern and brother Louis worked hard to keep Levi's business humming, and Levi acknowledged their contributions in 1863. Sometime during that year he changed the company name from simply "Levi Strauss" to "Levi Strauss & Co." It was now truly a family firm.

During the war, California gold was as essential as beef to the Union's war efforts. In order to obtain and secure good credit with allies Britain and France, gold was a vital backing for the government's currency. Between the start of the Civil War in April 1861, and its end in April 1865, Levi Strauss shipped $2,172,000 in gold to New York, worth $31 million today. Had the *Golden Gate* not burned and its cargo been lost, the figure would have been much higher. Levi's friends and competitors sent equally large volumes of gold, all of which led Ulysses S. Grant to say, according to legend, that California and its gold helped Abraham Lincoln win the war.

San Francisco's merchants also prospered because of the way currency was now handled. In San Francisco, specie or coins were the medium of exchange, but in the East, most merchants also accepted greenbacks or paper currency. Merchants in the city benefited from the fact that gold was the foundation for the specie they regularly used (now that a branch Mint was firmly in place).

If a merchant only accepted United States gold coin, he could exchange it for greenbacks when he did business back east. Paper money was highly discounted because it was not backed by either gold or government reserves. Like the difference between American and foreign currency, a gold dollar was worth $1.70 in greenbacks. A San Francisco merchant could buy $5,000 worth of goods from a New York supplier, but if he paid in gold, he would only pay about $2,940 for them. In 1863 greenbacks were only worth fifty cents in gold. In order to keep greenbacks from circulating into the local economy, the city's merchants met in November of 1862 and agreed to only accept gold as the medium of exchange. Anyone who paid for goods in greenbacks on par with gold would be hounded and forced to pay for any future goods in advance—and in gold.

This adherence to the gold standard, along with the ability to provide supplies to meet demand outside of California, meant San Francisco's merchants (as well as those in the gold country) could sometimes make enormous profits. Some people felt the city's businessmen were morally reprehensible for profiting from a long and bloody war. Some also complained that the wealth was not shared with the general population.

Many people, moreover, both within and outside the city, felt that Jewish merchants had taken the most advantage of the gold/greenback situation, even long after the war was over. An unnamed man from Quincy, Illinois, who was living in San Francisco at the time, wrote a long letter to his hometown paper in 1872, describing the city's people and culture in great detail. He spent a lot of time on the topic of Jewish commerce and mentioned Levi and his company in particular: "The Jews of San Francisco are very wealthy, but much of their money was made during the war, when all they had to do was to purchase goods at cost as the difference between greenbacks and gold made an immense profit, in addition to which the usual profit to their country customers. I will give you one example: it was considered doubtful whether the leading dry goods house here, Levi Strauss & Co., would be able to continue business at the commencement of the rebellion. It is now worth three millions."[6] It is impossible to verify this writer's figure.

The merchants had a lot of supporters, though. Many saw the city's prosperity as healthy, and with merchants paying for goods up front, they did not build up enormous debt that could hamper overall progress after the war was over. With the city already in good shape, it could easily see even greater investment by eastern capitalists in its future.

Levi Strauss put his money behind something else during the war years. In 1861 the United States Sanitary Commission was founded to help clean up the unhealthy camps where Union Army soldiers had suffered more deaths from disease than from battle. The commission opened hospitals, organized supplies, and educated government officials. Between 1862 and 1865, Levi Strauss & Co. donated $1,800 to the commission ($30,000 today). The citizens and other merchants of San Francisco were equally generous. By the end of 1862 California gave $500,000 in gold to the San Francisco branch of the Sanitary Commission, half of which came from the city itself.[7] A local Unitarian minister, Thomas Starr King, was the greatest orator against slavery and for the Union ever seen or heard by anyone in California. He was also the biggest booster of the Sanitary Commission, and was responsible for drumming up much of the generous donations throughout the war years.

Tuesday, November 8, 1864, was Election Day, and the city's business community felt as one that it should close its stores, warehouses, and factories for the occasion. On November 6, two display ads appeared in the *Daily Alta California* stating that "we, the undersigned, business men of San Francisco" agree to close the city's places of business so that "we and those in our employ may devote one entire day to the successful service of our country and its preservation as against an armed rebellion. We recommend a similar action throughout the cities and towns of California."[8] The ads listed the names of over 350 local firms and 19 manufacturers. Levi Strauss & Co. was on the merchant list, sharing space with other dry goods firms and with just about every type of business found in the city.

The men and women of San Francisco's commercial district took the re-election of Abraham Lincoln very seriously, and it showed. Lincoln received the majority of the city's votes, and when the news came over the telegraph wires that he had won, thousands of people, who had stayed up until after midnight waiting for word, hung out of windows, waved flags and handkerchiefs, and wept.

When news of Lee's surrender came on April 9, 1865, the city erupted with joy again, but five days later, even as celebratory bunting still hung along the walls and windows of downtown businesses, came the shocking news of Lincoln's assassination. The red, white, and blue that draped the city turned quickly to black, and on April 20, fourteen thousand people marched through downtown San Francisco to Union Square, to hear a memorial address.[9]

Even after the war was over, Levi Strauss demonstrated his fierce Union loyalty, whether in the service of his business or as an expression of his personal beliefs. In the years after 1865, Union veterans organized into a group called the Grand Army of the Republic (G.A.R.). They held regular reunions, called "Encampments," and met all over the country, and wherever they went, the host city went all out to honor them. In 1886, the 20th encampment was held in San Francisco. Employees at Levi Strauss & Co. headquarters decorated the outside of their building with colonial paintings of a soldier and a sailor, with a mammoth badge of the G.A.R. between them, and the words "Welcome G.A.R." with colored draperies flanking the pictures. Levi Strauss himself was on the Executive Committee for the event, which raised funds for the veterans. The company donated the equivalent of $6,000 to the organizers and won third prize for decorations.

The tireless yet exhausted Thomas Starr King died of diphtheria and pneumonia in March 1864. Everyone in the city knew how hard he had worked to bring citizens around to the idea that the Union was sacred and worth preserving. His fund-raising genius on behalf of the Sanitary Commission meant that thousands of soldiers benefited from the organization's care and skill. In 1888, when the city was collecting money to commission a statue of the Unitarian minister, Levi Strauss & Co. donated $250 ($6,400 today) to the fund. The statue was designed by Daniel Chester French, who later sculpted Abraham Lincoln for the memorial in Washington. The Starr King statue was placed in Golden Gate Park (near the Tea Garden) and was dedicated in October 1892.

In 1867, two years after Appomattox, Levi moved the dry goods inventory and his offices to a four-story (plus basement) bonded warehouse at 14–16 Battery Street, on the southeast corner of Pine. The building was large, the interior spacious, and the exterior beautiful. It was the perfect headquarters, perfectly reflecting Levi's success, and the business would remain there until April 18, 1906.

The man and his company now carried real weight in the city. In May 1868, architect John P. Gaynor, who would later go on to design the magnificent Palace Hotel, ran an ad in the *Daily Alta California* in order to drum up more business. In it he listed a number of references, including Levi Strauss & Co., stating that he built extensively for the firm.

In fact the move to 14–16 Battery Street was not the first major real estate transaction that Levi undertook in the 1860s. Sometime before 1867 he acquired a piece of property at the corner of First and Mission Streets, in the industrial district, which he and David Stern sold in February of that year. In early 1868 the company bought a building at Kearny Street and St. Mark's Place (now called Maiden Lane), just a few months before it was badly damaged in the sizeable earthquake that struck San Francisco on October 21. In the words of the *Daily Alta California*, the structure was "cracked through and through."[10]

Over the next decade, Levi bought and sold more property all over the city, from a lot in the manufacturing sector south of Market Street, to a small structure used for storage between Taylor and Jones, close to Union Square. Prosperity, and the new opportunities for business that always found their way to San Francisco, gave Levi the confidence to keep investing in real estate. He was smart enough to see that the city would continue to dominate the coast as its commercial hub.

One of those opportunities was the 1859 silver strike in Nevada, called the Comstock Lode. It sent mercantile hearts aflutter. Many of San Francisco's businessmen started to speculate in silver stocks, and they weren't the only ones. The discovery aroused the kind of fever that the city hadn't seen since the early days of the Gold Rush. Mark Twain said it best: "Stocks went rising; speculation went mad; bankers, merchants, lawyers, doctors, mechanics, laborers, even the very washer-women and servant girls, were putting up their earnings on silver stocks, and every sun that rose in the morning went down on paupers enriched and rich men beggared. What a gambling carnival it was."[11]

There is no evidence that Levi Strauss went in for silver stocks until 1864, when he bought 121 shares of the Peytona Gold and Silver Mining Company, located near Virginia City, Nevada. He held these shares until about 1868, when the stock was no longer listed, though in its heyday it was a large enough company that it had headquarters in San Francisco. Like most ore strikes, the Comstock enriched only a few. And, in this case, the greatest discoveries in the region were made in the early 1870s. Even so, the *Daily Alta California* estimated that by late 1863 San Francisco residents owned about $25 million in silver stocks.[12] In 1869 most of the city's merchants, including Levi, accepted silver as well as gold for payment of goods.

Levi and his fellow merchants gained something even more valuable than silver speculation from the Comstock discovery: new retail customers. Towns great and small were springing up all over Nevada. Men were moving in, and they needed dry goods, groceries, hardware, and other necessities. Between 1863 and 1872, Levi Strauss & Co. opened new accounts in Virginia City, Austin, Goldfield, Dayton, Gold Hill, Genoa, Ophir, Silver City, and the state's capital, Carson City.

During the same time period, Levi expanded his customer base up and down the West Coast, only venturing beyond this region and Nevada in 1869. In that year, the company sent its dry goods to Montana, with Helena becoming the first city to carry Levi Strauss & Co. products. A major gold strike in 1864 had made Helena the shining center of Montana and, as with Nevada, the discovery made for more opportunities for commerce and for Levi to expand his geographic base.

For example, Levi made more connections in Oregon, expanding to Portland, Salem, Eugene, Jacksonville, Corvallis, McMinnville, Roseburg, and Coos Bay. Lumber, small manufacturing, and farming had opened up Oregon to the wider world. Levi also recognized the importance of the Pacific Rim to San Francisco commerce, and in the decade between 1863 and 1873, he cultivated retailers in Victoria, Canada; Mazatlan, Mexico; and Honolulu, in the Kingdom of Hawaii.

He looked for customers farther south as well. In 1869, Arizona City (renamed Yuma in 1873) was the hub for the transport of goods to the military forts scattered throughout Arizona Territory. The most important retailer in the region was Blumenthal and Landsberger, which had an auction house and shipping center in San Francisco, and became a Levi Strauss & Co. customer that year. The retailer's Arizona City store carried a huge inventory of dry goods, liquors, crockery, oil, medicine, saddles, musical instruments, and guns.

During the Civil War, San Francisco's Jewish leaders—most of them merchants —felt they needed a place where they could get together and discuss issues of mutual interest. They also knew that this kind of socializing would be important to the younger men growing up in or just coming into the city, as a way to keep them from succumbing to the temptations of the Barbary Coast (likely recalling their own youth in the previous decade when they had to wrestle with the same temptations). In 1864 a writer for the Jewish paper *The Hebrew* proposed that a "house of refuge" be organized for men of commerce and men of learning to enjoy books, "debates and games of chess."[13] Jews from the German states had helped to found *vereins* or German cultural societies in the 1850s, but Jews in San Francisco now thought the time seemed right for a place of their own.

The Concordia Society was incorporated on January 10, 1865, with the stated object being "the promoting of social intercourse, cultivating literary taste, and diffusing useful knowledge among the members thereof."[14] The president was Israel Steinhart, a clothing wholesaler; the vice president was Levi Strauss. Brother Louis was a director. The club's first headquarters were in rented rooms in Odd Fellows' Hall, at the corner of Bush and Kearny. The Concordia, like the Masonic organizations that other Jews belonged to, both in San Francisco and New York, did truly become a place of both social comfort and a sounding board for business. Members were also very loyal to their club mates, as Levi soon demonstrated with his personal bank account.

In January 1868 Levi Strauss paid a considerable amount of his own money—not the company's—to help out a fellow merchant and member of the Concordia Society, Hermann Robitscheck, who served as the club's treasurer in 1867. The money was for bail, because his club mate was in jail for murder.

Robitscheck worked for J. Isaacs & Co., a wholesale stationers located at the corner of Sansome and Merchant Streets. Sometime around 1865 a friend and wholesale marble merchant named Joseph Eisner decided to spend a couple of years in Europe. Robitscheck was given power of attorney by Eisner to manage his financial affairs, and he sent Eisner regular payments and reports about his work. In December 1867 Eisner came back to San Francisco, satisfied that his friend had taken good care of his investments.

The men went out to dinner one evening soon after Eisner's return and drank quite a lot of claret. They went back to the office of J. Isaacs to look at another set of books, and Eisner noticed that some of the notes taken in for credit had not yet been paid. He became enraged, even when Robitscheck assured him the payments would be forthcoming on the next Steamer Day. Eisner refused to accept his explanations and, reaching into a desk drawer, pulled out a derringer, aimed it across the desk, and shot Robitscheck, shattering his arm.

Robitscheck fell to the floor and then heard the sound of another shot. Staggering to his feet, he was appalled to see Eisner on the ground with a bullet hole in his forehead. Eisner was still alive, and Robitscheck, ignoring his own wounds, ran out to get help. Despite badly broken bones, he recovered in a few days, but Eisner eventually died.

Local opinion and witnesses quoted in the *Daily Alta California* concluded that Eisner had shot himself, out of remorse for having apparently killed his friend.[15] That would have been the end of the story, except that members of Eisner's family, hearing rumors that his will had benefited Robitscheck at their expense, petitioned the court to exhume Eisner's body. After the disinterment a surgeon concluded that the bullet wound had not been self-inflicted but that it had been fired by another party. It wasn't suicide. It was murder. Robitscheck was arrested and charged with the crime.

In late January 1868 Judge Dwinelle agreed to set bail for the accused in the amount of $20,000 (about $345,000 today). The amount was put up by six prominent local businessmen, including Levi Strauss and three other Jewish merchants. In the end, the Grand Jury did not indict Robitscheck, and the case was dismissed on February 29.

Sharing his prosperity with a fellow merchant, Jew, and Society member was part of who Levi was as an observant Jewish man and loyal friend. However, this was only the beginning of what would be a lifelong relationship between Levi and both the city's and the nation's legal system.

CHAPTER 8

OUR SOLID MERCHANTS

L ike most of us, Levi first walked into a courtroom as a juror. And he had all the necessary qualifications. He was over twenty-one, had become a citizen, and had lived in California for over six months. Prospective juror names were chosen from voter poll lists, the first voting records in California, which means he was also a regular voter.

He caught a prominent case for his first time in the jury box. Thomas N. Cazneau, brigadier general of the California militia, had a longstanding feud of some kind with Zebedee M. Quimby, a watchmaker and jeweler. The two men "had for some time been mutually disgusted with each other, and had previously had difficulties."[1] On the night of November 21, 1858, they happened to meet in Blum's clothing store on Montgomery where, after exchanging a few heated words, Cazneau raised his cane and struck Quimby three times on the head and face. Quimby tried to fight back but didn't have a weapon. Cazneau was arrested, indicted, and put on trial on February 22, 1859.

The city's residents followed the case closely, given the prominence of the accused. And, in the end, the jury, including Levi, took only one day to decide Cazneau's fate. On the 23rd, the jurors found the general guilty, and he was sentenced to pay $1,200 or spend 350 days in jail. By the following year he was working as an insurance adjuster, so it appears Cazneau paid his fine. In reporting the conclusion of the case, the *Daily Alta California* echoed the sentiments of the jurors by describing it as one in which "the public peace was violated and the law insulted."[2]

Nine years later, Levi served on a jury in a case that put Cazneau in the shade: the trial of Andrew Jackson Stevenson, accused of raping Martha MacDonald at the Cosmopolitan Hotel in February 1866, while she was at the hotel without a chaperone. The Stevenson trial began in January 1868, and it rivals any "he said/she said" case of our own time. Allegations against MacDonald of immoral character, bastardy (she had a child after the alleged rape), and insanity contrasted with Stevenson's apparently unblemished citizenship and upstanding activities. He was a wealthy businessman who owned a substantial property downtown called the Stevenson's Building, and who claimed that he had been entrapped. The case was heard for ten days in the courtroom, and after thirteen hours of deliberation, the jury found him not guilty.

The verdict, coming on the heels of testimony that had been "very generally read and commented on by the public at large," was not a surprise.[3] And it indicates something going on under the surface of San Francisco's wide-open civic personality: the city would not tolerate women stepping out of societal norms without punishment. Merchants counted on order within society to keep business flowing. Without a solid demonstration of a woman's good character, witnesses, or other irrefutable evidence, no jury would convict a man who made substantial contributions to the city's prosperity.

In January 1864 Levi served on the Grand Jury for the first time, a civic duty he would take up again throughout the rest of his life. He was becoming a man of substance and influence, which would not only serve him well as his business grew but also give him a platform to help shape San Francisco's future.

One guaranteed way to make an impact in a city is to get involved in politics. Beginning in the Civil War years, Levi started to use his money and his reputation to further Republican politics in San Francisco and in California.

He started small. In June 1863 he was one of forty men, including quite a few fellow Jewish merchants, to put up funds for a $20,000 bond that Sheriff John S. Ellis was required to post in order to be re-elected. Ellis, a former general of the National Guard, was well liked among the city's business elite for his integrity and capability, and he was re-elected in July. Levi also was a bond holder for the election of county clerk William Harney, who ran and won his seat in 1871.

As for party affiliation, Levi was a member of the short-lived, but for a time influential national Union Party, composed of a disparate group of thinkers whose only common goal was the preservation of the Union in the years before the Civil War. He was among a number of pro-Lincoln and, after the president's assassination, pro-Johnson supporters who called for a convention of Union party members in the fall of 1865. Their platform was a vague listing of platitudes about the life and legacy of Abraham Lincoln, calls for new president Johnson to follow his example, and comments about opposing the "restoration of civil power in the rebellious States until the President and Congress shall be satisfied that it will be wielded by truly loyal majorities therein."[4] Party members, in their convention of 1867, were vocal about the issue of anti-Chinese immigration, labor, and voting rights in the city (something that Levi and his company would be faced with very soon). Schisms in the Union Party soon led to it being folded into the newly reorganized Republican Party.

During its 1865–66 session, the California State Legislature passed the Registry Act. Any man who wanted to vote in future elections had to officially register his name on a list. The act was intended to prevent fraud, and naturalized citizens had to produce their original naturalization papers in order to register. Levi, Louis, and David all signed up in 1866.

Levi Strauss & Co. closed its doors again for a presidential election, on November 3, 1868, along with another long list of businesses. Republican Party candidate and winner Ulysses S. Grant barely carried California, with Levi and most of his fellow merchants voting a straight, now-Republican ticket.

These same merchants were also getting more organized as a commercial body. They created associations that would bind them together no matter what their political affiliations—or their competitive relationships. The first was the Chamber of Commerce. Founded during the chaos of 1849, the purpose of the chamber was to bring order to the free-for-all that characterized early San Francisco commerce. Its by-laws and constitution were modeled on New York's chamber. It set commission rates, created arbitration boards, and standardized city rates for freight and wharfage fees to make San Francisco's port more competitive along the Pacific Coast. The merchants of the chamber also pushed for better mail service and for assistance with harbor improvements. Those requests went straight to Washington.

The reason for the chamber's creation was best stated by Hinton Rowan Helper, a North Carolina native who later became a rare and outspoken opponent of slavery in the South in the antebellum years. He lived in San Francisco from 1851 to 1854, hoping to strike it rich, but went home disillusioned and bitter. In 1855 he organized the letters he had sent to friends and family into a long narrative, which he published in a book titled *The Land of Gold: Reality versus Fiction.* Among the many awful things he said about San Francisco included this assessment of the way the city's merchants conducted their business: "Whatever they do is done in a helter-skelter, topsy-turvey sort of way. They never take time to do a thing well, but are always going and coming, or bustling about in such a manner, that one would suppose they are making preparations for some calamitous emergency, rather than attending to the every day routine of an established occupation."[5]

Levi joined the Chamber of Commerce sometime before or during the Civil War. In May 1866 he was elected to the Committee on Arbitration, to serve a three-month term. This committee heard the two (or more) opposing arguments concerning disputes about business methods, pricing, debts, and so forth. The members did their best to help the parties settle their differences rather than resorting to the courts. They were used most frequently by merchants seeking damage claims.

The city also had a Merchants Exchange, which dated back to the early Gold Rush years. In 1865 there was a movement among some downtown merchants to merge the exchange and the chamber, but some men, opposed to the merger, reorganized the exchange, publishing their names—Levi Strauss & Co. among them—in the *Daily Alta California* as supporters of this new effort. The following year the exchange offered stock for sale, and Levi Strauss & Co. was among the subscribers.

San Francisco wasn't the only thing in Levi's life that was prospering. Between 1859 and 1865, Fanny and David Stern, his sister and brother-in-law, had four more children: Louis (1859), Harriet, or Hattie (1861), Abraham (1863) and Lillie (1865), the last child. There were now eight Stern siblings, ranging in age from fourteen to infant.

In 1864, Levi was living with Fanny, David, and the children in their large home at 317 Powell Street, at the southeast corner of Post, just up the block from where the St. Francis Hotel is located today. Sadly, the postwar years also brought death to the family. Levi's younger half-sister Mary, wife of William Sahlein, died in New York in 1866, only forty-five years old. And in January 1869, his mother, Rebecca Strauss, who had held her biological and step family together for so long, passed away at the Stern home at the age of sixty-eight. Later that year, in July, Levi went to New York and spent about a month, very likely working with Jonas, to settle their mother's affairs.

Despite these sorrows, and the pressures of business and family obligations, Levi found time to enjoy the city's pleasures. Less than twenty years after the Gold Rush saw scruffy miners wandering its muddy streets, San Francisco was now the kind of place where important artists and performers wanted to go. One of them was George Felix Benkert, a composer, pianist, and, soon, one of John Philip Sousa's teachers. Benkert arrived in San Francisco in May 1866, and was expected to give a piano concert, but came down with a mysterious illness. While he recuperated, a contingent of businessmen placed an ad in the *Daily Alta California* congratulating him on his recovery and asking him to "name an early day for your first Concert, assuring you of an appreciative audience to welcome your appearance in public."[6] Among the signatories was Levi Strauss, who was in the audience at the Academy of Music, on Pine and Montgomery Streets, at Benkert's June 7 concert.

Levi Strauss & Co. also increased its donations to needy causes. Between December 1861 and January 1862 a series of catastrophic floods inundated the city of Sacramento. Hydraulic mining during the Gold Rush years had sent tons of sediment into the Sacramento and American Rivers, which surrounded the city and other small towns in the region. During an unprecedented rainy season of two months, the water built up against a city levee and had no place to go. People drowned, homes were lost, property was destroyed, bridges washed away. This also meant that jobs were lost, stores had no inventory, livestock was killed, and food was scarce.

On December 12 a large group of San Francisco citizens met spontaneously in Platt's Hall, at the corner of Montgomery and Bush, where the Mills Building is today. There they organized a subscription drive to aid the people of Sacramento, collecting everything from cash to commodities. The Howard Benevolent Association of Sacramento was in charge of accepting and distributing the aid, and among the donors to the organization was Levi Strauss & Co., which gave an unknown volume of clothing in early January 1862.

In foreign affairs, Levi closely followed the news from Europe during the Franco-Prussian War of 1870–71. The German state of Prussia, tired of France's domination of Europe since the days of Napoleon, went to war with that country and eventually triumphed, leading to the creation of a unified Germany. Although the German citizens of San Francisco were the most vocal in their support for Prussia's side, Jewish merchants from Bavaria and other states were also hoping that their former homeland would defeat France. Levi Strauss & Co. was a subscriber to the "German Sanitary Fund," which functioned much as the Sanitary Commission had during the Civil War. The firm donated $100 to the fund in August 1870. More telling is the company's donation of $50 to the French Relief Fund in February 1871, soon after the armistice.

At war's end, cities across the United States that had sizeable populations of German citizens threw parades called "Peace Jubilees." San Francisco was one of them, holding its jubilee on Wednesday, March 22, 1871. Levi and many of his fellow merchants closed their businesses that day or at least kept them closed for the duration of the parade.

Closing doors on a business day was actually a vexed subject in San Francisco and throughout the nation. The reason was the Sunday Law.

In the early to mid-nineteenth century many American cities had a law on their books requiring businesses to close on the Christian Sabbath. This was a problem for Jewish merchants, who generally closed their places of business on Saturday, the Jewish Sabbath. Closing on Sunday as well meant that observant Jews, at least, lost two valuable days of business.

In 1855, William W. Stow, a Santa Cruz County congressman, gave an invective-filled speech to the California Assembly about the need for the Sunday Law. He accused Jews of only coming to California to make money and then leaving the state with their riches, never investing in the place where they made their fortunes. Stow had no sympathy for Jews, and said that if it were up to him, they would be eliminated not only from the country but from the whole state. Prominent San Francisco Jewish leaders immediately wrote letters and articles denouncing Stow and his language. Less extreme supporters of the law said they weren't targeting Jews but only trying to keep society civil by affirming Christian values. Some Jews argued in return that by observing their own Sabbath they were demonstrating exactly what legislators had in mind with a Sunday Law in the first place. But many closed on Sunday in order to maintain their good standing among their customers and fellow citizens, knowing that the law would be contested in court. California's Sunday Law was found unconstitutional in 1858, re-enacted in 1861, and was finally abolished, but not until 1883.

Whether Levi closed his shop on Sundays to follow the law or not is unknown. However, in October 1865, he and twenty-one other wholesalers ran an ad in the *Sacramento Daily Union* affirming that they would, for the foreseeable future, close their businesses on Saturdays. As wholesalers, they stood to lose less than men who had retail stores, since much of their business was done with traveling salesmen. Only San Francisco customers would need to drop in to the warehouse on Sacramento Street to look at the dry goods inventory. But this does tell us that Levi was observant enough to want to spend the Sabbath appropriately.

A few years earlier, Levi had taken another occasion to express his opinion as a Jewish man, but in a quite different way.

San Francisco had no shortage of newspapers, and they covered every possible ideology, demographic, ethnic group, and opinion. The *Daily Alta California* was the voice of the business community, for example. And in the latter half of the nineteenth century, the city had two Jewish papers, the most influential—and controversial—of which was *The Gleaner*. It was founded in 1857 by the Polish-born rabbi Julius Eckman, who had come to San Francisco in 1854 and was known for his deeply Orthodox teachings. He was one of the religious leaders who denounced Stow in writing during the Sunday Law controversy.

With *The Gleaner* Eckman hoped to "promote our material and moral welfare as a people."[7] Although he claimed not to speak for all Jews, he was influential enough to be seen as the mouthpiece for that group. When he began to publish his personal pacifist views in *The Gleaner* at the outset of the Civil War, many Jews got nervous. Men who were committed to the preservation of the Union, either personally or through membership in the Union Party, objected to the general opinion that there was a "Jewish vote" and that Eckman spoke for all Jews.

On October 6, 1862, a group of "Many Jewish Subscribers" wrote a letter to the *Daily Alta California* denouncing this assumption:

> The attention of several of your Jewish subscribers has been repeatedly called to the rantings of a paper called the *Gleaner,* and as the old gentleman who edits it happens to be one of that faith many persons erroneously suppose that the peculiar ultra views which proceed from that paper are but the echo of his Jewish brethren's ideas. While they have proved harmless, his brethren have been perfectly willing that he should, if he chooses, follow in the footsteps of the Emperor Norton.[8]

Undaunted, Eckman published an article on June 10, 1864, titled "Our Superiority." Among its many inflammatory elements was the statement "We reiterate it. We claim for the Jews more virtue and more humanity, as we claim for them more penetration and more intelligence." Eckman then went on to criticize life in the United States, saying that America was "a nation running riot with itself."[9]

The article caused eruptions of outrage throughout the business district and beyond. Writing a letter wasn't enough this time. On June 17, two hundred firms, merchants, and individuals published "A Card" in the *Daily Alta California* to express their frustrations with Eckman, his paper, and his opinions. In a long narrative, the men said that the article filled them "with indignation and disgust as an open and flagrant violation of truth." The writers also defended their adopted country against Eckman's slander, saying that he insulted "a noble, generous, and highly cultivated people, of whom we are proud to form an integral part, and with whom we are intimately connected by the holiest ties of fraternal love, patriotism, and nationality."

The final sentence before the list of signatories stated "We, therefore, collectively and individually, disavow the sentiment and language of said article and thus refute it, as a slander revolting to our feelings, alike as Americans and Israelites."[10] David Stern's name was on the list, and so was Levi Strauss & Co. Levi didn't sign the card as an individual Jewish man but as the head of a business that he also felt had been slandered. Being a merchant was not just what he did, it was who he was. Many of the other signers did the same thing. This repudiation of the "Jewish vote" not only reflected their personal opinions but was also crucial to commercial success.

Such success was not always smooth. Even the most efficient and profitable companies could have problems, especially with their employees. Levi Strauss & Co., like other firms, needed clerks to work the warehouse and salesmen to hawk the dry goods in the surrounding states and territories. Having staff sometimes meant having problems.

In 1866, for example, newspapers in San Francisco and Sacramento began to report on an embezzlement at Levi Strauss & Co., described as a "defalcation on an immense scale, throwing even those in New York into the shade."[11] Confidential clerk (or bookkeeper) G. S. Goodman allegedly took $500,000 in currency from the company and then fled the country. This was first reported on October 12, and on October 13, the papers reported that Levi Strauss & Co. denied anything was missing. Even so, it placed an ad in these same journals saying that Mr. Goodman had ceased to be a company employee on October 5, and had no authority to transact any business in its name. The news even crossed the Atlantic, with the *Anglo-American Times* of London reporting the story on November 3, along with the first mention of the amount of money allegedly stolen.

Announcing that Goodman was persona non grata would seem to verify the rumors (though the dollar amount seems exaggerated). Denying a loss of this magnitude was obviously a calculated strategy for keeping customers from worrying that Levi Strauss & Co. was lax in its bookkeeping. After November there is no news of Mr. Goodman, who apparently managed to evade the law and the journalists with whatever money he got away with.

The embezzlement did not harm the reputation of the man or his company, though, and it did not keep Levi from moving into important positions in other corporations. Between 1867 and 1870, Levi joined the corporate boards of the Occidental Insurance Company, the National Insurance Company, and the National Fire and Marine Insurance Company. He was a trustee of the newly incorporated Eastland Coos Bay Coal Mining Company and a stockholder of the Bank of California. He also bought $30,000 worth of County Hospital bonds for eighty-seven cents on the dollar.

The Goodman incident didn't affect the company's credit rating, either. R & G Dun, despite their feelings about Jewish companies, agreed that Levi Strauss & Co. was a good risk. Its August 1871 report on the company read:

> Composed of Levi & Louis Strauss (bro's) & David Stern—their brother-in-law. Israelites, ages 40 to 45. All married. Have been long established and very successful, do the most extensive business in their line here for which they have more than ample means. Manage well and carefully. Are steadily adding to their means. Have also a house in N.Y. under the style of J. Strauss Bro's & Co. own a good deal of R[eal] E[state] here, estimated from 1 to 2 millions and in the highest standing. Generally discount their bills and it is said never give a note. Very wealthy and abundantly good.[12]

Despite the false assumption that Levi and Louis were married men (both were not), the report is precise about the company's business practices. Also of interest is the way it describes the relationship between Levi Strauss & Co. and J. Strauss Brother & Co. From the beginning, the San Francisco venture was meant to be the western branch of the original family firm, headed by Jonas and headquartered in New York. Levi was still sending gold back to his brother, but the astonishing profits of his company, and his own rising influence, made his venture the more important of the two.

More telling is the fact that Nathan Strauss, Jonas's son, now in his early twenties, came out to San Francisco in 1863 to work with his uncles at the Battery Street headquarters. He lived at the Powell Street address with the rest of the family. By this time the New York end of the business was simply a supplier of dry goods and clothing to its more prominent western half. The youngest brother was eclipsing the oldest, moving closer to becoming the patriarch of the family business.

Five years after moving to 14–16 Battery Street, the wholesale warehouse of Levi Strauss & Co. was a familiar and respected fixture. So much so that the *San Francisco Chronicle* sent a reporter to the firm in early February 1872. The paper regularly profiled local merchants that they felt were "solid and honorable." Stating that he happened to be in that part of the city a few days earlier, the reporter stepped through the front door and searched out "Nat" Strauss, "our genial and wide-awake friend." The profile opened with a brief dialogue between the two men:

> "Suppose," we said, "that a CHRONICLE man should step in and 'interview' you, what would be the consequence?" He replied, "We are not in the habit of being interviewed by newspaper men, but if you desire to walk in and take a look at our establishment, you are at perfect liberty to do so."[13]

This meeting was undoubtedly prearranged, and the interview authorized by his uncles, but "Nat" seems to have done a good job. No doubt the lively and younger Strauss would make a better impression than his elders on the reporter, who had nothing critical to say about the company. Nor was that his intention, as the article was meant to be part of a laudatory series of commercial profiles.

Nathan took the reporter on an extensive tour of each floor, the size and contents of which were reported in fine detail: wholesale clothing, domestic and dry goods, foreign dry goods, packing and storage, and the expensive and newly installed hydraulic elevator. The office in the rear of the first floor was a large, comfortable room for the "principals and book-keepers," who had a good view of the wholesale clothing department just outside.

The balance of the article described where the dry goods came from, where the company had its customers, the large force of employees (sales-men, bookkeepers, clerks, assistants, porters and teamsters), how quickly they filled orders, and how well respected the "principals" were. Although he didn't name them, the reporter assumed his readers knew who these men were, especially the company's founder.

The reporter was especially taken with staff efficiency:

> If a city merchant should call at 8 o'clock A.M., he might make purchases to the amount of $50,000, and have every article delivered in his store by 1 o'clock in the afternoon of the same day. If time is money, there is no need of argument on this point.

He liked the headquarters interiors as well:

> They moved into their present establishment five years ago, and a short time since expended $25,000 in painting, varnishing and refitting it in general. Everything within looks clean and orderly: the various departments have capacious chandeliers, which throw a fine flood of gas-light through the building, and in the daytime there is an abundance of clear light from the numerous splendid windows which adorn the building to the east and west.[14]

The article also used the surprisingly modern corporate concept of "empowerment" when talking about how business got done:

> If in the absence of the principals a purchaser should call in to buy $500,000 worth of goods, the chief salesman is empowered to act in every particular as if he was a member of the firm.[15]

When it appeared on February 11, the reporter titled his article with a phrase that must have been gratifying to Levi and his partners: "Our Solid Merchants."

This reputation was already well known outside of San Francisco as well. And Levi's good name would soon bring him an unusual business opportunity, a giant leap in profits, and the need to create an entirely new department for his Battery Street headquarters.

CHAPTER 9

"THE SECRATT OF THEM PANTS IS THE RIVITS"

J acob Davis liked to tinker.

Like Levi, he was a Jewish immigrant, and started his working life in the clothing business. And he was always thinking about how to improve the ways things were done, as well as how to improve his own life. An inventor at heart, he also found a way to re-invent himself.

He was born Jacob Youphes in 1831, near the city of Riga, when it was part of the Russian Empire. Riga had been a prize in many wars since its founding in 1201, and by the time Jacob was born, Riga had been on the maps of both Poland and Sweden. An important industrial center and Baltic seaport, Riga today is the capital of an independent Latvia.

Jacob learned the basics of tailoring when he was a teenager, and advanced to the level of a journeyman before he was twenty. In early 1854 he decided that his prospects looked brighter across the ocean. He landed in New York and worked as a tailor for about six months. He then met a storekeeper from Augusta, Maine, who likely told him about job prospects in the state. After moving north, Jacob worked as a pressman, or clothes presser, for six months with one employer and with another until August 1856. In his mid-twenties he heard the siren call of California, and making his way to New York via Boston, he took a steamer to Panama and then to San Francisco, arriving in September.

He got a job with Figel & Bro., on Clay Street, as a cutter and tailor. But

he was restless and wanted to see if the gold-bearing regions could transform his life, as they had done for others. So, after six months with Figel, he
headed to Trinity County, California, landing in the town of Weaverville.
He set up as a tailor, but he aimed his needle at the local merchants and
businessmen, not the raggedy miners who came through town on their way
to and from the diggings. He eventually bought a store from a local man
and tried his luck as its owner, but by the spring of 1858, he returned to San
Francisco. He wasn't there to stay but simply to find a steamer that would
take him to British Columbia. A gold strike on the Fraser River had created
another rush, and all eyes were turning north.

Between summer 1858 and autumn 1866, Jacob, who had already
changed his last name to Davis, lived in Fort Yale, Fort Alexander, Williams
Creek, and Victoria, going back and forth between these cities more than
once. Specializing in mining gear, he ran a store out of a tent, and then in
an actual building. He rode in pack trains to pick up and deliver his merchandise. He spent some time in San Francisco in 1859 collecting supplies,
and escaping the harsh Canadian winter. He also worked as a commission
merchant, invested in mines, and was part-owner of a brewery. In January
1865 he married Annie Packsher, in Victoria, and their first two children
were born in Canada.

Jacob sold his interest in the brewery in fall 1866, then took his family to
Victoria for two months. By the first week of January the following year, the
family was in San Francisco. There, Jacob invested in a coal business, but by
April that proved to be not only unprofitable, but it placed him deep into
debt. It was time to move again, to where prosperity might still be lurking.

All of these moves were a consequence of Jacob's relative success (or
not) in business. He always moved to towns or regions that revolved
around mining and the men who made money from it. He rarely if ever
tried mining himself and seems only to have been an investor. But when he
fell back on tailoring, the trade he knew best, he set up shop where mining
was either the economic backbone or at least a supporting industry.

Jacob chose one of the West's most famous mining towns for his family's
new home: Virginia City, Nevada. The massive Comstock gold and silver
strike turned this empty valley in Mount Davidson's shadow into the most

important, and richest, cities between Denver and San Francisco. In fact, Levi Strauss & Co. had retail customers for its dry goods in Virginia City by 1863, though that was after the city had become established and a bit notorious.

When Jacob installed himself as a tailor in town in the spring of 1867, Virginia City was at the height of its population, power, and fame. Jacob worked twelve hours a day or more in his tailor shop, and he also owned a cigar store with his brother-in-law, Simon Packsher. That didn't bring in the kind of money he wanted, so tailoring became his one and only source of income. He repaired clothing and made garments for local clothing stores.

He once said that during his time in Virginia City its population was about fifteen thousand people, of which "5,000 were miners, and about 5,000 of bummers, gamblers and prostitutes, and about 5,000 of business men, speculators and capitalists."[1] But despite hard work, and an apparent glut of potential customers, Jacob only stayed in Virginia City for a year. On May 8, 1868, he and the family headed about twenty-five miles north to Reno, with unintentional good timing. On May 9, the town of Reno was officially established.

The area was originally a stopover, complete with toll bridge, for people on their way to Virginia City. After the Central Pacific Railroad pushed through the Sierras to the adjoining meadows earlier in 1868, the company planted a town site and depot nearby. These drew a population still eager to get to the mining regions but eager as well to go into the businesses that supported mining and railroading. There were also livestock ranches and farms cultivating alfalfa a few miles outside of town. As a distribution hub for the Comstock, and with agriculture as part of its infrastructure, Reno had a bright future.

Jacob set up again as a tailor but also got back in touch with his former Canadian brewery partner, Frederick Hertlein. Hertlein came down to Reno, and the two men started up another beer-making business, which they named The Reno Brewery. However, Davis found that he could not serve two masters, and he soon abandoned the brewery business and once again began repairing and making new clothing for individual customers.

The people of Reno were not like those in Virginia City. Jacob described the town as "more of a floating population than anything else" He also called it "a very great place for teamsters."[2] A "teamster" was someone who drove a team of horses pulling a wagon full of produce, merchandise, or other goods. In Reno, these men loaded and offloaded materials on the railroad and hauled goods where the railroad didn't go.

Then, in spring 1868, another massive silver discovery was made, this time in the farthest eastern portion of Nevada, in the White Pine mountain range near Ely. A new rush was on, and men from all over the state, including Reno, needed to outfit themselves to try their luck yet again. By 1869, Jacob Davis realized he could take advantage of this opportunity, and began to specialize in making tents, wagon covers, and horse blankets. Stage companies bought the covers, teamsters bought the horse blankets, and prospectors bought the tents.

The business was steady but not that lucrative. Nevertheless, for a long time Jacob had been thinking about some ideas he had for a few clothing-related inventions. In 1870 he began to tinker in earnest, and by the summer of 1871, he had invented a process to fasten buttons with a screw, which he tried and failed to patent. He had more luck with his next two inventions: an ironing and stretching board, and a folding clothes press, both of which he did get patented.

Back in January, Jacob had made a pair of pants for a local laborer. With inventing and improving on his mind, he decided to add a little something extra to the pants to please his customer, and then didn't think much more about it. But other people soon would.

One of the fabrics that Jacob used most often in making wagon-covers and tents was something called "duck" or "ducking." It was a sturdily woven cotton fabric, similar to canvas in appearance but much stronger. For these purposes, it had to be. But he also used duck to make pants for the teamsters in town, or sometimes he used denim, the sturdy, indigo-dyed fabric traditionally used for work wear. And although the duck was described as "white," it was actually more ecru in color.

In September 1870 Jacob needed to buy more fabric but didn't know of any place locally where he could get it. His brother-in-law Simon, along with one his wife's cousins, knew about Levi Strauss & Co. During that month these relatives were in San Francisco and went to the company's wholesale warehouse and headquarters on Battery Street, where they bought the amount of duck fabric that Jacob needed. Simon paid for the goods, and then Jacob later reimbursed him. He was happy with the quality and placed another order on credit with Levi Strauss about a month later, this time for other fabrics.

Sometime before the end of December 1870, a woman came into Jacob's tailoring shop on North Virginia Street. Her husband needed a pair of cheap pants, and as he was sick at the time, she came into the shop to place the order. He had worn out his last pair of trousers, and she hoped to get a new pair for him before the new year. Jacob told her he needed to have her husband's measurements, and she tartly replied that he "could not very well come as he had nothing to put on." So he told her to get a string and measure him around the waist, and also measure the inside of another pair of pants (presumably a pair that was not completely in tatters). She did so, gave him the string, and he promised to get the pants made as soon as possible, asking her to pay the $3.00 fee in advance.[3]

As it happened, he didn't get to this order until the first week of January. The woman told Jacob her husband was pretty rough on his trousers, and she asked him to make the pants as strong as possible. Using the duck fabric he had bought from Levi Strauss & Co., Jacob sewed up the trousers, thinking about how he might make them sturdier. As he recalled, "I was making horse blankets and covers for the teamsters at the time, and had used rivets for the straps in the blanket. . . . Those straps were not sewed with seams—but were just riveted together. So when the pants were done—the rivets were lying on the table and the thought struck me to fasten the pockets with these rivets. I had never thought of it before."[4]

A rivet is nothing more than a mechanical fastener, intended to be permanent, and not removable, like a button. Both the word and the function have been used since medieval times, from knightly armor to mighty bridges to World War II liberty ships built by "Rosie the Riveter." But rivets can also be small and serve many non-industrial uses: to fasten leather straps on horse blankets, for example. It makes sense that a man like Jacob Davis, having a mind already primed to see the ordinary in extraordinary ways, would find another use for this everyday item in his working life. He thought a rivet would be "a good fastening for a pocket."[5]

The woman came back to pick up the pants and was delighted with them. Jacob saw her husband walking by his tailor shop wearing the pants soon after, but then never saw him again.

Jacob decided to add rivets to some of the pants that he made for the local laborers, and in February produced ten pairs for some Reno teamsters. Then, in March, he made about a dozen pairs for the men working for the county surveyor, Andrew J. Hatch. And pretty soon the white duck pants with the dark metal pieces on the pockets were seen all over Reno.

Jacob had many friends, and he was quick to strike up conversations with the men who came into his shop, as well as those he encountered when he patronized some of the other stores in town. In the summer of 1871 he met Jacob Sheyer, a Carson City dry goods merchant, who came into his Virginia Street shop one day. Sheyer mentioned that he had seen some of the riveted pants on the surveyors who were fanned out all over Washoe County, and he complimented Jacob on his invention.

Jacob's business was rather casual, and he didn't keep very good records of the sales of his riveted pants until October, and even then, it was hit and miss. But he did complete some very important paperwork on the 14th of that month: he became a naturalized citizen.

After spending some time in San Francisco, Jacob Sheyer came back to Reno the following spring. He ran into Jacob Davis one evening in a cigar store owned by a Mr. M. Mose. Also on hand were a Mr. Cantrowitcz and a tailor named Rossak. The men began to talk about Jacob Davis's patented ironing and stretching board, which Rossak had licensed to use in his own business. They also talked about Jacob's famous riveted pants.

Sheyer thought Jacob should put rivets in the duster he had with him. A duster was a long coat made of linen, canvas, or waxed cotton, and it was worn by cowboys, gunslingers, or anyone wanting to keep his clothing from being soiled. Rossak sewed some pockets onto the duster, and Davis attached some rivets down at his shop. Sheyer was pleased, and walked out of the shop with a few loose rivets in his hand, which did not please Jacob, but he didn't say anything about it.

Based on his past experience, Jacob thought he might be able to patent his new style of pants. But his success as an inventor was not adding to the family bank account. Applying for a patent was not cheap, and by the spring of 1872, Jacob's wife Annie was at her wit's end with how much time and money he had put into inventions that did not live up to their billing. In tears, she begged Jacob not to go down that road again. He knew he had to try to patent his process, though. He was afraid someone else might steal his idea, which he was sure was a moneymaker. So he decided to take a different route.

This time he would get a partner.

On July 5, 1872, Jacob Davis sent a letter to Levi Strauss & Co. in San Francisco. Enclosed with the letter was a check in payment for a recent order, with a request to credit any outstanding amount to his account. He then described a package he had also sent, via Wells Fargo Express:

> I also send you by Express 2 ps. Overall as you will see one Blue and one made of the 10 Oz Duck which I have bought a great many Peces of you, and have made it up in to Pents, such as the sample the secratt of them Pants is the Rivits that I put in those Pockets and I found the demand so large that I cannot make them up fast enough I charge for the Duck $3.00 and the Blue $2.50 a pear. My nabors are getting yealouse of these success and unless I secure it by Patent Papers it will soon become to be a general thing everybody will make them up and thare will be *no* money in it. Tharefor Gentleman I wish to make you a Proposition that you should take out the Latters Patent in my name as I am the Inventor of it, the expense of it will be about $68, all complit and for these $68 I will give you half the right to sell all such Clothing Revited according to the Patent. . . . Please answer these as soon as possible, these looks like a trifle hardly worth speakeing off But nevertheless I knew you can make a very large amount of money on it if you make up Pents the way I do.[6]

There is no way to know what kind of conversations went on between Levi and Louis about this astonishing offer. Levi might have sent a telegram to Jonas back in New York, to get his opinion, but at this point Levi may not have either wanted or needed the approval of the company's aging patriarch. Sometime before July 10, Levi gave orders to someone (likely the company attorney) to write up an agreement with Jacob Davis:

> We wish to have the right to sell all goods manufactured under this Patent for our own account. We want to restrict Davis from selling his half of Patent for Goods manufactured on this Coast to any other person on this Coast and Territory and he shall not have the right to assign or sell without our consent, we having the privilege of buying the Patent from Davis. The proceeds of sale of Patent rights outside of the Pacific Coast and Territory shall be equally divided between ourselves and Davis.[7]

Jacob Davis sent back the signed agreement on July 12. He felt sure that the U.S. Patent Office would quickly issue the patent, and he offered to go to either San Francisco or New York to oversee the manufacturing of the riveted clothing. And he made sure that Levi Strauss understood one more thing: "It is not the Rivits alone that will sell them well, but also properly Cut and made.[8]

There were at least seven agencies in San Francisco that helped people with the patent process, and Levi Strauss chose Dewey & Co., on Montgomery Street. Alfred T. Dewey, George H. Strong, and J. L. Boone not only ran the agency but also printed the *Pacific Rural Press,* a magazine aimed at farmers and ranchers that regularly published lists of the patents issued by Dewey & Co. to Pacific Coast inventors. On July 29, the completed patent application and samples of the riveted pants were packaged up and sent to Washington. The new invention was described as an "improvement in fastening seams."

While waiting for the good word from Washington, Jacob kept on making pants for the locals, and sometimes for men who lived further afield. On August 4, he made four pairs of pants for Wadsworth, Nevada, storekeeper James A. Ferguson, who then sold them to his customers. Four days later, the papers were officially filed in the patent office. And from almost the day that Jacob signed these documents, he marked his pants with the phrase "Patent Applied For." Whether this was on a removable label, a permanent label, or written in ink somewhere is unknown.

Levi and Jacob were both fortunate and unfortunate in the timing of their patent application. The nineteenth century was experiencing a burst of technological innovation, and the patent office was a busy hive of overworked examiners. In 1871 alone, 19,472 applications were submitted for new "utilities," or inventions, of which 11,687 were granted. This was the era that saw the invention of the safety pin, the elevator, the typewriter, and dynamite. The clothing world hadn't seen many new innovations, but what did get patented was game-changing. Elias Howe created the first truly functional home sewing machine, and Isaac Singer improved on his design. The two men then fought over patent rights, with Howe coming out on top. When Howe's rights expired in 1867, Singer (and a few others) took the sewing machine to the next level, and Singer made the leap to commercial use.

At the same time, the historical period known as the Second Industrial Revolution was in full flower. Its greatest influence was in the forty-year span that began around 1870 and was fueled by the need for a new, mechanized America. After the horrors of the Civil War had faded, the U.S. economy began to recover and thrive. The new territories in the West were bursting with exploitable natural resources. With new populations moving west, along with the northern migration of newly freed slaves, markets for manufactures also grew. Immigrants became the cogs of the labor force, and the transcontinental railroad made it easier to distribute the piles of goods produced in the new factories springing up all over the country.

Invention mirrored both industry and changes in the way people lived their lives. The telephone made business move faster and also helped individuals stay connected in a way they never could before. Electric light illuminated factory floors, as well as the simplest of homes. Typewriters transformed communication and gave women new opportunities for work.

Riveted work trousers fell directly into this period of technological transition. The West, poised to be more important to the nation than just the sum of its mines, required a lot of men to work with their hands, and to wear collars of blue, not white. Subsisting near the bottom of the wage scale, laboring men needed pants that didn't have to be continually replaced because they were torn at the seams or the pockets. The rivets provided an economic benefit beyond strong sewing. When a man didn't have to give up a day's pay

to travel many miles to find a store in order to replace his torn pants, he benefited in the most material way. Jacob Davis alluded to this in his patent document, but perhaps he should have made his point a little stronger. Because
on August 14, 1872, the Patent Office rejected his application.

According to the examiners, the army had been using rivets in their
shoes for years, so the use of a rivet for pants was not considered substantially new. Another man named Elijah Adams had filed for a shoe patent
that used an eyelet, and that was also refused, for the same reason. But even
though it was rejected, Adams's idea was similar enough to Jacob's that it
"anticipated" the riveted trousers.

In October, Levi Strauss hired attorneys A. H. and R. K. Evans of Washington, D.C., who specialized in patent law, and asked them to appeal the
decision. They addressed the Adams case, arguing that there was a great
difference between the two ideas. Adams used an eyelet (or rivet) that gave
"independent" strength to various parts of a shoe. Jacob's rivet, however,
was used to "protect" the seams in wearing apparel (and definitely not
shoes). The two attorneys made a strong case that riveted trousers were
distinct from shoes made with eyelets, meaning that Adams had invented
something that bore no resemblance to what Jacob had come up with.[9]

On October 15, the application was rejected again. The examiner
brought up those army shoes, and then made a vague reference to having
seen sailors' canvas pantaloons fastened by rivets. He concluded by saying
that buttons served the same purpose, so Davis had not created anything
"patentable." Ten days later, another examiner took up the cause and came
up with even more reasons to throw out Jacob's application. Apparently
two men named C. C. More and L. N. Williams had both patented pro-
cesses using rivets to fasten cloth together.

While Levi and Jacob were enduring this waiting game and receiving
nothing but bad news, they both still had to get on with their lives and
work. Levi continued to take in shipments of dry goods from New York,
with six ships carrying his merchandise arriving from Panama between July
and December. He served on the Grand Jury in October, along with prominent bookseller and stationer Isaac Upham.

Jacob kept on making his riveted pants for the working men of Reno and throughout Nevada, always making sure that "Patent Applied For" appeared on each pair. And he kept on buying his fabric from Levi Strauss & Co. He also began to order rivets from the company, though where they came from is unknown. In January 1873 Jacob received a shipment of rivets that were too long; he wanted ¼-inch rivets, but he got 5⁄16-inch ones instead. He wrote to Levi about his order and told him he was also low on thread, which Levi Strauss & Co. could get at any place where sewing machines were sold. And, finally, he asked the company to send him "1 Pece of the Haveyest Blue Dennim for Overalls you can get."[10]

He then went into greater detail about the denim he wanted. "I would like to have Blue Dennim to wagh about 8 9 and 10 ounces to the yard and be 29 Inches wide and it must be Intirely without Starch and Applyable the Collor should be something of the inclosed Sample."[11] (During this period, the weight of a fabric such as denim was based on the number of ounces in a square yard.) He was making the riveted pants out of both duck and denim, and told Levi in the same letter that he was going to keep on making his trousers for the wholesale trade whether they got the patent or not. He nudged Levi again about the paperwork and reminded him that a patent for "17 years is worth a large Fortune."[12]

On March 30, Jacob completed an order for twenty pairs of riveted pants for a storekeeper named Prichard of Palisade, in Nevada, near Ely. Teamsters working in this area had seen other men wearing the pants and had asked Prichard to start carrying them in his store. That same day Jacob wrote to Levi again, asking for more duck fabric, specifically pieces that were not from the outside of the bolt of cloth, as these often got damaged in shipping. He signed his letter and then added a P.S. "Please wake up Dewey & Co. about our Patent. I cannot supply the demand with my present sistom of working alone."[13] Whether Levi needed Jacob's urging or not, he apparently was successful in waking up Dewey & Co. Something had shifted, and for the better, because by April 26, 1873, Jacob Davis, his wife Annie, and their five children were living in San Francisco, settling in at 407 Folsom Street, between Fremont and First.

Dewey had likely advised Levi and Jacob to amend the original application to make the language stronger about the distinction between riveted trousers and riveted shoes. The new paperwork was submitted on May 7. Jacob (or, rather, his attorneys) spent a lot more time talking about the rivets and their uses for "pants, drawers, or other article of wearing apparel which terminates at the pockets."[14] He (or they) went on to explain, "By this means I avoid a large amount of trouble in mending portions of seams which are subjected to constant strain. . . . As a new article of manufacture a pair of pantaloons having the pocket openings secured at each edge by means of rivets, substantially in the manner described and shown, whereby the seams at the point named are prevented from ripping as set forth."[15]

The examiner who reviewed the paperwork on May 10 was almost convinced, but he cited two other patents that used rivets. He felt there was still doubt about the patentability but thought there was now a stronger case. Dewey & Co. and Jacob Davis responded to this quickly, reminding the examiner that Jacob was not saying he was the first person to ever use rivets on any article of wearing apparel. But he still claimed to be the first to use them on *trousers*.

And this time it worked. On May 17, Levi Strauss & Co. paid the necessary fees to the Patent Office. And on May 20, 1873, Patent Number 139,121 was issued in the names of Jacob W. Davis and Levi Strauss & Company of San Francisco, California. The official patent documents read: "As a new article of manufacture, a pair of pantaloons having the pocket-openings secured at each edge by means of rivets, substantially in the manner described and shown, whereby the seams at the points named are prevented from ripping, as set forth."[16]

Putting on its publisher's hat, Dewey & Co. included the rivet patent in its "Telegraphic List of U.S. Patents Issued to Pacific Coast Inventors." The listing appeared in the June 7, 1873, issue of the *Pacific Rural Press,* and read as follows: "FASTENING POCKET OPENINGS.—Jacob W. Davis, of Reno, Nev., assignor to Levi Strauss & Co., S.F., Cal."[17] Breathing a sigh of relief, Levi and Jacob now had the exclusive right to make and sell clothing strengthened with rivets for the next seventeen years.

Jacob Davis's move to San Francisco can only mean one thing: Levi intended for him to run the manufacturing end of the business. As a tailor, Jacob understood how to put garments together, and he must have also convinced Levi that he would be able to manage multiple sewing-machine operators in a factory, as well. The fact that the Davis family moved to a working-class neighborhood in San Francisco tells us how Levi viewed his new employee. He probably paid Jacob well but not well enough for the tailor to join his employer on the other side of Market Street, on Union Square and beyond, where prominent merchants like Levi were now living.

The Davis house at 407 Folsom was in the South of Market neighborhood. It was surrounded by all the amenities a family could need and was just far enough away from the burgeoning manufacturing district to be comfortable. Within walking distance were a grocer, butcher, baker, and a carpenter's home, and the Davises were probably very comfortable. Their house was only about three blocks from the factory, and another two to company headquarters, so Davis could walk to work if he wanted to.

Levi made the transition easy for Jacob. On May 27 he paid him $1,000 for the home and tailor shop on 31 North Virginia Street in Reno. At a modern-day value of nearly $20,000, this must have gone a long way toward drying Annie Davis's tears over the time and money spent on her husband's latest invention.

In the June 28 issue of the *Pacific Rural Press,* the patent was lauded in a regular column called "Notices of Recent Patents":

> Simple as this device seems, nevertheless it is quite effective, and we do not doubt that this manufacture, of overalls especially, will become quite popular amongst our working men, as the overalls are made and cut in the style of the best custom made pants. Nothing looks more slouchy in a workman than to see his pockets ripped open and hanging down, and no other part of the clothing is so apt to be torn and ripped as the pockets. Besides its slouchy appearance, it is inconvenient and often results in the person losing things from his pockets. Levi Strauss & Co. of this city are sole agents for the new manufacture, and will soon place them in the market in large quantities, so that our miners, farmers and workingmen can supply themselves with superior overalls.[18]

They didn't know it, but Levi Strauss and Jacob Davis had just invented the blue jean.

CHAPTER 10

PATENT RIVETED CLOTHING

Why did Jacob Davis turn to Levi Strauss when he needed a partner to finance the patent? No documentation survives to give us a hint. When he began to think seriously about applying for a patent, he reached out to Levi first, an act that signaled a certain level of trust. He had started buying fabrics from Levi Strauss & Co. in the fall of 1870, so by spring 1872, he knew that Levi Strauss & Co. carried quality textiles and was generous with its credit terms. He also knew enough about Levi as a person to entrust him with his money-making idea.

Levi's company wholesaled its dry goods to stores all over Nevada, in towns as close to Reno as Carson City and Virginia City. There may have been customers in Reno itself. Merchandise purchased from a San Francisco house was expected to have a certain level of quality, and when the company name was also the name of the owner or founder, opinions about a company's products naturally carried over to the man whose name was on the paperwork. Other San Francisco wholesale merchants were in the same position and also had good reputations: Henry Neustadter, of Neustadter Brothers; Daniel Murphy and Adam Grant, of Murphy, Grant & Co.; and Leonard Heynemann, of Heynemann & Co., among others. In other words, although Jacob didn't know anything about Levi personally, he knew about the quality of his products and the integrity of his business. The name alone was enough.

Levi had taken just a few days to accept Jacob's proposal for partnership and to agree to finance the patent, and for many good reasons. One of the most critical was the way that San Francisco was being transformed from a place where goods just passed through, and into one where goods were being made.

The city always had an industrial sector, even as far back as the 1850s. Foundries and machine shops went up first, necessary for repairing the ships and steamers that were so vital for early commerce. Later in the decade, gold mining moved from individuals using pans and rockers to organizations managing large-scale hydraulic operations. The new facilities required heavy equipment, but it was too expensive to bring in from eastern manufacturers. So, companies such as Union Iron Works and Pacific Foundry stepped in and began to make everything from wire to blasting powder. They set up shop in the area known today as South of Market, close to the shoreline and the port, in what would one day be the city's powerhouse manufacturing district.

Northern California sawmills provided lumber, and as agriculture grew, local firms began to process the bounty coming from the Central Valley. Boots, shoes, tack, and rope came off the loading docks of San Francisco factories, rather than from the cargo holds of inbound steamboats. California's isolation during the Civil War also contributed to the rise of local industry.

And although many feared that the completion of the transcontinental railroad in 1869 would mean that San Francisco's prime location would no longer be its calling card, the reverse was actually true. The railroad forged new links to the East, and at the same time steam was replacing sail as the locomotion for sea travel. San Francisco continued to dominate the Pacific Coast as a center for distribution in all four directions. The raw materials of agriculture and mining went through the city to their final destinations, while finished products for the increasingly fine homes sprouting all over the West came into port for distribution throughout the city and its surrounding towns.

Clothing production started small in the late 1850s as well, but it increased steadily over the next decade. An estimate of the value of the clothing produced in San Francisco in 1866 came to nearly one million dollars.[1] Everything from underwear to work pants to suits in the French style came off San Francisco's sewing lines, and the clothing was sold throughout California and nearby mining regions. The local clothing manufacturers were aware that their products had to compete with the fine goods that were still being brought in from New York and Europe, and that their customers ranged from miners to bank presidents. They took pains to make sure the quality of their goods was at least equal to the competition.

One of these manufacturers was Weidenrich & Lehman, whose factory was on Sansome Street near Commercial, in the heart of the financial, rather than industrial, district, a geographic anomaly that would persist until the mid-1870s. Their clothing was described in an 1867 article about local factories in the *Daily Alta California:* "An examination of the coats, etc. sent out of this establishment will satisfy the most fastidious in matters of wearing apparel that San Francisco is not at all behind London or Paris in giving style and elegance to the appearance of the outer man."[2] The same article also pointed out that clothing for the working man was being produced in the city as well: "Mr. William Banks is engaged in making clothing suitable for miners, sailors and laborers."[3]

Although garment production was expanding by the late 1860s, not everyone thought it was a good bet. Wages for the men and women who cut and sewed the clothing were among the highest in the country, due to a shortage of skilled labor. A lot of men wanted to try their luck with mining before immuring themselves inside a factory. Women often worked out of their homes, rather than in factories, but they still commanded top dollar. Merchants and investors were not sure that manufacturing was the best way to see a return on their money, so they instead put their energy and resources into real estate, mining stocks, or their own firms, if they had one. Levi also took this path, though there is no way to know if he thought about adding clothing production to his commercial repertoire before 1872.

By the time he was twenty-four years old, Levi had already been on three hazardous ocean voyages, any one of which could have meant death rather than safe harbor. These experiences could have made him more willing to take risks, but he trod well-worn paths in his early years in San Francisco. He set up his wholesale business in the same manner as his fellow Jewish merchants before him. He also had older brothers to answer to, with the responsibility of a family business sitting firmly on his shoulders. He acted cautiously and conservatively, both on the job and in his activities within San Francisco.

However, he did take a few commercial risks. He supported the actions of the Committee of Vigilance, and he stood up in defense of a friend who was wrongly accused of murder. He expanded his retail presence beyond the borders of the United States. Nothing in these actions indicates that he sought out risk for its own sake, though.

But he knew the clothing business, and he knew it from the hem up. When Levi's deep knowledge of his customers' needs met Jacob's riveted pants, it's no wonder Levi jumped on the opportunity and made his decision so quickly. For twenty years he had been importing and distributing a vast array of clothing and dry goods. By 1872 his retail base stretched from Montana, Nevada, Arizona, California, and the Pacific Northwest, to Canada, Mexico, Hawaii, and Japan. He knew what kind of people needed what kind of clothing, and where they needed it. In the 1850s and 1860s, Levi's company imported and distributed a wide array of workwear: flannel shirts, sack coats (simple work jackets), hickory shirts (of heavy blue-and-white striped fabric), boots, buckskin gauntlets, calico shirts, jumpers (a cross between a jacket and a shirt), leather gloves, duck pants, denim pants, and miners' check shirts. It also sold ladies' shawls, fine linens, and dress shirts.

And even though the West now had great cities with great houses filled with very rich people, it still had plenty of small towns, constantly booming mining regions, vast landscapes of lumber, seaports cluttered with cargo, and a working class that kept this enormous machinery humming. Levi believed that the need for sturdy work clothing was not going away. He saw it in his own financial records. As the 1870s began, he still sold the flannel shirts and duck pants of previous decades, but he also began to sell dusters, waterproof dusters, denim jackets, army blankets, and jumpers made of tough cotton duck.

He knew that riveted pants would get snatched up by the storekeepers who served the swarming populations of laborers in the West. Jacob had already told him how word of his new trousers managed to travel around

Nevada alone. In short, Levi had an eye for opportunity and the means to jump on it. It would have been less in character for him to pass on the idea than to champion it.

That new kind of work pant is called the blue jean today, but in 1873, and for at least the three previous decades, the term meant something very different.

"Jean" was an all-cotton, or cotton-and-wool-blended twill fabric, and had been made in American textile mills since the eighteenth century. (The jury is still out on the theory that the word "jeans" comes from "Genoese," and refers to pants worn by the sailors of that Italian city.) Clothing made of jean fabric was designated as such: jeans pants, jeans coats, and so forth. It was a rather light-weight fabric, typically used to make clothing for working men but not expected to last very long. It was usually made in a slate blue or bluish-black color, and sometimes garments were called "blue jeans pants" or "blue jeans coats." In other words, the fabric became an adjective. By the 1840s work pants called "Kentucky jeans" were being made in that state but also copied elsewhere because their style and fabric tended to be popular with laboring men. In the 1850s Levi himself imported and distributed "jeans pants."

In 1884, Mark Twain described the clothing that the character known as the "Dauphin" was wearing when he first met Huckleberry Finn: blue jeans britches (stuffed into boots) and a blue jeans coat with brass buttons. Throughout the nineteenth century, and even into the twentieth, everyone knew that "jeans" meant clothing made of a very specific fabric but not the sturdiest in the world. And they knew who it was for.

In 1878, the San Francisco Chronicle printed an article about the men who speculated in mining stocks and about how representatives of all classes ended up together at the low end of the economic thermometer when most stocks inevitably failed. The process made San Francisco society "wonderfully democratic," the article said. "Never since the fall of Adam," it concluded, "has there been such a tumbling to low levels and mixing of starched linen and blue jeans."[4] Everyone reading this article would know that "blue jeans" meant working-class clothes, which were the perfect contrast to the concept of stiff linen worn by the wealthy men of the city's financial center.

So, when Levi and Jacob discussed their patent riveted pants in 1873, they knew they had to use a different word with their customers and in advertising. And that word was "overalls." Today this word conjures up the full-length denim or chambray garment with straps that buckle over the shoulders, worn by farmers, Okies, and country singers (both in reality and in stereotype). But in the nineteenth century, "overalls" was a word that meant sturdy pants worn by cowboys, lumberjacks, and other laborers. It also meant a rather oversized garment that was worn over regular trousers as a type of protective garment, sometimes called "waist overalls." Jacob might have seen his first riveted pants worn this way in Nevada, but he also saw them worn just as regular pants, as we do today.

Jacob and Levi used both "pants" and "pantaloons" in the language of the patent application, and the drawing accompanying their description shows trousers that aren't too baggy and aren't too tight, and that are obviously not being worn over another pair. The men did not use the word "overalls" in the paperwork because they did not want too narrow of a definition of the new product. Casting their net wide gave them a greater chance of getting the patent, and "pantaloons" covered a lot of ground. But once they had the patent in hand, they wanted their future customers to be able to wear the riveted clothing in any way they wanted. They knew men would understand what they meant by "overalls."

Levi and Jacob also understood that the product they were about to put on the market was both familiar and new. They did not come up with a new design for the actual pantaloons or overalls. Jacob, as a tailor, knew how to make a garment that men would want to wear, that they were used to wearing. What was new was the rivets. Customers could see them there, reinforcing the pockets, but the pants weren't so strange that men would not want to try them. The rivets were simply an addition to the typical work pants they were used to buying, and if the storekeeper did his job well, these customers would want to buy the riveted pants instead of the unriveted ones.

The word "overalls" itself has been used since at least 1782 in the United

States, and the phrase "heavy blue denim overalls" can be found in clothing advertising as far back as the 1850s. Although duck cloth was also used in the production of overalls by other manufacturers, Levi and Jacob decided that they would produce their pants in both duck and denim. Jacob had already used both back in Reno, but neither of the men could have imagined how popular the latter would become. And soon.

The origin of denim—both the fabric and the word—can cause even the most genteel textile historians to get into overheated arguments with one another. Most agree that the word comes from the French "serge de Nîmes," meaning a serge or twill type of fabric woven in the town of Nîmes, about 450 miles south of Paris. A fabric with this name was known in France before the seventeenth century. There was also a fabric called "nim," and both were wool blends.

But serge de Nîmes was known in England well before the end of the seventeenth century. This begs the question: had this fabric been imported from France, or was it a homegrown English fabric? Textiles were often named for a specific geographic location, even though they were made elsewhere. Consider "Kentucky Jeans," for example, which were made in many places that were not Kentucky. So the name and the fabric originated in France.

Serge de Nîmes was made of silk and wool, but denim has always been made of cotton. What we have here is a relation between textiles that is in name only, though both are a twill weave. That is, a fabric whose threads, upon close inspection, run along the diagonal, rather than straight up and down like a grid.

Textiles and their names often have murky and unresolved origins. For example, the real origin of the term "serge de nim," or "serge de Nîmes," could be a fabric that resembled the part-wool fabric called "nim." "Serge de Nîmes" was better known, and the term potentially was mistranslated when it crossed the English Channel. Savvy British merchants may have given a zippy—and perhaps better known—French name to an English fabric, most likely for marketing purposes.

One thing we do know, thanks to the *Oxford English Dictionary*, is that "de Nîmes" had been Anglicized to "denim" in England by at least 1695. But not all the time. "Serge de Nim" was used to describe some trousers in 1705, for example. However, by the time this fabric—by now made of cotton—moved across the Atlantic, its name was only, and always, denim.

One of the first printed references to the word "denim" in America was in 1789; a Rhode Island newspaper reported on the local production of denim (among other fabrics). The book *The Weavers Draft Book and Clothiers Assistant,* published in 1792, contains technical sketches of the weaving methods for a variety of denims.[5] Denim was one of the first fabrics to come out of America's fledgling textile industry in the eighteenth century, and it would never have gotten off the ground without British innovation and an early example of industrial espionage.

Britain was well known for its woolen cloth, thanks to a climate and landscape admirably suited for raising sheep. But in the mid-eighteenth century, men such as Richard Arkwright and others began to mechanize the production of cotton cloth, rather than importing it from India, the source of both raw and finished cotton goods. By the end of the century, only the picked cotton itself came into England, and fine, homegrown fabrics were rolling off new water- and steam-powered machinery.

This first Industrial Revolution created an insatiable demand for cotton in England's colonies across the Atlantic. This was worrisome for British producers. For nearly a century England had laws in place that prohibited its various technologies from leaving the country. Once textile machinery proved to be essential to the British economy, tougher laws were enacted to prevent diagrams, models, or machinery from passing beyond its borders. The list of prohibited exports also included the men who knew how to build and operate the equipment. One man managed to run this blockade, and in doing so, helped create America's own textile industry.

His name was Samuel Slater, and he was an overseer at a cotton mill owned by Jedediah Strutt. He chafed at his place on the economic ladder and felt that England's enormous textile output couldn't last forever. He thought the industry and his own future lay in America, but he could not leave the country as the employee of a textile mill with deep knowledge of its operations.

So, in 1789, he disguised himself as a farmer and lost himself in London before booking passage to the colonies. He had everything he needed in his head: the plans for a water-powered spinning machine, which he had memorized down to the last spinning head. Within a year, financed by the forward-looking (and slave-trade invested) Brown family of Providence, Rhode Island, he started to build factories for making cotton yarn.

Not all of the cotton in America was home-grown at this point, though it had been cultivated in the colonies since 1786. The invention of the cotton gin in 1793, mechanizing the tedious process of separating clean fibers from seeds, not only made cotton production a very American operation, but it drove the expansion of the plantation South and the entrenchment of the slavery system. Between 1800 and 1820 cotton exports from America to England grew from nearly 18 million pounds to a phenomenal 128 million.[6]

The raw materials moved north to become finished goods, with New England rapidly becoming the center of fabric production in the country. And, from the beginning, both denim and jean fabrics were staples on the weaving floor. George Washington, a champion of the new country's textile industry, toured a Massachusetts mill in 1789 and spent some time watching denim being made.[7] The pages of American newspapers in the decades before the Civil War were filled with advertisements for clothing made of "blue denim" or bolts of "denims" fabric for sale. Sometimes a color wasn't even specified, though from the 1840s to the 1860s both blue and brown denim were sold from Honolulu to South Carolina.

The color, whatever it was, came from how the warp, or top yarns of the woven goods, was dyed. The warp formed the front of the fabric and consisted of two yarns or strands together, working as one. The weft or fill yarn—one strand only—was white or some lighter color, and was the underside of the fabric. And whether denim was blue or brown (or any other color), the fill flitted like a ghost among the brighter-colored warp, giving denim a multidimensional shade that few other fabrics could match.

Duck, the other traditional textile for workwear, was simpler. It was a plain weave, two warp yarns woven over two fill yarns of the same color in a straight, not diagonal formation. The word comes from the Dutch, *doeck,* meaning linen or linen clothing. Duck can be woven from either linen or cotton, and though it looks like canvas or sailcloth, it is lighter in weight, while still sturdy enough for tailors like Jacob Davis to use it for men's working pants.

Denim could be made in any color, but blue was the most popular and the most advertised. And thanks to an eighteenth-century woman who desperately needed a cash crop to support her family, that blue came from a home-grown source: indigo.

Indigo, both the plant and the dye extracted from it, is ancient, and before it was the color of everyday wear, it was the color of royalty and power. Egyptians, Hindus, Mayans, and the early Christians used this shade of blue in their clothing and their art. The plant itself is of the genus *Indigofera,* and two species (out of hundreds) are used to make the dye: *Indigofera tinctoria* is native to India and Asia, while *Indigofera suffruticosa* is found in Central America. The dye is extracted from the leaves through a complicated fermentation process.

The ancient historian Herodotus mentioned the blue dye and its use in the Mediterranean regions around 450 BC. Portuguese and Italian merchants found good sources of the dye in Egypt and Persia, and indigo became an important commodity on the trade routes between the Far East and southern Europe. Dyers in England, France, northern Italy and Germany could use a local plant called woad to obtain the blues they wanted, but it paled (literally) next to the richness of indigo. By the seventeenth century the Dutch and British were trading massive quantities of the dyestuff from India and from colonies in the West Indies and the Americas. India, by the way, is probably the origin for the word "indigo" itself.

The plant, no matter the species, needs hot, humid weather to grow and thrive. Some traders felt that Asian indigo was superior to the dyes from the New World, but cultivation of American indigo didn't get going until a young woman named Eliza Lucas Pinckney planted some New World seeds near her home in South Carolina.

Born to English parents on the West Indian island of Antigua around 1722, Eliza Lucas went to school in England and then left the Caribbean with her family in 1738. War was coming to the island, and Eliza's mother wasn't well, so the Lucases moved to South Carolina, where they began to manage three plantations that Eliza's grandfather owned. They lived on the smallest of the three: six hundred acres and located about seventeen miles from present-day Charleston.

Eliza's father was still involved with political movements on Antigua, and after a year, he was recalled to serve in the British Army during a trade war between England and Spain, with the unintentionally hilarious name of the War of Jenkins' Ear (so named for a British captain who lost his ear during the conflict). He remained on Antigua, eventually serving as lieutenant governor, and died in 1747.

In the meantime, Eliza, who later married Charles Pinckney in 1744, was in charge of the family's land and livelihood. She and her father regularly corresponded about the plantations, which were rapidly falling into debt. She wanted to find a crop that would pull them out of their financial hole, and her father obliged by sending her some indigo seeds. It's not clear which species she planted, and she wasn't the first person to try cultivating indigo in the colonies. However, she was the first to make indigo production a paying commodity, due mostly to good timing. Rice was a more profitable crop in the South, needing the same growing conditions as indigo. But in the 1740s the price of rice fell, and because of the War of Jenkins' Ear, indigo supplies from the Caribbean were cut off.

Eliza shared the seeds of her successful crop with others throughout South Carolina. By 1746 over 100,000 pounds of processed dye had been sent to England.[8] By the 1750s both species of indigo were being grown in the Carolinas, though it was a valuable cash crop for only about fifty years. During the Revolutionary War indigo was embargoed and could not be exported, and its fortunes fell as quickly as they had risen. Indigo was replaced by cotton, a crop that yielded much bigger profits and, as it turns out, historical influence.

Levi had regularly sold bolts of fabrics to his customers, one of them, of course, being Jacob Davis. No one knows which textile mills these came from, but since the majority of fabrics were woven in New England, it is very likely that the duck, denim, calico, and other fabrics came from that region, via Jonas in New York. However, when it came to the denim for the patent riveted overalls, there was really only one place to go. New

England itself hosted the greatest concentration of textile mills by the mid-nineteenth century, and it was the Amoskeag Manufacturing Company of Manchester, New Hampshire, that specifically commanded the attention of merchants like Levi Strauss.

Manchester sits at the Merrimack River, which lured settlers and traders beginning in 1722, with the town of Derryfield incorporated there in 1751. While the river was envisioned as the perfect conduit for goods headed to places like Boston, the treacherous Amoskeag Falls were in the way. (*Amoskeag* is an English corruption of the word *Nemaske*, meaning a place of fish, or abundant fish, and used by the local Penacook Indians.) However, in 1807 a local entrepreneur and merchant named Samuel Blodget championed the construction of a canal to circumvent the falls, which proved to be a boon to the now-thriving little town.

Blodget had visited the great English industrial city of Manchester soon after the end of the Revolutionary War, and by 1810 had succeeded in getting Derryfield renamed Manchester. The name fulfilled its ambitions when other local men began to construct cotton-spinning mills near the river. In 1831 a consortium of money men from Boston funded the creation of a new enterprise, incorporated in 1831: the Amoskeag Manufacturing Company. During the following decade, machine shops and foundries were built at the site so that the company could be as self-sufficient as possible. A company town was built up around the spinning complex, which eventually encompassed houses, parks, churches, and schools. Constructed of locally made bricks, the imposing red buildings dominated both landscape and life.

In 1851 the company displayed its fine fabrics—including denim—at the Great Exhibition in London, winning out over many homegrown products. Amoskeag textiles were now recognized for their quality, and the mill for its astonishing output. In 1854 the company produced twenty million yards of fabrics, including denim.[9] In the late 1840s the machine shops actually made locomotives. In 1859 trains were put aside in favor of the production of steam-powered fire engines. The San Francisco Fire Department bought four of them in 1866. And by the time of the Civil War, the word Amoskeag was used in advertising for both fabrics and clothing, the guarantee of a quality product.

The raw cotton fueling Amoskeag's spinning machines came from the South and was, of course, cultivated by slave labor. And despite New England's reputation for being a hotbed of abolitionist agitation in the antebellum period, the owners of the great mills ignored the source of their wealth or were sometimes invested in it themselves.

If Levi bought cotton fabrics from the Amoskeag Manufacturing Company in the period before emancipation, he had to have known about the industry's reliance on slave labor, as well. As with voting and other politically charged topics, Jews did not think as one when it came to slavery. Many Jews living in the South before the Civil War defended the institutions, and some were slave owners themselves. There is no way to know how Levi felt about slavery, but any fabric purchases before the war had this taint upon them.

Levi had to look east for his fabrics because there were no textile mills in the West that could make the type and quantity he needed. Cotton wasn't grown in California until just before World War I, and the only mills in the area cranked out woolen cloth, not denim and duck. Jonas, living in New York, could find sources for fine fabrics in his part of the country, to be shipped to Levi out west. Within a couple of weeks after relocating his family to San Francisco—on May 10, 1873, to be precise—and with foreknowledge that the patent would be granted, Jacob began to make the first riveted pants in his new city, for his new employer.

The company has an oral tradition about the first pants made in San Francisco. It is based on an interview with an elderly employee named Bill Hindshaw, who was hired in 1898 and interviewed in the 1960s. He stated that the initial batch of riveted overalls was made by women working in their homes. Women had been doing this kind of work in the city for at least a decade, so his recollection rings true. Jacob may have done the riveting after the pants were sewn up, but we just don't know.

In any case, Jacob delivered the first batch of duck and denim pants to the Battery Street headquarters on June 2. They were immediately added to the company inventory, and salesmen were instructed on how to sell the new products to customers in their territories. It didn't take long: the first sale of duck pants was on June 5, and denim on June 19.

Because of the rivets, and the additional labor time needed to apply them, the pants commanded top dollar. The wholesale price was $19.50 per dozen, with Levi Strauss & Co. seeing between 33 and 40 percent in profit. Storekeepers therefore paid about $1.65 before adding their own profit margin. Traditional overalls hovered around 50 cents a pair in the mid-1870s, so salesmen and counter men had to do quite the selling job to convince potential customers that pants with rivets were worth the extra dollar or so.

On July 15, Levi Strauss & Co. started manufacturing the overalls in a factory at 415 Market Street, between Fremont and First, just a couple of blocks from the headquarters. This part of town was given over to a number of industrial enterprises. The building at 413–415 Market was also home to Horatio N. Cook, who dealt in leather hoses and fire suppression supplies, and was the agency for the Douglass Artificial Limb. Another tenant, Van Winkle & Davenport, imported iron, steel, heavy hardware, and Cumberland Coal.

A month after Levi Strauss & Co. got its factory up and running south of Market, an experiment took place farther west, on the steep grade of Clay Street. August 2, 1873, saw the first successful run of another classic San Francisco symbol: the cable car.

CHAPTER 11

TOWERS OF STRENGTH

Hiring workers for the factory was as easy as placing an advertisement in the *San Francisco Chronicle*. And the women who answered the ad knew that if they got the job, they were required to bring something highly unusual to the factory.

> Wanted—Fifty First-Class Female sewing machine operators, who can bring their own machines with them; either Singer's No. 2 or Grover & Baker's No. 1, for sewing heavy work. Steady and remunerative employment, at 415 Market street, upstairs."[1]

The emphasis on the word "female" in this and other ads is not a surprise. Men who worked in sewing factories did the strenuous jobs, such as cutting the denim, maintaining the equipment, stoking boilers, and keeping the floors swept. Having mastered at home the use of sewing machines now that they were more affordable for the average household, women were the most desirable workers in a factory setting. Many women already made good money on their own as seamstresses and dressmakers. And although the mental image of women dragging machinery along Market Street is a little disconcerting, outfitting a full factory with enough Singers, Grover & Bakers, or Howes to make the anticipated output of riveted overalls would have been very expensive.

By the time Levi and Jacob hired those first few women to sew the first few overalls, San Francisco was already on its way to becoming the ninth leading center of industrial production in the United States, a distinction it would reach by 1880.[2] The biggest boom was in clothing, boot and shoe making, and, interestingly, cigar making. These industries were the largest employers in the city by 1880, as well.[3]

For now, Levi and Jacob relied on the women of San Francisco, their personal sewing machines, and their first-class skills. The women did have to learn a few new methods, however, especially if they were not used to working with the heavy denim. The fabric was unwieldy, was harder on needles, and the indigo likely meant the women left the factory at the end of the work day with blue-tinted fingers.

Whether in denim or duck, the riveted work pants required the most basic type of construction, with typical workwear details. The overalls had a waistband with a "cinch" or two-piece strap of the same fabric as the pants themselves. A simple two-pronged metal piece was sewn onto the left strap. By pulling the straps together, and forcing the prongs into the other strap, the wearer could adjust how tight (or not) the pants would fit. They were also held up by six suspender buttons placed strategically around the waistband.

A leather patch was sewn underneath the cinch or on the right hand side of the back of the waistband. Embossed on the leather (likely from cattle rather than other livestock) was the company name, address, and language about Levi Strauss & Co. being the sole proprietors and manufacturers of the Patented Riveted Duck & Denim Clothing. At the bottom was a place for waist and length, hand-written in black ink during the first few years.

There were two hand pockets in the front, and the right-hand one was also fitted with a coin or watch pocket. The back of the pants sported just one pocket, on the right. The leg pieces were cut on the selvage or "self-edge" part of the denim or duck, which meant that if the cuffs were turned up, the white edge of the denim, or a black line on the duck, was visible on the outside.

Cuffs, especially on the denim pants, generally had to be turned up, because the fabric was not preshrunk; that was an innovation many decades in the future. Any customer who wore denim pants, even before the riveted ones came on the market, knew that he had to get the pants oversized, to allow for shrinkage, depending on how much he planned to wash the pants, or at least get them wet. Unless he "stacked" or simply crumpled the pant legs on his boots (if he wore them), they would drag on the ground. Early photographs show men wearing the overalls both ways: cuffed or crumpled.

These first overalls had eleven rivets: two holding down the cinch, two on the corners of the back pocket, two each on the front pockets, two on the watch pocket, and another at the base of the button fly. The rivets were stamped with the company's initials, followed by "SF" for San Francisco, and the month and date of the patent.

No one knows where Levi Strauss & Co. obtained the rivets that went on the pants, but it is certain they were made of copper. Where that metal came from is also a mystery. Arizona was a big copper producer, but the copper boom there came after the 1870s. Michigan is a likely source, but the actual supplier is, so far, elusive. Why this metal was chosen over any others is also unknown.

Applying the rivets in the early days was probably done by a man with a couple of tools, and the rivet itself was actually a two-piece affair. A nipple-like piece was fitted through the hole of another that looked like a washer. These pieces had to go through the very heavy denim, and though a man with a chisel and a hammer-like tool called a maul could manage this, it's likely rudimentary machinery took the place of the one man/one rivet system fairly soon.

The thread used to sew up the overalls was an orange shade, and over the decades people have speculated (and published) that the color was chosen because it matched the color of the copper rivets. This is a nice theory but with nothing to back it up. The only thing we know about the thread color comes from a letter that Jacob sent to Levi on January 6, 1873. The patent had already been rejected, and Jacob continued to press Levi to keep trying. In the meantime, he still bought fabric and sundries from the company, and continued to make and sell riveted pants. In his letter he asked specifically for "Orange color" machine thread, though he did not say why.

The buttons on the denim pants were a zinc alloy and were stamped with the full company name, followed by "S.F. Cal." They were the traditional, and very modern-looking, "shank" style, and were also made of two pieces that fit together. In the 1870s they were probably attached by hand using a tool that looks like a pair of pliers, but by the 1880s, this fastening could be done with newly patented machinery. The duck pants, by contrast, had sewn-on buttons. It's possible a woman highly skilled in sewing on buttons could apply these just as quickly as a man applying the shank buttons with a hand tool.

The pants had one final flourish: stitching on the back pocket, consisting of two curves, made up of two parallel lines each, resembling an "M." Along with just about every other detail on the pants, the reasoning for the stitching was lost in the fires of 1906. The most logical explanation, and one based on the history of workwear in general, is that the stitching was meant to help distinguish the pants from the other denim overalls that shared shelf space in a men's mercantile or general store. While the rivets certainly made the pants unique among the competition, other products might have had pocket stitching that was familiar to regular customers. Back pockets were sometimes lined with blanket flannel or other fabrics, and the stitching could have been used to hold it in place; in fact, Levi Strauss & Co. introduced its own line of blanket-lined clothing sometime before 1876. But perhaps having a particular design on the back pocket was another instance of making a product that was both new and familiar. Other overalls had pocket stitching, and men were used to seeing that. So Jacob and Levi may have chosen to add this extra step to the riveted pants in order to blend innovation with tradition.

By December 1873, when both riveted overalls and riveted duck-hunting coats were now on the market, the company sold over 1,800 dozen riveted goods, which comes to over 20,000 individual pieces. Working men from California to Montana were snapping up the products—emphasis on working. Economic distinctions continued to be rigidly defined by clothing in the nineteenth century. Everyone knew that denim overalls—riveted or not—adorned working men alone, and there was also a view that these trousers were a western phenomenon. In July 1873 a former member of Congress from Minnesota, Ignatius Donnelly, was trying to get reelected. According to a story in the *Sacramento Daily Union*, Donnelly tried "to fool the Western farmers into sending him back to the House of

Representatives. He wears a hickory shirt, blue denim overalls and plantation shoes without stockings."[4]

But there was one westerner who did not wear overalls or riveted clothing of any kind:

Levi Strauss.

As a successful business owner, as the man whose name was on the company letterhead and the leather patch, and who was rapidly becoming the
patriarch of his extended family, Levi would never have worn a pair of riveted
work pants. His uniform was a black suit, a white shirt, a silk tie, and a top hat.

Jacob Davis probably didn't wear the overalls either. Levi brought him
to San Francisco to get the production of the riveted products up and running. As a foreman or a manufacturer—the titles he used to describe himself in city directories—Jacob was in a position of authority. And while his
suit was less expensive than Levi's, and his tie wasn't made of silk, Jacob
had moved past his hand-to-mouth tailoring days, and his upscale clothing
reflected his new status.

Negotiations over the rivet patent and his working relationship with Jacob
did not take up all of Levi's time in the early 1870s. He still had a big dry
goods business to run, and he also was putting more energy into outside
business interests.

He chose his activities wisely, and his fortune not only grew but gained
notice. On October 11, 1874, the *New York Times* published an article titled
"San Francisco Millionaires." It was a reprint of an article first seen in the
San Francisco Bulletin: a "carefully prepared list of individuals and firms in
San Francisco whose reputed wealth exceeds $1,000,000." There were over
fifty men and sixteen companies on the list. The writer referred to the individuals as "towers of strength," and Levi was listed as a millionaire in his
own right. Though the company wasn't listed, it was worth much more.[5]

Levi shared this millionaire's list with a formidable collection of San
Francisco personalities whose interests represented nearly every enterprise
that had shaped the city, and, to a great extent, the American West.

For starters, there were the founders of the Bank of California: Darius
Ogden Mills, William Ralston, and William Sharon. Ralston, who also

owned the splendid Palace Hotel, took the fall when the Bank of California failed in 1875. One day he went for his morning swim in San Francisco Bay and drowned, giving rise to suspicions of suicide.

Also on the list were two of the Bonanza Kings, men who made fortunes in the Nevada silver rush: James Flood and William O'Brien.

Henry Miller and Charles Lux were the Cattle Kings, whose wealth came from land and beef. Their rival, James B. Ali Haggin, was the son-in-law of attorney (and millionaire listee) Lloyd Tevis, the president of Wells Fargo Bank, who also had interests in water systems and mining. In the nineteenth century, Tevis was the very definition of a "capitalist."

Peter Donahue built the first iron foundry in San Francisco: Union Iron Works.

And last but not least (certainly in their own minds) were three of the Big Four: Leland Stanford, Charles Crocker, and Mark Hopkins. These former store owners ran the powerful Central Pacific Railroad, which would be joined in 1885 by the even more powerful Southern Pacific (SP). Stanford was later a president of the SP, had already been governor of California, would be a U.S. senator in the following decade and, of course, would create the university that bears his name.

Levi's enterprises, like those of his contemporaries, were varied in scope and level of risk. Where he had been simply a stockholder in the previous decade, he was now a major investor, and in some very interesting organizations. Taking on the manufacturing and marketing of the riveted pants— and succeeding—seems to have given Levi the freedom to move even further away from simply wholesaling dry goods. His assets bore this out. The *San Francisco Chronicle* printed a list of the property assessments for the city's businesses in 1877. Levi Strauss & Co. had $245,000 in merchandise and $5,000 in cash (together amounting to over $5 million today).

Someone had taken note of his prosperity a few years earlier. On April 15, 1873, burglars tried to break into the company warehouse and headquarters on Battery Street. They started to cut away part of the back door but couldn't do enough to get into the building, so they just took off. When workers came in the next day, they spotted the damage, called the police, and arranged to have it repaired. The intruders were never caught.

Levi's success also convinced him to take stronger action in organizing his company. On May 27, 1874, Levi and Louis signed copartnership papers for Levi Strauss & Co., including Jonas Strauss and William Sahlein as the other half of the partnership. Louis had power of attorney for the two New Yorkers, and he and Levi appeared before a notary on June 10.

Confidence in business allowed Levi to take on new ventures in far-flung locations. Back in 1869 another wealthy German immigrant named Isaac Lankershim, who owned vast acreage in southern California, purchased sixty thousand acres in the San Fernando Valley and formed the San Fernando Valley Farm Homestead Association. Levi may have been an early stockholder. Then, on January 8, 1875, Levi, Lankershim, and five other capitalists from northern and southern California filed articles of incorporation for the San Fernando Sheep Company, which was organized to buy, sell, and raise sheep and other livestock, as well as raise crops.

The sheep were already in place before the company was formally incorporated—40,000 of them by 1873. The firm sent their first clip of wool to New York in March 1875 (a "clip" refers to the wool taken from a herd of sheep). They shipped 8 bales of wool that year, a bale usually running about 400 pounds. By the following year 11 bales went east. In May 1877, the *Pacific Rural Press* reported that the company's clip was probably the largest in the United States, weighing in at 331,000 pounds of wool, a value of $50,000 (over $1 million today). The entire crop was shipped to Europe.

But there was trouble brewing. A recent and severe drought meant financial death to many livestock owners, and Lankershim's group was not immune. He had started to plant some of the land in wheat, but it didn't produce as expected, either.

In June 1879 Levi and fellow merchant Louis Sachs took the train to Los Angeles, staying at the Cosmopolitan Hotel for a few nights. They were likely there to talk with Lankershim about a new venture, or at least a renamed one. In February 1880 Levi, Louis, and four other money men (including Lankershim) incorporated the Los Angeles Farming and Milling Company, subsuming the old San Fernando Valley Ranch Company and its sheep business.

Lankershim died in 1882, and his son realized that the property now covered with wheat and barley could turn a greater profit if it was developed, since more people were coming to Los Angeles and the area was experiencing one of its many residential booms. Within a few years this land became known as Toluca, and is today North Hollywood.

Levi's involvement with the enterprise after Lankershim's death is murky, though he was the vice president of the Los Angeles Farming and Milling Company as late as 1900. One thing is clear, however. He didn't get involved in any business venture that was not tied to the development of the state or its industry. For example, about the same time Levi was investing in southern California sheep, he was doing the same with northern California wool.

In December 1875 Levi and Joseph Brandenstein—whose son Max would soon be the "B" in the famous MJB Coffee—purchased the Mission and Pacific Woolen Mills, at Folsom and Fifteenth Streets in San Francisco. A third interest in the company was then conveyed to Leopold Cahn, owner of the Pioneer Woolen Factory. The following year Levi and Brandenstein sold the rest of the stake to Cahn, and the name was changed to Mission Woolen Mills, with Levi retaining stock in the firm. Levi Strauss & Co. was doing good business making blanket-lined riveted pants and coats, and no doubt received an excellent price on the wool used for linings.

Levi also put his voice and his name to causes that would either further the expansion of trade or prevent it from being restricted. One of the earliest was his support for the Hawaiian Reciprocity Treaty of 1875.

The U.S. government negotiated this treaty with the Kingdom of Hawaii in late 1874. Among its many articles were provisions for removing tariffs on commodities coming to the United States from Hawaii, and also removing them from goods going the other direction. Among these goods were fabrics, linens, and other dry goods. Levi had good retail customers in Honolulu who bought these items from his inventory and arranged for their shipment to Hawaii. The Reciprocity Treaty would keep that relationship a lucrative one.

The treaty was signed on January 30, 1875, but had to be ratified by both Hawaii and the United States. King David Kalakaua, monarch of the kingdom of Hawaii, pushed the ratification through on April 17. On March 3, the leading merchants of San Francisco had sent a petition via telegraph to the two senators who represented California: Newton Booth and Aaron A. Sargent. The men representing the companies listed at the bottom of the petition—including Levi Strauss & Co.—respectfully requested that Booth and Sargent support the Reciprocity Treaty and advocate for its ratification. On May 31, the United States followed King Kalakaua's example and voted yes.

Many issues loomed large for San Francisco's wholesale merchants in the years following the Civil War. One of the most annoying involved business failures and bankruptcies, illegitimate ones, that is. Although the Chamber of Commerce had tried to arbitrate between merchants and their customers when retail stores went under or bills went unpaid, there was a lot of grumbling that many of these "failures" were not failures at all. Settlements were sometimes out of proportion to what the retail merchant could actually pay. That is, sometimes retailers had hidden assets that could have gone toward paying off debts, but there was no organization in place to investigate each case. So, in 1877, a group of wholesalers formed the Merchants' Protective Association, renamed the Board of Trade of San Francisco the following year. Levi Strauss & Co. was one of the founding companies, and Levi served as the association's first treasurer in 1877.

San Francisco history sometimes played a part in how Levi approached his business. He was very concerned about the dangers of fire, for example, no doubt having heard the horror stories of the 1850 and 1851 conflagrations. And he had good reason to be worried.

On March 21, 1875, a Levi Strauss & Co. storage shed on Tyler Street, between Taylor and Jones, was destroyed by fire, along with nearly four hundred packing boxes. The loss came to $1,000, and ten days later two boys, John O'Brien and John E. Walker, were arrested and charged with arson. It's not clear how old these "boys" were, but they were certainly underage, since they were "given passes to the Industrial School" as a punishment. In other words, they were sent to an early version of juvenile hall.[6]

On June 13, 1875, there was another fire at a company property, which may have been the headquarters. The location of the fire didn't make the newspapers, but Levi's response did: on July 5 he threw a banquet in honor of the Fire Patrol, to thank them for stopping the blaze and saving the building.

The company regularly sent money or goods to fire relief efforts in other locations, too. Levi Strauss & Co. sent $100 to a committee helping out those affected by the great Chicago fire of 1871. A check for $250 was sent to Portland after that city's fire of August 1873, and the same amount went to Virginia City, Nevada, in late 1875 for its fire relief committee.

In April 1879, Levi, along with over one hundred mercantile firms and individual merchants, sent a letter to the San Francisco Board of Supervisors, protesting its decision to remove limits on the number of wooden buildings that could be erected in the financial and industrial districts. The policy change, the merchants argued, "permits the erection of large frame buildings to be occupied as mills and manufactories and other hazardous occupations and is decidedly against the well-being and safety of the whole city."[7] It also threatened many of the men who signed that letter and whose own factories could be lost to fire. It's unclear from the surviving records, but the supervisors most likely ignored the merchants' plea.

Levi's concern about destruction of local property was not entirely altruistic. He had his own factory to worry about. And between the early 1870s and the end of the 1880s, Levi both amassed and sold an astonishing collection of real estate. In Bavaria his people were landless, but in America anyone could buy land and property. Both the state and the region were growing, and would continue to grow, and Levi made sure he was part of this expansion. His reach went even beyond U.S. borders.

When the Fraser River gold rush hit in Victoria, British Columbia, in 1858, a little community called Emory Creek was formed near the river. Emory Creek started out as a typical collection of tents and shacks. Its miners soon discovered that they were not going to find the piles of gold they expected. Most took off for shinier pastures, but speculators came into the area, noting that the creek could serve as a terminus for the riverboats plying the Fraser River. The area was quickly becoming interesting to the Canadian Pacific Railroad, and in 1879 the company chose the city of Emory (or sometimes Emory City) as its western hub.

A big real estate auction took place in Victoria, British Columbia, in March 1880. Up for sale were lots in Emory, and Levi Strauss & Co. purchased three of them. Two of the lots were on the old Cariboo Wagon Road, which went right past a sawmill that was in operation twenty-four hours a day. With the railroad setting up shop in Emory, chances were good that this investment would pay off.

It didn't. In 1881, the Canadian Pacific Railroad decided to relocate its western terminus to the town of Yale, a few miles away. By 1885 Emory was a ghost town, and unless Levi had acted quickly and sold out (it is uncertain whether he did), his property was soon close to worthless.

He had better luck farther south.

In 1874, after twenty years of legal maneuvering, the city of San Diego received clear title to what were called the "pueblo" lands. These 48,000 acres had been part of the Pueblo of San Diego, established by the government of Mexico after it gained its independence from Spain in 1821. The pueblo itself was granted its status by Mexico in 1834. But when California became part of the United States after the Mexican War, title to the lands had to be proved in American courts. Mexican citizens were rarely able to hold on to their property, and claims were generally decided in favor of American land owners and officials.[8]

In March 1883 a man named G. W. R. McDonald sold five acres in Pueblo Lot No. 1343 to Levi Strauss, for $5,000. Levi bought an additional piece of this lot in 1901, though what the company did with it after his death is unknown.[9] Levi saw how the city of San Diego was developing and believed in its promise, even as railroads and the military were showing great interest in its well-placed port.

Levi also snatched up real estate closer to home in San Francisco, and would do so for the rest of his life. In 1883 alone he was assessed $550,000 in taxes on his personal property, worth $13 million today.

Owning land or property comes with headaches beyond just the property taxes. In 1874 Levi held a $50,000 mortgage on the Pioneer Bank building at the corner of California and Montgomery Streets. Joseph C. Duncan, an officer of both the Safe Deposit Corporation and the Pioneer Bank, was supposed to pay up the mortgage by June 1877. He told Levi he was having some financial difficulty, and Levi agreed to reduce the mortgage by $35,000, with the balance payable in six monthly installments of $2,500 dollars each. The first was due on June 30, which Duncan paid, and he also made a payment on August 21. But no more money came in as the fall progressed, and Levi commenced a suit against him to collect the outstanding debt. By October the reason why Duncan defaulted became clear.

The Pioneer Bank failed on October 7, 1877, and within a few days everyone in town knew why: Duncan had used his position to embezzle from the bank to cover how badly he had managed its affairs. He then disappeared, and a massive manhunt failed to find him. On February 12, 1878, Levi won his case against Duncan, and he foreclosed on the former Pioneer Bank building.

Twelve days later, Duncan was discovered. He was caught in a boardinghouse on Kearney Street near City Hall, of all places. He gave a number of self-pitying interviews to the newspapers over the next few days, and among the people he blamed for his predicament was Levi Strauss. Referring to the defaulted mortgage payments, Duncan claimed Levi "came down upon me, and other creditors followed with relentless vigor."[10] Levi was also interviewed, and his response was published the day after Duncan's statement appeared, in the February 26 issue of the *San Francisco Chronicle* (on Levi's forty-ninth birthday, no less): "Mr. Strauss protests against the imputation of having dealt with Duncan with unnecessary rigor. On the contrary he made concessions that good business discretion would not have sanctioned, and Duncan was treated magnanimously rather than otherwise."[11]

Duncan went on trial for the first time in December 1878, but after four attempts to convict him, the case was dismissed in July of 1882. He and his wife, Mary Dora, divorced around 1880, and he then moved to Los Angeles, where he speculated in real estate and remarried. He did well for a while, but by the late 1880s that city's property boom had flattened, and he again lost everything. In 1898 he and his new family were on a ship bound from London to New York, when it crashed into rocks near Cornwall. The Duncans were among the dead.

The fascinating footnote to this story relates to Duncan's San Francisco family. The last of his four children with Mary Dora was born in the midst of the banking scandal, flight, and trials. Her name was Isadora Duncan, and she was one of the pioneers of modern dance in America. Her colorful and, to some people, scandalous personal life easily surpassed that of her notorious father.

In February 1874 Levi Strauss & Co. began to run display advertisements in papers such as the *Daily Alta California* and others in San Francisco. The text ran about the same in each:

CAUTION!

NOTICE IS HEREBY GIVEN, THAT WE are the owners of United States Letters Patent granted May 20th, 1873, for fastening Pocket Openings in Pantaloons by fastening the two pieces of cloth at the edge or ends of the pocket openings together with metal rivets or eyelets. We have commenced legal proceedings to protect our patent, and all parties and dealers are hereby particularly cautioned and warned against either making or selling pantaloons having our improvement attached to them, without our authority as we shall prosecute all parties so doing to the extent of the law, in such case made and provided.[12]

The legal proceedings mentioned in the ad concerned a lawsuit, the first of at least eight patent infringement suits filed by the company between 1874 and 1878 against manufacturers and retailers all across the country, from California to New York.

Levi Strauss & Co., as the patent holder for riveted clothing, was the only company allowed to make and sell pants, jackets, and other garments reinforced with metal rivets for the next seventeen years, until 1890. After that year, any company could take advantage of the expired patent and make as many riveted garments as it wanted. Patent law was designed so that an inventor could take economic advantage of his new creation, but only for a reasonable period of time. Hence the seventeen-year moratorium.

Invention, innovation, and technology were supposed to benefit the public eventually, and wise patent holders made hay out of their new products while they could.

But in the meantime the success of the riveted goods was a temptation to those who thought they could circumvent the law, or at least try to. The first was someone that Levi knew, who served with him on the Board of Trade, and whose rival dry goods and clothing business was just the next block over on Sansome Street: Albert Elfelt, principal in the firm of A. B. Elfelt & Co.

CHAPTER 12

HOME INDUSTRY

Sometime in early 1874, A. B. Elfelt & Co. began to manufacture and put riveted pants into the retail stores that carried its dry goods and other wholesaled clothing. Levi Strauss found out about this in the spring, and by June a lawsuit was in full flower. Once he was sued, Elfelt took his products off the shelves of his stores, but Levi Strauss & Co. proceeded with the lawsuit anyway in order to show San Francisco manufacturers that it was serious about its patent rights.

However, there were machinations going on below the surface of this case. Michael Reese was another local Bavarian who started life peddling merchandise around the gold country, and then made a massive fortune in San Francisco real estate. He was a friend of both Levi Strauss and Alfred Elfelt, as all of the men ran in the same commercial circles and probably worshipped together at Temple Emanu-El.

The night before the lawsuit got underway Reese visited Levi one evening at his home on Powell Street. He asked Levi to drop the case; though we don't know exactly what was said, this plea may have been to keep enmity from creeping into what had been harmonious relations among the city's merchants. And although Levi, in a later infringement case, said he had agreed to stop his lawsuit, the trial went ahead anyway.

Elfelt's lawyers did their best to try to demolish Jacob Davis's claim that he had invented riveted clothing, even taking depositions from people in Nevada who said they had seen men wearing riveted pants before Davis came up with his idea. This gambit caused snickers at the *Pacific Rural Press* newspaper, and one writer jumped in to defend anyone who used its Dewey & Co. patent agency: "It is always easy to find some one who is willing to swear to prior use after an inventor has made a success of his invention."[1] He then went on to belabor the point in a way that both defended Davis and touted the power of patents in general: "Davis, the patentee, was an independent inventor and, being also a sensible man, he did what any sensible inventor would do—secured his invention by patenting it. Further, after securing his patent he has succeeded so far in making a success that his riveted overalls have driven all of the common overalls out of the market; and the consequence is, he has the combined capital and influence of our wholesale clothing merchants pitted against him."[2]

The Elfelt case dragged on until February of 1875. And although it was settled in favor of Levi Strauss & Co., amounting to damages of $2,000, Levi later said he paid all of Elfelt's court costs. This may have been the deal he made with Reese. By allowing the case to go through the courts, and by demonstrating that Elfelt was in the wrong, Levi strengthened his hold on the exclusive rights to riveted clothing. He did this in a way that did not cause Elfelt any financial difficulty, but he later said that he only covered these costs because Reese asked him to. And, in the end, to use his own words, Levi and Elfelt were "just as good friends as before."[3] In fact, when Elfelt died in 1886, Levi was on a special committee of the Board of Trade charged with writing a resolution honoring his long service to San Francisco's mercantile community.

This experience may have made Levi and Jacob think harder about protecting the patent. By the end of 1874 the company was not only making riveted pants and hunting coats but also vests, jumpers, and jackets. At some point in the latter part of that year or early in 1875, the men filed paperwork with the patent office to reissue their patent. These new documents changed the description of what the rivets were used for.

In the original patent of 1873, the invention was titled an "improvement in fastening pocket-openings." In the reissued patent, Number 6335, granted March 16, 1875, the invention was for an "improvement in fastening seams." This has a very specific meaning. The wording of the rest of the new patent document was not substantially different from the 1873 version, but the emphasis on seams gave more latitude to how the rivet was used. In other words, by saying that the rivets strengthened the seams, and not just the pockets, the new patent allowed the company to make a greater variety of riveted clothing, in which the rivets were not just placed on the pocket corners. This would prevent another inventor from trying to patent a process that used rivets for purposes other than pocket-fastening.

The reissued patent added two years to the company's right to be the sole manufacturer of riveted garments. When it went into effect in March 1875, the original 1873 patent was, in the words of the patent office, "surrendered." The seventeen-year term began again, meaning that instead of the patent expiring in 1890, it would expire in 1892. The extra two years, from 1873 to 1875, would be very welcome.

Sales figures for the riveted products made this an even more important move. By the end of 1874 the company had sold nearly 6,000 dozen individual garments; these were counted by dozens because the stores had to buy them that way, or at least in portions of dozens. In 1875 the sales figure was over 7,000 dozen. And the products were still priced at a "premium" wholesale level:

> Riveted pants: $19.50 per dozen
> Jackets and jumpers: $21 per dozen
> Oversized pants: $24 per dozen
> Duck hunting coats: $50 per dozen
> Vests: $21 per dozen

Levi later explained the popularity and increase in sales this way: "the goods were made up excellently and gave good satisfaction to all who bought them, and the demand kept on the increase . . . and they have a wide-spread reputation."[4]

That reputation was helped along with advertising. Ads for the riveted products began to appear in the spring of 1874, and among the first papers to carry them was *The Independent,* from Helena, Montana. As a mining region, this city was the logical geographic choice to spread the word, and the ads used large type and lots of celebratory language:

IMPORTANT

To the Workingman, Mechanic,

Drayman and Miner.

Buy Levi Strauss & Co.'s celebrated

Patented Riveted Duck

AND

Denim Overalls

The bottom of the ads also included the following statement: "None Genuine unless bearing our copyrighted label."[5]

Dewey & Co.'s *Pacific Rural Press* was also an early advertising partner. And retail stores in San Francisco and Boise started to advertise that they carried the riveted products on their shelves early in 1874.

Levi not only looked after Jacob's stake in the patent but also his other financial interests. In May 1873 Levi bought Jacob's property at 31 North Virginia Street in Reno for $1,000. This no doubt helped the Davis family with the costs of moving to San Francisco. In March 1875 the Davises moved from Folsom to 911 Hyde Street, between Pine and Bush. This was about ten blocks or so from the factory and headquarters, and Jacob probably took hired or public transportation to work each day. But this relocation has a much greater meaning. He was making enough money to move away from the city's industrial sector, to a part of town becoming more residential, even though it was still conveniently close to the financial district.

Levi kept Jacob's former tailor shop and home in his real estate portfolio, and in June 1875 he sold the property back to Jacob for one dollar. Three months later Jacob sold it to Reno resident John McGinley for $1,200. Overall, Jacob saw a profit on his former home of about $200, worth about $4,500 today.

Strauss and Stern family matters of all kinds came up in the early 1870s. Happy news came first: Nathan Strauss, who sometime in late 1873 had moved back to New York, became engaged to Minnie Gladke, the daughter of wealthy clothing manufacturer Jacob Gladke. They were married

January 7, 1874. It's likely Levi did not head east for the wedding, because David Stern, his sister's husband and valued partner in the business, passed away on January 2.

He was only in his early fifties, and his obituary reported that he had been ill for many years. On January 3, the secretary of the Eureka Benevolent Society published a notice in the *Daily Alta California* inviting all the organization's members to attend David's funeral on Sunday, January 4, to be held in the family home at 317 Powell Street. They and many members of the Jewish community were in attendance, according to a report published in the *Los Angeles Herald,* which said that the funeral was "one of the largest ever witnessed in this city, the majority of the Jewish population turning out."[6]

R & G Dun, in a report dated January 3, said this about David's passing:

> The death of the Senior partner "David Stern" . . . has had no material effect upon the position of this house. His son will take his place in the firm if he has not done so already, and anything that may be withdrawn for the other heirs will not hamper them in the least as they have not only far more capital than their business requires but large outside investments in R.E. [real estate] are doing a large and prosperous business and are good for anything that they will buy.[7]

The son mentioned in this document was Jacob, the oldest boy, now twenty-three years old. He had joined the firm in late 1870 or early 1871, starting as a salesman.

Fanny was consoled in her grief by the presence of her brothers and her children, but in August 1874, the family home experienced an even greater loss. Henry Stern, her second oldest son, just eighteen years old, died on the first of the month. The reason for his death is unknown, but it could have come from one of myriad nineteenth-century causes: accident, disease, or infection; the list is long, and youth was not immune to such perils. Henry had been a promising scholar at University School, the college preparatory academy he and his brothers attended on Post Street, just a block away from their home. Both Henry and Sigmund won prizes for their academic work, and Henry had graduated and was possibly on his way to college.

Fanny was now a fifty-one-year-old widow and a bereaved mother of seven children, ranging in age from Jacob at twenty-three, to Lillie, nine. Even with the help and support of her brother and the servants the family employed, Fanny could not manage her new situation on her own. So she turned to the one solution taken by many women, of all financial circumstances, in her predicament: she remarried.

And she remarried close to home. Among those who grieved the death of Henry Strauss was his cousin Henry Sahlein, the older son of Fanny's sister Mary and her husband William. As Jonas had done with Nathan, William had sent his son to live with the San Francisco branch of the family, while he and daughter Rosa and other son Moses stayed in New York. Henry arrived at the Powell Street home between mid-1870 and early 1872, starting in the business as a "collector," and soon working his way up to salesman.

Sometime before March 1875, William, Rosa, and probably Moses were also living at the Powell Street home. And in July of that year, William and Fanny were married. If this sounds familiar, it should. It echoes Rebecca Strauss's quick remarriage to her husband's brother, which was very likely for convenience and economic necessity. Now around sixty years old, William was another male figure in the home, a good influence for Fanny's younger children. At the same time, Fanny could be the mother figure for William's only daughter. Fanny had no worries about her children's inheritance when she remarried, as David had left her in good financial standing. She also must have recalled how William had managed that extra bank account for her in New York twenty years earlier.

Later in 1875 or early the following year, the family packed up and moved to a larger home at 621 Leavenworth Street, at the southwest corner of Post. They needed the space, because there were fourteen Strausses, Sterns, and Sahleins now living together: Levi and Louis Strauss; William, Henry, Moses, and Rosa Sahlein; and Fanny, Jacob, Caroline, Sigmund, Louis, Harriet (sometimes called Hattie), Abraham, and Lillie Stern. There were also four female servants in residence. Caroline, the oldest Stern daughter, soon married Leopold Bachman, of Bachman Brothers, another wholesale dry goods firm, and they moved next door to number 619 Leavenworth.

Fanny and William's union was useful in another happy way. In 1879 or early 1880, Jacob Stern married William's daughter, Rosa, and they also made their home at 621 Leavenworth.

Sales of the riveted products continued to rise, and by the end of 1876, over 8,000 dozen pants, vests, coats, and jumpers had been sold. In late 1873 the company expanded into Colorado, and by March 1874 was also selling in Utah. By 1876 the riveted goods were on store shelves in California, Nevada, Colorado, and the territories of Utah, Montana, Idaho, Arizona, and New Mexico.

Jonas, back in New York, saw opportunities for sales from the East by this time, as well. In a reversal from the way the business had begun, he imported riveted clothing from San Francisco to sell to some customers in New York, and also began to cultivate some western retail stores not covered by the San Francisco sales force. By the end of 1876, however, Levi realized this didn't make good business sense. He recalled, "I told them it would not do to send the material out, manufacture the clothing, and then send it east; that they must commence manufacturing it themselves, and Jacob W. Davis started east for that purpose, in the latter part of 1876."[8]

It's possible that Jonas already had a small manufactory up and running for the production of some of the dry goods he sent to Levi. So adding the riveted clothing to the mix would not have been that difficult. But Jacob was needed to help the company obtain the right equipment to attach the rivets and to make sure the clothing met the same specifications and standards as the products made in San Francisco. Once under way, the New York house sold its products in Missouri and Wyoming, as well as to some local retailers.

Around the time that Jacob Davis arrived in New York, Levi faced another patent infringement case, and it turned out to be the longest and most complicated of all the cases he had to prosecute before the patent expired. On December 2, 1876, the papers for *Levi Strauss et al. vs. Henry W. King et al.* were filed in the U.S. Circuit Court for the Southern District of New York. Henry W. King and his partners had a clothing business in both New York and Chicago, under the name H. W. King and Co. The substance of the prosecution's complaint was as follows:

And it being also set forth in said bill that you, the defendants, have made, used, and vended to others to be used and sold, and that you are now making, using, and vending to others to be used and sold, pantaloons and other garments containing, using, and employing the above mentioned improvements [rivets], and substantial and material parts thereof, and which are an infringement upon said patent, and that your actions and doings are contrary to equity and good conscience.[9]

Levi Strauss & Co.'s case against King & Co. went beyond mere infringement. Unlike Elfelt, the company didn't stop making and selling riveted clothing when they were told not to. By continuing to infringe on the company's patent, King & Co. sent a message to other companies that they could do the same thing. Levi Strauss & Co. also saw a sharp decrease in sales once King's version of the riveted garments went on the market. By the end of 1877 the company had sold 3,600 fewer dozen products: that is, over 40,000 fewer individual pieces.[10] Levi's case, therefore, had two legs to stand on: patent infringement and a decrease in trade.

For their defense, King's attorneys used the same gambit as the Elfelt case: they argued that Jacob Davis's invention was not unique and that the way he used rivets in clothing was not patentable. No matter that the patent office disagreed. Twice.

King fought hard to win its case, which went on for nearly four years. Levi Strauss & Co. fought just as hard. Attorneys for both sides deposed over four hundred witnesses all over the country. On April 29, 1880, Judge Blatchford made his decision: "The court overrules the alleged defense, sustains the novelty and patentability of the invention, holds defendants to be infringers, and orders a decree against them for perpetual injunction and damages."[11]

For Levi Strauss & Co., this was more than just the end of a long court case. It was a vindication of the company's long assertion that it had invented something new and that this invention belonged to the firm both legally and morally. Even as the King case rolled along, other companies and individuals infringed on the patent: a Chinese man in San Jose named Kan Lun, also in 1876; Meyer and David Lindauer of St. Louis, in 1878;

and B. (possibly Berthold) Greenebaum, of Greenebaum Bros., another wholesale and manufacturing firm in San Francisco. Kan Lun stopped production of his goods right after Levi Strauss & Co. contacted him, while both Lindauer and Greenebaum went through the courts. The patent was upheld in every single case.

Now that he was a manufacturer, Levi had another set of employment challenges, and some far-reaching decisions to make. And they all had to do with a labor pool that was extensive, hard-working, and despised.

Among the many imports from Asia that passed through San Francisco were laborers from China. Most of them came into California in the 1850s to join in the gold frenzy. As they competed with white miners, they were marginalized, harassed, evicted. When a strike was played out, the Chinese went in and worked over the lower-yielding leftovers, called tailings.

Then, when uncomplaining workers were needed to build the west-to-east portion of the transcontinental railroad, the Chinese were there. Historians estimate that about ten thousand Chinese men worked to bore the tunnel through the Sierras and move construction of the line through Nevada and Utah. When the project was completed, some men stayed with the railroad to help build branch lines north and south. Others moved into the growing agricultural regions, working to clear land, dig drains, and harvest crops for white ranchers.

But as manufacturing grew mightily in the early 1870s, many Chinese moved to San Francisco, where other Chinese had set up shop as early as the Gold Rush years doing domestic work, and running restaurants and laundries. By the early 1860s San Francisco had about 8 percent of the Chinese population of California as a whole. By 1870 this had risen to 26 percent and up to about 30 percent through the rest of the decade.[12]

Chinese men were drawn to the city because of the growth of manufacturing during a time when the state and the entire country were suffering under the effects of what has been called the Long Depression. While the expansion of railroads was a boon to local and national industry and a source of jobs, its potential as a huge moneymaker was a temptation for shady speculators and reckless investors. In addition, more efficient production led to an oversupply with no one to buy the output. Companies began to finance railroad-building on credit, and by 1873 this edifice came crashing down as banks began to fail. Railroad and factory jobs were cut, and a nascent labor movement also held strikes as the decade lurched on. Currency reforms, regulation, and new taxes were among the solutions that eventually turned the crisis around by 1878.

San Francisco had its own home-grown crisis, as well. William Ralston had founded the apparently solid Bank of California in 1864. By the early 1870s he had begun to speculate heavily in Nevada mining stocks, and was also juggling investments in other financial schemes. The bank collapsed in August 1875 (and, as noted earlier, Ralston took his usual swim soon after and suspiciously "drowned"). The bank quickly reopened, but the damage was done. Many other local banks fell like dominoes, and San Francisco's capital began to drain away, leading to massive unemployment.

The Long Depression and the failure of the Bank of California meant that men flocked into town by the thousands to look for jobs. Manufacturers were also affected by these economic conditions; the costs of raw materials didn't go down, and finding markets for their wares in a period of overproduction was a challenge. So they had to do everything they could to keep costs under control. Some manufacturers had to shut their doors. Those who were left realized that the greatest savings were found in labor, and the Chinese were willing to take the lower wages that were now the norm.

Before the economic woes of the mid-1870s, the Chinese were seen as a "unique" people of strange and sometimes repulsive customs, but not as a threat to the majority. This changed by 1876 when the effects of the depression settled heavily on the city. The Chinese became an "other" that was in the way.

There was a dividing line among the marginalized and unemployed in San Francisco. Men of many countries and unshared languages—whether Irish, Italian, German, French, or myriad others—felt solidarity with one another in their situation as job seekers. Many Chinese were out of work too, but they were not included in this brotherhood. Appearance, language and, very important, religion, made laborers keep the Chinese at arm's length. Chinese worship seemed even more strange than Jewish worship, the latter being tolerated because of the tenuous relationship between Old and New Testaments.

City laborers also knew that many Chinese were only working to make enough money to go back to China, unlike themselves, who wanted work so they could stay in California, to start or feed a family, to become Americans. This raised an impenetrable barrier between what could have been potent political allies. Instead, the Chinese became a dangerous threat.

But not to the merchants, at least at first. They knew that the growth of manufacturing, and the continued growth of San Francisco, would have to rely on labor that was cheaper than it had been in the years before the Civil War. Manufacturers did not immediately object to hiring Chinese in their factories, or indeed any foreign laborers, who worked for lower wages than American-born workers. The high cost of importing raw materials justified finding savings on the production line. Often Chinese were hired through a middleman from the "Companies," Chinese-led organizations who recruited workers and placed them in various industries, with payments going to them for disbursement to the individual workers.

But as more men were out of work, and more Chinese were getting paychecks, anti-Chinese sentiment began to bubble. "Anti-coolie" clubs were formed to agitate against the hiring of Chinese by industry employers of any kind. Inflammatory articles on all sides of the question appeared in local newspapers, and in 1876 Levi Strauss & Co. was brought into this fray.

On April 8, 1876, the San Francisco *Daily Morning Call* published an article about local firms that hired Chinese in their factories, and those that didn't. The reporter noted that "there are several firms of white citizens that employ Chinese labor, and have trained the Chinaman in arts of industry from which the Caucasian is being ousted, because he cannot work so cheaply for the capitalist. Among these may be cited Levi Strauss & Co., employing 500 Chinese."[13] The next day, April 9, the *San Francisco Chronicle* published an article in response, titled "Justice to a Worthy Firm":

> It was stated in the *Call* of yesterday that the well-known wholesale and manufacturing house of Levi Strauss & Co. of this city, employ 500 Chinese. The statement is not at all true. Levi Strauss & Co. employ only *one* Chinaman, and he is employed for labor which white men

have again and again tried and failed to do. It is work which requires great strength-the cutting of the material for the patent-riveted clothing, overalls, etc. . . . The firm would be only too glad to give the place to a white laboring man if they could find one to take and keep it. . . . They adopt the wholesome motto of encouraging home manufacture and home production, wrought and brought forth by the honest toil of the white working people or of citizens.[14]

The important word in this statement is "home." Since the 1850s the concept of "home industry" had been floating around the city and the state as a whole. In those early days, it meant increasing the production of home-grown agriculture, wool, and dairy products in California, rather than importing them from nearby states or territories. After 1869, when more products arrived from New York and Europe on the new transcontinental railroad, "home industry" meant rejecting these goods in favor of those now being made in the city. By mid-decade "home industry" was about labor, not just about commodities, and about white labor in particular, in industries as varied as candle-making and piano construction.

Levi Strauss & Co. seems to have taken home industry as its credo in these early days. In this, as in many issues facing the city in the nineteenth century, Jews did not think as a bloc about the Chinese. Those who needed workers and who were struggling hired Chinese workers to keep overhead under control. Being outsiders themselves, Jews could have perceived that the Chinese were suffering under many of the constraints that they did. But the Chinese were more "other" than the Jews were, and when it came to success in business, Jewish employers, no less than their Christian counterparts, followed whatever path they needed to keep that success intact.

No less a personage than Rabbi Isaac Mayer Wise understood economic necessity. Writing in the *American Israelite* in 1877, after a visit to San Francisco, Wise summed up his observations about the vexed question of the Chinese: "It is the Chinaman who does the factory work, the house work, the farm work, the railroad work, all sorts and kinds of manual work. But it is equally true that this cheap labor builds up California, and San Francisco especially. Factories here in order to compete with Eastern establishments must have cheap labor, hence it is necessary to engage Chinamen."[15]

In that same April 1876 *Daily Morning Call* article, Einstein Brothers & Co., importers and manufacturers of shoes and boots, were called out for hiring Chinese, which they then stopped doing, claiming they would only hire white men in the future. Einstein would probably have continued to keep Chinese laborers on the books had they not been shamed in the newspaper. Levi himself felt compelled to refute the allegation that his factory was swarming with five hundred Chinese laborers.

Offering products for good prices while catering to social prejudice was a thin line all San Francisco manufacturers had to walk. And there is no way to know how personal feelings entered into the equation. We don't know if Levi refused to hire Chinese out of prejudice or because of social pressure. Perhaps it was good marketing; being able to claim that his clothing was a production of "home industry" and "white labor" could lead to greater sales. In any case, it would seem he had the means to pay the higher wages that white men and women commanded: $3.00 to $4.00 per day for male workers, $2.00 to $3.00 per day for female workers, compared to $1.00 or $1.25 for Chinese labor.

Beginning in the late 1860s at least four Chinese-owned stores on Dupont Street, in what was becoming known as Chinatown, carried the company's dry goods. By the 1880s, Levi also sold to the Sun Sun Wo store in Coulterville, California, in Mariposa County, near today's Yosemite National Park, where there was a large and thriving Chinese community. So it would seem that Levi had no personal animosity toward the Chinese, certainly not in having them as customers. But as with the decision to start manufacturing in the first place, he knew what would be best for his business, not only financially but culturally.

Murmuring resentment toward Chinese labor exploded in the summer of 1877. Irish-born Denis Kearney, a former seaman and owner of a San Francisco drayage business, yearned to go into politics to express his socialist leanings. He and other speakers held a mass meeting in a vacant sandlot next to city hall and began to harangue against the Central Pacific Railroad, in solidarity with men who were striking against eastern railroad companies on the other side of the continent. Fearing the same would happen if local crowds were whipped up, the city police came out in force.

Agitators of other stripes wandered the fringes of the mass demonstration, including an "anti-coolie" club, which demanded that the speakers say something against the Chinese. When told that the meeting was about other topics, the men grabbed sympathetic listeners and crashed into Chinatown, wrecking laundries and other nearby businesses that had even the most tenuous connection to the Chinese. The rioting lasted for three nights, and several men were killed, forcing local leaders to call up former members of the Committee of Vigilance. Armed with hickory pick-handles, the force patrolled the streets until it felt order had been restored. Encouraged by this response, Kearney added an anti-Chinese platform to his new Workingmen's Party, and the entrenchment of prejudice into city politics was complete.

Feelings remained high for the rest of the year. Annie Bosworth, a dressmaker who boarded at 317 Powell Street after Levi and his family moved to 621 Leavenworth, wrote about the sinister atmosphere in a diary entry for November 26, 1877: "Rough times are anticipated—vicious looking faces are seen on the street. It is an anxious time for the inhabitants of this city."[16]

In speeches that continued into 1878, Kearney denounced the companies which hired Chinese. He and others of like mind kept on holding meetings in the sandlots. At a May 12, 1878, gathering, Sergeant at Arms M. H. O'Connor "denounced several firms as being employers of Chinese labor. He advised the men to give up wearing jumpers and overalls until they were made by white labor."[17] Since Levi Strauss & Co. had gone on record as being firmly committed to home industry, it's possible O'Connor was referring to a competitor. But for men like Kearney and others, any firms even suspected of using Chinese labor were tarred with the same brush. Levi and his firm, like the rest of the city, would continue to face the Chinese question in the following decades.

This photo of the house in Buttenheim, Germany, where Levi Strauss was born, dates to the nineteenth century. The building, looking much the same today, is now the Levi Strauss Museum and houses exhibits about Levi and the company, as well as revolving exhibits about denim, Jewish life, and other related topics.

A young and serious Levi Strauss posed for his first photograph in San Francisco, when he was getting his wholesale business off the ground. The photo likely dates to the late 1850s or early 1860s.

In 1867, Levi Strauss & Co. moved to an elegant building on Battery Street near Pine, in the heart of San Francisco's financial district. This was the firm's headquarters until April 18, 1906.

On May 20, 1873, the U.S. Patent and Trademark Office issued Patent Number 139,121 for an "Improvement In Fastening Pocket-Openings." This is the official announcement of the patent, granted to Jacob Davis and Levi Strauss & Co.

From 1873 until 1892, the copper rivets were stamped with the company's initials and "S.F." for San Francisco, along with the patent date of May 1873. After the patent expired, the date was removed, leaving only "L.S. & Co." and "S.F.," the design that is still used today.

The first jeans, made in 1873, were called "XX." This early pair is from around 1879.

As a prominent San Francisco businessman, Levi Strauss posed frequently for his portrait. This photo dates to the 1870s.

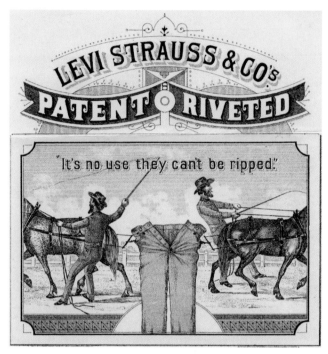

The company first used the Two Horse logo on its pants in 1886, and the image also was used for print advertising, such as in this flyer from around 1887.

In 1890 the company introduced a less expensive version of the 501® riveted pants, assigning them the lot number 201®. The new number appeared on the linen—not leather—patch sewn onto the new style.

Levi posed for this portrait around 1890, one of the last photographs taken of him.

More than just a figurehead, Levi Strauss was a daily and integral part of the business. In 1897 he let his image be used for this humorous flyer, which illustrated just how sturdy his riveted denim pants were.

Levi Strauss & Co. took every opportunity to show off its new riveted clothing line at mercantile trade shows throughout San Francisco and the West. The location of this 1898 company booth is unknown.

Company invoices from the nineteenth century included the lot numbers or names of the great variety of riveted products. This document from 1898 features the lot number 501®, initially used around 1890 to replace "XX" as the name for the first blue jean..

Among the many promotional flyers printed by Levi Strauss & Co. was this item from 1899, which illustrates a variety of the company's products, from children's bib overalls to a sturdy coat for teamsters. The back of the flyer describes the clothing's quality and reliability. Salesmen gave these flyers to their retail customers before the days of printed catalogs.

In 1892, Levi Strauss & Co. introduced its Guarantee Ticket, sewn (and later stapled) onto the back of the jeans. Made of linen-backed oilcloth, its printed text testified to the strength of the riveted pants along with a guarantee of quality. This version of the Guarantee Ticket, printed in 1899, includes the celebrated phrase "For Over 26 Years"—a reference to the patent date of 1873.

Levi Strauss & Co. employee get-togethers, like this 1899 picnic on Angel Island in San Francisco Bay, were common in the nineteenth century, just as they are today.

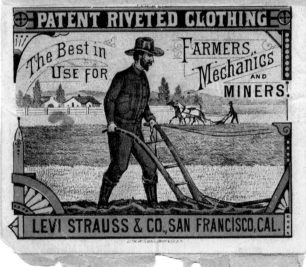

Trade cards were one of the first "gifts with purchase" in the nineteenth century, and Levi Strauss & Co. printed various trade cards for distribution to its consumers. These featured brightly colored illustrations of some of the company's products, and consumers received the cards when they bought a pair of jeans, a jacket, or a shirt. These 1899 cards emphasize the company's full array of denim and cotton duck clothing.

Working men in nearly every western industry wore the riveted denim pants. These agricultural workers from Elk Grove, California, near Sacramento, posed for the camera around 1900.

During its early years, Levi Strauss & Co. printed many flyers, which promoted its products and described how they were made. Traveling salesmen carried and distributed them to customers throughout the West. This flyer, from around 1900, emphasizes the concept of Home Industry by depicting American women working in a clean, airy sewing factory.

H. H. TOLAND   JAMES LICK   S. C. HASTINGS
LEVI STRAUSS   MRS. PHEBE HEARST   D. O. MILLS
A. K. P. HARMON   J. C. WILMERDING   H. D. BACON

OUR BENEFACTORS

Levi Strauss appears on this page of "Benefactors" in the University of California, Berkeley, yearbook, Blue and Gold, from 1900. He began to sponsor scholarships at the university in 1897, and they are still in place today.

A contented Levi Strauss pauses in the midst of a relaxing day with friends and family, probably in Atherton, south of San Francisco.

CHAPTER 13

VERY STRONG OPINIONS

Levi's experience in protecting the patent for riveted pants helped him decide to give trademark protection to some of his other products, too. On June 17, 1878, the company applied for and was later granted a trademark for the "word-symbol" HERCULES, used on blankets. On that same day, the firm applied for "the arbitrarily selected words THE GRIZ-ZLY and the figure of a bear," also used on blankets.[1] This would indicate that the company had come out with its own line of blankets and was contracting for blankets to line some of the riveted clothing, as well.

Concerned that the Grizzly trademark might be used by potential infringers, Levi appeared in 1881 before a notary to sign an affidavit he was filing with the State of California. In this document, he swore that the company was the exclusive owner and claimant of the trademark (presumably both the word and the bear design), and that it was used on "Grizzly clothing for Farmers, Miners, Mechanics and Hunters."[2] But the most important trademark was a few years into the future.

In the meantime, Levi expanded the riveted clothing business. Even though the clothing was only distributed in the West, with a couple of stops in some midwestern states, Levi still wanted more people to know about it.

In May 1876 the first major world's fair in the United States opened in Philadelphia, called the "International Exhibition of Arts, Manufactures and Products of the Soil and Mine." Its colloquial name was the Centennial Exposition, and it celebrated the one-hundred-year anniversary of the

Declaration of Independence and, more important, one hundred years of American progress.

Manufacturers from all over the country exhibited their products at the fair, and Levi Strauss & Co. was among them. San Francisco's IXL Auction House, with locations on Kearny, Sacramento, and Commercial Streets, advertised heavily in Bay Area newspapers, touting itself as a "Retail Agency of Levi Strauss & Co's Patent Riveted Goods on Exhibition at the Fair." Having a presence in Philadelphia was a selling point for both manufacturer and retailer.

The company was also expanding its advertising in general, placing display ads for its products, and the warning about patent infringement, in more California newspapers, as well as in Nevada, Arizona, and Colorado publications.

There were new reasons to advertise by the end of 1877, because more riveted clothing was coming off the production line at the Market Street factory. Besides the basic overalls, vests, and jackets, there were now blanket-lined pants and jackets, in duck and denim; ulster coats; hunting suits; a denim overall with a pocket for a folding ruler riveted onto the left thigh; and an entire line of heavy-duty clothing for boys. Levi had also started advertising that his clothing was made of Amoskeag denim, a quick way to convey the quality of the denim, to store owners at least. Well-trained salesmen could explain what it meant. The introduction of the riveted clothing to the company's inventory contributed to mind-boggling sales of $3 million by the end of the 1870s.

Jacob Davis was busy with his duties as superintendent of the factory, but he still came up with ideas for new inventions. On January 15, 1878, he received Patent Number 199,273 for another "Improvement in Pantaloons." This time, the invention was a means for reinforcing the seat and knees of a pair of pants with a patch of the same fabric sewn inside of it. As Jacob explained in his patent application, "When pantaloons manufactured for and sold ready made by the trade are worn out on the seat or knees it rarely happens that pieces of the original fabric can be obtained for patching them, so that they must either be thrown aside or else patched with pieces of a different quality and color. There is, hence, always a sacrifice either of economy or appearances." The idea was that when the knee or seat wore out, the fabric from the inside would already be there, and the ragged edge of the hole would be sewn to the fabric, making a cleaner-looking patch. And there were other advantages: "The knee-patches also serve to protect the knees of the wearer, and keep them warm and dry, when they might otherwise become cold and wet. . . . My improvement is particularly useful and applicable for boys', youths', and men's pantaloons of the cheaper grades."[3]

No records of Jacob's interesting new pants have yet been found.

What we do know is that sometime before 1880 Jacob moved his family again, and this one was quite a step up. The Davises now were living at 1635 Sacramento Street, between Polk and Larkin. His moving farther west from the financial district indicated he had more spare money to work on new inventions without causing Annie Davis any more anguish. This home was also farther from the factory, but by using either public transportation or maybe even his own carriage, Jacob no longer needed to walk to work. He was coming up in the world.

Levi's business was doing the same. Beginning in 1874, he expanded his definition of "customer" and began to pick up government contracts for his dry goods. The U.S. government had used private companies to provide goods of all kinds as far back as the Revolutionary War, and by the mid-nineteenth century firms were regularly bidding against one another to win contracts with myriad government agencies. Levi found his niche with two of them: the Indian Service, and the Boards of Prisons for California and Arizona.

The United States Indian Service was founded in 1824, and in 1849 it was transferred to the newly created Department of the Interior. Today it is called the Bureau of Indian Affairs. After the Civil War the purpose of the service changed; Native Americans were now seen as "wards" of the nation and not inconvenient sovereign peoples. They were dependents, the responsibility of the United States, but not yet its citizens. Under President Ulysses S. Grant, especially, the government felt it owed a debt to these First Peoples for the many wrongs that they had suffered. And to right these wrongs, the Indian Service began to create programs to give them the tools they needed to eventually blend into the fabric of American life, even as it required them to give up their cultural traditions. Tools included goods, such as dry goods: fabrics, clothing, bedding, and so forth. Commodities freely given (but not as charity) would mold new character and change traditional behaviors. Indians were to be converted through commerce.

In 1874 Levi Strauss & Co. received its first government contract: to supply dry goods to the agency for distribution to the Hoopa tribe in northern California's Humboldt County. This was two years before the creation of its reservation. In 1878 the company won another contract for reservations in California, Nevada, Oregon, and Washington Territory. After that year, the company ceased supplying the Indian Service, either by choice or because it was outbid.

At the same time, the company was also winning contracts for the prison system in California, with the first one awarded in 1875. Levi Strauss & Co. was named the supplier of clothing and dry goods for the state prison at San Quentin, north of San Francisco, which was opened in 1851. The next contract was signed in 1884, and the company became a regular supplier to San Quentin for the balance of the 1880s. In addition to clothing, it also provided blankets and bolts of fabric.

Other customers were even more interesting than prisons, and some ended up there. Or should have.

Michael and Joseph Goldwasser, immigrants from Russia via England— where they changed their name to Goldwater—wandered around the West after their arrival in San Francisco in the 1850s. By the 1870s they had settled into storekeeping in Arizona, both together and singly. Joseph regularly went to San Francisco to pick up merchandise for himself and a partner. In early 1881 he found himself the topic of conversation and of front page news in the city. According to one account, "The wholesale merchants on Sansome, Battery and Front streets, particularly those of Hebraic extraction, are just now wonderfully anxious to see Joseph Goldwater, a commission merchant engaged in the purchase of goods for Arizona, who left very suddenly for the land of the rattlesnake and tarantula a week ago."[4]

Goldwater had made extensive purchases on credit from the biggest firms in San Francisco, including Levi Strauss & Co. He then hightailed it back to Arizona apparently unable or unwilling to pay for the goods. He had been on good terms with the city's wholesalers, so no one expected any trouble. This time, however, he turned the merchandise over to a partner in Yuma, with no intention of paying his creditors. Newspaper accounts of subsequent events read like a sensational western novel.

A U.S. marshal and a few other lawmen went to Yuma to either retrieve the goods or arrest Goldwater and his partner, a man named Lyons. The *Sacramento Daily Record-Union* reported, "The defendants have men barricaded on the premises, armed with shotguns, who declared that they would resist service at all hazards." The marshal, for his part, said that he "will serve the process regardless of consequences. If resistance is offered by the mob there will surely be bloodshed. The posse are all determined men."[5]

When this force of law showed up, the armed resistance turned into quiet acquiescence, and Goldwater was arrested and taken back to San Francisco. By early April the matter had been "amicably arranged," and Goldwater was released. Despite the high drama, Levi, as well as the principals of the other defrauded firms, were used to dealing with defaulting customers, and very likely Goldwater and Lyons simply arranged to either return the goods or make some sort of payment. The Goldwaters continued to do business in Arizona, and their name rose in prominence in the following decades. Joseph's great-nephew became a U.S. senator and, in 1964, candidate for President. His name was Barry Goldwater.

A few months after this affair was settled, events elsewhere in Arizona also made headlines. Levi Strauss & Co. had a number of retail customers in Tombstone, the town built on silver in the southern part of the territory. Levi may even have run into Charles A. Morse, who ran the Tombstone Consolidated Gold and Silver Mining Co. offices in San Francisco, just the next block over on Sansome Street. Among Levi's customers in Tombstone were Shaffer & Lord, P. W. Smith, McKean and Knight, and Michael Calisher, who had storefronts in or around the center of town, within spitting distance from a place called the O.K. Corral. On October 26, 1881, shots from the most famous gunfight in the history of the American West rang out from that spot, heard by many who were shopping or attending to shoppers. The Earp brothers and Doc Holliday did not wear Levi's riveted overalls, but it's entirely possible that the "cow-boys" who died that day, and those who didn't—Frank and Tom McLaury, Billy Claiborne, Billy Clanton, and Ike Clanton—did own a pair or two.

And there were other connections between Levi Strauss and the "town too tough to die." The woman with whom Wyatt Earp spent his life after the shootout was Josephine Marcus, who grew up in San Francisco and whose family worshiped at temple Sherith Israel. When Wyatt died in 1929, Josephine buried him in Hills of Eternity cemetery in Colma, south of San Francisco, just a few gentle hillocks away from Levi's tomb, in Home of Peace.

Levi and his fellow merchants were the targets of fraud again in 1884. In April an "elderly, respectable-appearing" woman, who called herself Hannah Fagan, visited the various wholesale firms in downtown San Francisco soliciting money to aid one of the local kindergartens. She said she was working with the wife of a reputable local man, and when she showed up at Levi Strauss & Co. the employees gave her ten dollars and some of the dry goods, "none of which, needless to say, reached the little kindergartners."[6] The woman, who also went by the name of Dufficy, was well known to local police and had run a similar scam two years before, but escaped punishment. She was arrested after this second scam and claimed it was a case of mistaken identity, but ran out of luck when the company's employees positively identified her as the culprit.

The following year fraud took a dangerous personal turn for Levi Strauss. Antonio Gagliardo was a storekeeper and Levi Strauss & Co. customer from Calaveras County, California, one of the state's gold-bearing regions. After his business failed, he declared bankruptcy and took off for Los Angeles. Recalling that Levi, his former supplier, was wealthy and highly regarded, he wrote him a letter, asking him to "use his influence" to help him get a clerking job in a store somewhere. Touched by the man's plight, Levi sent him $50. Instead of gratitude, Gagliardo became enraged. He wrote Levi again and told him he had ten days to help him get a job or he would "blow his head off."[7]

Levi's Italian American acquaintances, many of whom knew Gagliardo, told him to have the man arrested, but Levi said his former customer was simply "overexcited by his troubles." However, when he learned that Gagliardo had made his way to San Francisco, Levi finally decided to tell the chief of police, who picked the man up and tossed him in jail. The case was thrown out of the police court, though, at the beginning of April. Levi refused to prosecute because the defendant "promised to refrain from carrying his sanguinary promises into execution."[8] In other words, he promised not to shoot Levi, and Levi believed him. His belief in Gagliardo was well placed, as the man left the city soon afterward and never came back to San Francisco.

Murder and mayhem were always part of the city's history, and once again Levi was called for jury duty for another spectacular trial in February 1881. Isaac Milton Kalloch was charged with the murder of Charles deYoung who, along with his brother Michael, ran the *Daily Morning Chronicle* newspaper. Kalloch's father, Isaac Smith Kalloch, was a flamboyant Baptist minister who preached against the Chinese, the railroad, and the *Chronicle*. When he decided to run for mayor, deYoung, who backed the other candidate, printed scurrilous material about Kalloch's adulterous activities. Kalloch responded with equally nasty rumors about deYoung's mother and the rest of his family. On August 23, 1879, deYoung ambushed Kalloch and shot him, but he survived and was elected mayor in September, likely on the sympathy vote. The *Chronicle* continued to print attacks on Kalloch, and his son, Isaac Milton, decided to retaliate.

On April 3, 1880, Isaac Milton Kalloch strong-armed his way into Charles deYoung's office and shot him dead.

Speedily arrested, jury selection for Kalloch's trial began in February of the following year. When Levi was called into the box to be questioned about his fitness for service, he said that he was from Germany, had no family (meaning he wasn't married), and that he had "a very strong opinion in this case, which testimony would not remove."[9] He wasn't the only prospective juror to say this, and the others were also prominent men of business. What this meant was that Levi would never vote to acquit Kalloch, no matter the provocation or clever maneuvering on the part of his defense attorney. He was excused.

Henry E. Highton, a prominent British-born attorney hired to defend in the case, eventually won Kalloch's acquittal. He produced a witness who said that he heard seven gunshots, and because Kalloch's gun was a six-shooter, the only conclusion was that deYoung fired first, and Kalloch shot back in self-defense. Two years later father and son left San Francisco for Washington Territory to work as attorneys themselves.

Republican and presidential politics now occupied more of Levi's time. In September 1880 he was on the Committee of Four Hundred, charged with helping to organize details for President Rutherford B. Hayes's visit to San Francisco. On September 17, Hayes was the guest of honor at a banquet given at the home of Nevada senator William Sharon, who had a country home called Belmont, south of San Francisco. After a quick stopover to visit Governor Leland Stanford first, the presidential party arrived and had a splendid dinner. Among the guests, according to the *San Francisco Chronicle,* were "Mr. and Mrs. Levi Strauss." Because Levi was on the committee, he was also a guest, and apparently he brought a female companion. She could have been his sister Fanny, one of his nieces, or a female acquaintance whose name we will never know. It's also possible the reporter mixed him up with another couple whose name was left off the list. In any case, it is interesting to speculate on how amusing he might have found this mistake when he read it in the newspaper.

As plans were being made for the visit, Levi attended a mass Republican rally at the Grand Opera House on September 11, where he (among over fifty other men) was elected a vice president of the event. California senator and former governor Newton Booth, considered one of the era's finest public speakers, gave a rousing speech in support of James A. Garfield, the Republican candidate for president in the election to be held that November. But he spent more time excoriating the Democratic Party, dredging up its Confederate roots and calling it the party of obstruction. And although Garfield did not win California's electoral votes, he did win the presidency.

Levi's commitment to the Republican Party—which dated back to the administration of Abraham Lincoln—meant that he was asked to perform a task of great honor the following year. Barely four months after taking office, President Garfield was shot by an assassin on July 2, 1881, and he lingered until finally succumbing to death on September 19. A number of cities held symbolic funeral services for the slain president, and quite a few of them took place in San Francisco. Mercantile and benevolent associations held their own "obsequies" during the last week of September, but there was a huge ceremony on September 26, so that everyone in the city could share in the mourning. A procession wound its way through the streets south of Market and ended at the Mechanics' Pavilion, on 8th and Mission. A funeral coach representing Garfield was guarded by honorary pallbearers during the observance, and Levi Strauss was among them. He shared this distinction with other loyal Republicans who ranged from military men to merchants.

The following month Levi began his duties as a collector for the Garfield Monument Fund Association, which gathered donations throughout the business district for a memorial to the slain president. Levi and two other men, A. P. Williams and W. W. Montague, were responsible for calling on the merchants on Battery Street from Market to California; Williams was a partner in Livingston & Co., wine and liquor importers, and Montague's business was importing and wholesaling stoves, ranges, and iron mantels. The Garfield monument, placed southeast of the Conservatory of Flowers in Golden Gate Park, eventually cost $28,000, and was unveiled on July 4, 1885.

Sponsoring monuments was not the only thing that Levi wanted to do for San Francisco. Over the years he had quietly given his time and money to organizations and committees that benefited the city in myriad ways. He also gave to Jewish benevolent organizations in town and to disaster relief agencies all over the world. In doing so Levi was participating in the customs of both charity and philanthropy. Today those terms are nearly interchangeable, but in the nineteenth century they had distinct definitions.

Philanthropy meant advocacy for causes large and small, from prison reform to municipal improvements. Charity meant personal service to others, from small groups to a single individual. As American power and wealth grew after the Civil War, the word "millionaire" was used more frequently, and the men who matched this description turned to philanthropy when their fortunes were secured. Rockefeller and Carnegie fall into this

category. Levi, who had always given money where it was needed, also
began to give more as he entered his forties and his business entered its
maturity. But California millionaires were a different breed, and Jewish
ones even more so. Hubert Howe Bancroft, who lived in the city and wrote
numerous books of history and examinations of everyday life, observed
that Californians exhibited great "generous impulses," as demonstrated
especially by the help given to early immigrants and by the contributions to
the sanitary fund during the Civil War. And he singled out Jewish citizens
for their generosity: "Nationality exercised a powerful influence in drawing
men together. The Hebrews set the brightest example in establishing five
[benevolent] societies by 1855, the first dating to 1849."[10]

Levi had supported the Jewish orphanages and benevolent associations
since his arrival in San Francisco. But he saw needs outside of the institutions of his faith, and they were all around him. By the late 1870s the greatest was unemployment.

In the summer of 1877 thousands of out-of-work men gathered in meetings and marched in rallies throughout San Francisco, trying to get the city
to understand how desperate their situation was. Some were followers of
Denis Kearney, and focused their rage on the city's wealthy, the police, and
the Chinese, using the rhetoric of violence to spread their ideas. The *Daily
Alta California*, the newspaper most sympathetic to commerce, condemned
these men, saying that the city's "capitalists" were famous the world over
for their generosity. The paper suggested that the city and the state find
work for these unemployed men in ways that would benefit not only the
laborers but California, as well. It also reminded its readers that the recent
state legislature had cut off funding for these kinds of projects, such as the
improvement of Golden Gate Park and other public works. Such work was
"not only advantageous to the public, but a necessity."[11]

By the end of October a number of prominent citizens had banded
together and met with Mayor A. J. Bryant in order to come up with a systematic solution to this problem. The group was made up of men of business from nearly every industry, and included some of the city's biggest
names: Leland Stanford, president of the Central Pacific Railroad; stock-
broker Mark L. McDonald; mining millionaire Alvinza Hayward; and

Committee of Vigilance founder William T. Coleman; plus a Mr. Wheeler, who represented the Grange, a national organization founded just two years earlier to support innovations in agriculture and promote the social and economic welfare of farmers.

By November 6, a variety of committees were formed within what was now called the General Relief Committee. Among them was Ways and Means, and among its members was Levi Strauss. He shared his duties with other businessmen, from D. J. Staples, president of Fireman's Fund Insurance, to W. F. Whittier, whose company imported paints, oils, and mirrors, and operated the White Lead Works. Grocers, bankers, miners, and ironmongers rounded out the group. Levi was also a canvasser again, this time to gather donations for a relief fund, the committee's main objective. He and others in charge of soliciting donations for his district reported to the *Daily Alta California* that "the merchants in nearly every instance responded readily to the appeal for aid. It is believed that a large sum of money will be raised."[12]

One of the committee's goals was to pull together enough to open a Labor Exchange, where men could register and look for work in one place. They were successful, and quickly so. The exchange opened for business on November 21. By March 1878 hundreds of men found temporary or long-term employment as woodchoppers, cooks, carpenters, dishwashers, farmers, and blacksmiths. There was also an exchange for unemployed women, who found "light work" (housework, for the most part). The Labor Exchange was in business until the spring of 1881, when both the city and the country had finally pulled out of the Long Depression.

The businessmen of San Francisco had many motives for creating the Labor Exchange. For some, philanthropy was part of how they conducted their lives. But they had also felt the chill hand of revolution on their necks in the 1870s, when concerns about Chinese labor, international communism, and immigration in general formed the topic of many a club room conversation. No matter the motivation for their efforts, finding work for the unemployed was good for San Francisco. When it became clear that work could be found, even more desirable laborers would make their way to the city. Some men also found permanent work outside of the city, thanks to the Labor Exchange, demonstrating that California in general was a good place to live. Happy workers bought more consumer goods. And happy workers did not march in the streets threatening mayhem. The benefits of the General Relief Committee extended far beyond labor and well into management.

This is just one example of Levi taking on what I call "municipal philanthropy." For the rest of his life he would seek out, or respond enthusiastically to, people and organizations who had San Francisco's—and California's— welfare uppermost in their minds, especially when that welfare was good for business.

At the same time he was serving on the General Relief Committee, he was also participating in the work of the California Immigrant Union. Incorporated in 1869, its purpose was to encourage the emigration of laborers, farmers, and other workers to California from Europe and from the eastern states." The organization was also committed to helping immigrants make the journey to California. Many prominent local men were officers or on the honorary committee of the union: Charles Crocker, one of the railroad's Big Four and president of the Southern Pacific Railroad; California governor Henry Haight; cattleman Charles Lux; and former governors John Downey and Leland Stanford. A number of foreign consuls general, representing Italy, Peru, Denmark, Sweden, and Norway, were also affiliated with the Immigrant Union, as they saw opportunities for their countrymen in California. Levi was a director in 1877, though how long he remained with the organization is unknown.

In these ways Levi was deepening his commitment to philanthropy. Unemployment and opportunity for advancement were societal problems that needed remedy, and groups of like-minded men made this happen in ways that benefited the needy, but also enhanced their own reputations. Without diaries or letters, it is impossible to know how much of Levi's involvement stemmed from concern for the overall problem, or how much he believed that fixing this problem would benefit San Francisco. Given where he put his time and his money, it was probably a little of both.

When it came to charity—donating money for a single, specific organization or person—Levi continued in the vein he had already established, and also branched out a bit. Sometimes he gave in his own name, and sometimes it was through his company. In 1874 the YMCA took up a collection of money and goods for their refuge for indigent young men, and Levi Strauss & Co. donated a large pile of bedding. Between 1874 and 1885 the company also gave donations to assist flood victims in Louisiana and Hungary, holiday supplies for San Francisco's Old People's Home, and five hundred dollars to the German Hospital. Sometimes donations were for happier occasions; in 1875 the firm donated one of its riveted hunting outfits as a prize for a National Guard shooting contest.

Levi's charitable commitments were especially geared to education and the young, and these ties would only grow stronger. In 1880 Levi was a benefactor for the California Institution for the Instruction of the Deaf and Dumb, which was located in Berkeley but had been founded in 1860 in San Francisco. How much or for how long he supported the institution is unknown, and as we will soon see, it did benefit greatly from another Strauss family member.

On January 19, 1881, the *San Francisco Bulletin* ran an article titled "Funeral of Levi Strauss." It described the merchant's services and his burial at Home of Peace cemetery south of San Francisco.

The next day, the *Bulletin* ran another article, titled "Not Buried":

> Through one of those unaccountable typographical errors which will occasionally creep into the columns of the most carefully prepared newspaper, it was made to appear in the *Bulletin* last night that *Levi* Strauss, of the firm of Levi Strauss & Co., had been buried. . . . The name of the deceased should have been *Louis* Strauss. Of course no one acquainted with the firm or the family was deceived by the error.[13]

The family was no doubt horrified by the error, deep in the midst of their grief. Louis had died at the family home on Leavenworth Street on January 15, at the age of sixty-four. He and his older brother Jonas had started the family firm in their new country, and Louis had worked quietly, managing the business and the relationship between his brothers as he traveled back and forth from San Francisco to New York beginning in 1853. By 1873 he was in California for good, and had moved into the Leavenworth home with Levi and the rest of his family. He was a director of the Concordia Club and a member of Fidelity Lodge number 190, of the Free and Accepted Masons, of which Levi was also likely a member.

Louis's funeral took place on January 18. His pall bearers were members of his lodge, and at least sixty others also attended his funeral. Other bearers were from the Eureka Benevolent Society. The service was held at the family home, which was traditional, and conducted by Dr. Elkan Cohn, of Temple Emanu-El. So many merchants attended the funeral that the vast majority of the city's wholesale businesses closed for the afternoon.

In his will Louis left $10,000 to the Pacific Hebrew Orphan and Home Society, $5,000 to the Jewish Orphan Asylum of New York, $5,000 each to the Roman Catholic and Protestant Orphan Asylums of San Francisco, and $5,000 to the school for the "deaf and dumb." In each case, the bequest became known as the Louis Strauss Fund, and there was also a hall named for Louis at the "deaf and dumb" school.

He left the bulk of his estate to his nieces and nephews, emphasizing that the money paid to his married nieces was for them alone, and not to be managed by their husbands. Like Levi, Louis had never married. So it may have come as a surprise to the family when his will and an 1879 codicil were read. This codicil stipulated that a Miss S. Davidson, described by one newspaper as a forewoman in the Levi Strauss & Co. factory (others said she was just an employee), was to receive $5,000.

This was Susanna Davidson, who was listed as a widow in the 1876 city directory. She worked as a bookkeeper for Levi Strauss & Co. in 1877, and she disappeared from the directories after that year. What's conclusive about her identity is that she lived in the same building on Hyde Street as Jacob Davis and his family. It was probably a multi-flat structure, though neither she nor anyone else named Davidson was living there before 1876. Perhaps she moved there after her husband died and was able to get her job through Jacob and his connections. She would have met Louis at the Battery Street headquarters, though what the nature of their relationship was or why he left her such a substantial amount of money—nearly $125,000 today—will never be known.

CHAPTER 14

THE BEST INTERESTS OF THE PEOPLE OF THIS STATE

J ust a few weeks later, on February 26, William Sahlein, business partner and twice a brother-in-law, died suddenly after undergoing surgery, at around sixty-five years of age. Sadly he expired on Levi's fifty-second birthday. The business was then closed for the day while the family dealt with their sudden sorrow. William's estate went to the children from his marriage with his first wife, Mary Strauss, except for a few legacies to other Sahlein relatives. And he had one more important request: to be buried in Cypress Hills Cemetery in New York where Mary was also buried.

Business matters intruded on mourning, but they had to be taken care of. On March 21 Levi appeared before notary William Harney representing himself and his brother Jonas, for whom he had power of attorney. With the death of two members of the firm, and two estates to settle, he and Jonas filed documents of partnership as Levi Strauss & Co. with themselves as the sole partners of the firm. Jacob, the oldest Strauss brother, apparently remained in London, although it is impossible to know for sure, since he disappears from the historical record.

Among Jonas Strauss's ten children were two daughters: Henrietta, born in 1855, and Rosa, born in 1862. By the time of their father's death, they were living in San Francisco, truly the center of the family business. Henrietta had married Joseph Kahn in New York, and by 1879 the couple had relocated to California, where he worked in the shoe industry. Rosa Strauss married Ralph Brown, whose family were agents for Oregon woolen mills and clothing manufacturers in San Francisco; their ceremony took place in New York in June 1883.

Levi continued to make the lists of the "rich men of California," sharing column inches with Leland Stanford, James Flood, and the other usual suspects. One of those lists appeared in 1883, which was a rather quiet year for the business, but it did include some personal enjoyments. In October Levi attended an engagement party for Ida Elkus, the daughter of customer and friend Louis Elkus of Sacramento. There, he gave Ida and her fiancé a large floral arrangement. He conducted some more real estate transactions in San Diego, and was likely not pleased that the assessment of his personal property amounted to over $500,000 (the amount on which his taxes were based).

On January 8, 1884, Levi's beloved sister Fanny died, at the age of 60. Except for the three years he spent alone in San Francisco, Levi and Fanny had either lived in the same house or within shouting distance from each other, ever since their childhood in Buttenheim. He never gave a public statement about her death, but it's easy to imagine how hard this loss must have been for him. The *Daily Alta California* praised Fanny for her charity work, noting that "her many kindly acts will long be remembered by the needy and suffering, who were the recipients of her bounties."[1] The funeral was held on January 10 at the Leavenworth Street home.

Other obituaries and her will give us a sense of where Fanny put her time and her talents. She was on the Ladies' Visiting Committee of the Pacific Hebrew Orphan Asylum, and bequeathed $15,000 to the organization. Of this figure, $5,000 was to be spent on the orphans themselves, with the balance to be used to build an Old Ladies' Home. She left complicated cash bequests to her children and grandchildren, and then directed that a portion of her estate be put back into the family business. And, finally, she allotted $3 per month to the widow of Henry Dreschfeld. He was a real estate agent, notary, and insurance representative, and after his death in the 1860s his wife apparently took up embroidery work to make money. Fanny may have been a customer and may have wanted to help support the lady in her old age. This is especially plausible given the funds she left to build the Old Ladies' Home.

In October, Fanny's daughter Lillie was engaged to Albert Scholle, whose relatives were also San Francisco dry goods and clothing pioneers. The couple had planned a big wedding, but because of the loss of Lillie's mother earlier that year, they decided on a smaller ceremony, which took place in February 1885.

Then, on November 5, 1885, seventy-year-old Jonas Strauss passed away in New York.

For many years J. Strauss Brother & Co., the founding family business, had taken second place to its powerhouse California branch. R & G Dun made this clear in its credit reports. In June 1873 it described the business as "a California house with a branch here." "Here" meant New York, where the company maintained the "buying office and manufactory." But even as a subordinate to Levi Strauss & Co., the firm was described as "an old good house" and "a strong, rich house," with good credit and a good name.[2] The business had done well enough that Jonas and his family moved a bit uptown from Kleindeutschland as early as 1863. West Fourteenth Street was close to what is known today as the Meatpacking District, but it was still an improvement.

Among Jonas's obituaries was a notice in the *New York Tribune*. It stated, strangely enough, that he had worked as a clerk in the courts of Bavaria, which is so impossible that one wonders how the reporter came up with this notion. Otherwise, the notices stressed his fortune and his charity. He was a founder of the Hebrew Orphan Asylum, and "he made generous outlays for charities throughout his long life, giving also a good share of personal attention to the progress of benevolent work."[3] He left money to the orphans and then directed his executors to distribute money to other charitable institutions as they saw fit. His own children also received large bequests, and his wife Sophia was well provided for. Jonas was buried at Salem Fields cemetery in Brooklyn, which was administered by Temple Emanu-El. After her death in 1891, Sophia was laid to rest there as well.

The death of the founder and firm's senior partner meant some financial scrambling back in San Francisco. In August 1886 Levi auctioned off eight or nine pieces of property throughout the city. On January 3 of the following year, Levi, along with his four nephews Jacob, Sigmund, Louis, and Abraham Stern, signed new copartnership papers, indicating that probate and all other legal issues surrounding Jonas's death were likely settled.

It was important to get on this good footing because big changes were happening in the riveted clothing business. Sometime during 1885 Levi Strauss & Co. opened its own factory at 32½ Fremont Street, just around the corner from the leased space at 415 Market Street. It was clear by now that the success of the copper riveted pants and other garments was not a fluke. The pants, and the copper rivets, were now well known, and were even the subject of puns printed in national papers. In the wake of the King patent infringement case, the *Boston Post* made a quip as it quoted a Cincinnati newspaper: "'Can a man's attention be riveted with copper rivets?' asks the Cincinnati *Commercial*. It can, if the rivets are sharpened and put where he will sit upon them."[4]

Between 1884 and the early 1890s product distribution expanded to the states and territories of Oregon, Washington, Texas, Idaho, and Alaska: all places where sturdy clothing was needed. And there was more variety to choose from. In 1889, for example, the company came out with "Spring Bottom Pants." These were flared trousers—"spring" meant flare—made of various shades of a lighter-weight denim, including one with a gold-colored fill yarn. They had beautifully finished hems and were lined around the waist, and although they were riveted, they were meant to be a cut above laborers' trousers. Advertisements showed a man, holding a cigar, wearing the Spring Bottom Pants with a crisp white shirt, a tie, and nicely shined boots. He was likely meant to be a factory superintendent, a bookkeeper in the office of some light industrial business, or other similar occupation. He was the man who supervised the men who wore the heavy-duty riveted overalls.

But before adding to the product line, Levi added something to the products themselves. In 1886 the leather patch on the overalls and other products was redesigned. In place of the company name, address, and language about the patent was now a finely drawn image of two horses, each attached with harnesses to either side of a pair of riveted overalls. A man with a whip stood next to each horse encouraging them to tear the pants apart, which is obviously a futile effort. Above the men and horses was a banner saying "Copper Riveted," with the patent date in a space below. This "Two Horse" design was quickly registered as a trademark (about which Levi had to give a deposition in 1889), was used on products and paper advertising, and is still in use to this day.

Without historical records to tell us what Levi's thought process was, it's impossible to know why the company decided to make this change, and at this particular time. But it's very likely the Two Horse design was a pre-emptive strike against the competition he knew would pop up once the patent expired in 1892. A specific design that could be associated with the company's riveted overalls, five years ahead of the event, could go a long way toward keeping customer loyalty when competitors' products hit store shelves.

It also had a cultural function. Some new westerners were either illiterate or did not speak English as their first language. Many people navigated their world through symbols—think of the three balls outside of a pawn shop, or the striped barber pole—and a man could go into a store and ask for the overalls with "the two horses" on the label. This was instant brand recognition, and, within a few years, the name for the product itself: the Two Horse Brand.

In 1887 the Two Horse design was stamped on the back of the envelopes the company used to send out its invoices. About the same time Levi Strauss & Co. started to print up flyers about the riveted clothing that salesmen could carry with them and give to their retail accounts. One of these had multiple messages: it featured the Two Horse design, the phrase, "It's No Use They Can't Be Ripped," and a bold "Made By White Labor" statement just below it. This told a storekeeper everything he needed to know.

Employees at Levi Strauss & Co. enjoyed many activities that we associate with modern corporate life. One of the more consistent was the company baseball team, formed as early as 1886. In September of that year it beat the Murphy, Grant & Co. team in an inter-company baseball game, and a commemorative medal was struck and given to all employees. Two years later,

Murphy, Grant & Co. got their revenge. The *Daily Alta California* reported the outcome: "At Oakland yesterday morning the Levi Strauss & Co. baseball club was signally defeated by the Murphy, Grant & Co. baseball club. The latter club toyed with their opponents and finally won by the score of 9 to 7."[5]

The pressures of life, which also never change through the generations, affected those who worked for the company, too. Terrence Pettit had been a Levi Strauss & Co. salesman but either quit or was fired because of his drinking. His wife divorced him, then remarried him when he promised to reform, but he couldn't give up his habit. In despair, he poisoned himself and died on the street at Seventeenth and Howard on May 28, 1885.[6]

Annie Smith was twenty years old and worked as a seamstress at the Fremont Street factory. She lived at home and was a quiet, considerate young woman, who always showed up on time and worked hard. No one thought she was keeping company with any particular man. Then, around April 26, 1891, she became so ill a doctor was called to the house, and after he examined her, Annie confessed that she had had an abortion, which was illegal at that time. She refused to name her seducer (or lover), or the doctor who performed the procedure, and on May 4 she died of peritonitis. The police were called, then the coroner, and there was an inquest to find out who was responsible for "the latest victim of criminal malpractice."[7] No one was ever held to account for Annie's death, and no one at the company was asked to comment publicly.

Levi Strauss & Co. also employed outside firms to provide services that it couldn't do in house. One of these was printing. Every time the company filled an order, the details were handwritten on an invoice, and as early as 1858, Levi had hired lithographers and printers to create eye-catching designs for his paperwork. The city's first print shops were actually a side business of some of the local papers, like the *Alta California,* which printed a variety of materials in addition to its own news sheet. The first printer that Levi Strauss & Co. used (that we know of) was O'Meara & Painter, on Clay Street. Founded in 1854, the company designed a blue invoice blank featuring an inked drawing of a ship, a wharf, and tall commercial buildings. This was meant to show retailers that Levi Strauss & Co. was a substantial, growing enterprise, despite being very new in the business. John O'Meara was elected State Printer in 1857, and then died in 1860. His partner, Jerome B. Painter, changed the name of the business to Painter & Company, and it became one of the leading type foundries in the country.

Right after the Civil War, Levi Strauss & Co. used Bogert, Bourne & Auten of New York for its printing, though it's not known why. But by 1869 or so, it was back to the myriad printing possibilities of San Francisco: Winterburn & Co., which had a staff of twenty-eight by 1880; W. T. Galloway; and Payot Upham. The most interesting, however, was G. T. Brown & Co. Grafton Tyler Brown, the company's founder, was a brilliant and successful commercial artist and printer. He also happened to be African American, but he passed as white. Despite having to disguise a part of his identity, his life and career personified the opportunities of Gold Rush–era San Francisco.

By the 1870s, Levi Strauss & Co. invoices were still beautifully designed, but the company did not need to work so hard for name recognition as they had a couple of decades earlier. And by the 1880s, the company's creative energy went into flyers and other advertising pieces, which were used to help sell the riveted clothing.

Levi had found his business niche—actually, many of them. With the copper riveted pants and other products firmly established as part of the company's regular inventory, Levi concentrated on keeping up with his government contracts. He supplied the Army Quartermaster Corps with heavy gloves in 1886, and won the dry goods contracts for San Quentin Prison in 1887 and 1888, and the contract for "striped flannel" for Folsom Prison in 1890. The company bid to be the supplier of riveted overalls and gingham overshirts for the county hospital in Fresno that same year.

He also kept tabs on the many trade and tariff issues that would affect his business. He continued to believe that Hawaii was an important trade partner for the United States. In April 1885, Levi, along with many other San Francisco merchants, signed a petition to the Postmaster General to put a Hawaiian mail route out to bid, due to increased commerce between the islands and the mainland.

On February 28, 1887, Levi attended a special Board of Trade meeting to discuss what to do about California Assembly Bill 55, "An Act to Protect the Manufacturing Industries of the State," which was awaiting the governor's signature. Despite its positive-sounding title, this piece of legislation caused panic among the city's merchants. The main provision of the bill required manufacturers to label or stamp their company name and location on everything they made, whether clothing or canned goods or anything in between. Violation of the law would be a misdemeanor requiring fines of up to $500 and even jail time. The authors of the bill were vague about what this would do for commerce other than saying it would be a benefit to the state. The sticking point for the merchants was the extra time and cost of adding a corporate name and city to each item, which would allow eastern companies, already selling their products at lower prices around the city, to move in and completely undercut local manufactures.

Levi and four other merchants were asked to serve on a special committee to draft a petition to Governor Washington Bartlett, urging him to veto the bill. The day of the Board of Trade meeting they retired to another room and came back shortly with a special resolution. Among the many "Whereas" statements was this clause:

> WHEREAS, the provisions of said bill appear to be unconstitutional, unjust, oppressive and detrimental to the manufacturers, the commerce and the best interests of the people of this State . . .[8]

The committee arranged to meet with the governor to present the resolution within the next day or so. On March 7, Bartlett vetoed the bill, and his veto was sustained by the legislature. Whether he made this decision because the committee members were especially persuasive or because Bartlett had lived in and served as San Francisco's mayor for some time and understood the merchants' argument, is unknown. But Levi and his colleagues must have wiped their collective foreheads.

What's interesting about Levi's participation in this process is that he was already putting his name and place of manufacture on his products. From the moment they came off the production line, "Levi Strauss & Co." and "San Francisco, Cal." were stamped on the leather patch on the riveted overalls and, eventually, nearly every other garment. Even the rivets had "L. S. & Co."

on them, along with the May 1873 patent date. For Levi, this was a business decision designed to make sure that his products would continue to be purchased after the patent expired. But as one of the authors of the petition, he saw the bigger picture for his fellow businessmen, and hence the problems with A.B. 55. Many products were labeled with a manufacturer's name, but even more were not. Forcing this extra task and cost on industries for whom it was not important was "unjust" and "oppressive." Levi knew that every business in the city needed to be healthy in order for all to thrive.

In October 1890 a new tariff bill was passed in Washington, named for its Republican sponsor in the House of Representatives, Ohio congressman (and future president) William McKinley. The bill increased the tariff on foreign imports, which was generally supported by most businesses as it helped boost trade with local markets. However, the higher prices for foreign goods that could not be matched by domestic ones meant that working people could either not afford them or had to dig deeper into their pockets to do so.

The day after the bill took effect a reporter for the *Daily Alta California* wandered around San Francisco and asked local merchants what they thought about it. Lazarus Dinkelspiel's dry goods firm opposed it, saying it was an oppressive tax on Americans and one that would not stimulate trade. Some tobacco merchants thought it would be beneficial, while others thought it would cripple imports that they relied on. Levi Strauss was also interviewed.

When the reporter showed up, Levi was allegedly reviewing the text of the tariff bill. He said that he was only just now learning about its provisions but that he was disposed on the whole to take a conservative view, meaning he would wait and see how the bill affected national commerce. However, he also said he thought the bill would not necessarily make locally produced goods automatically cheaper. Then the article concluded: "Mr. Strauss is expecting advices from his New York correspondents, which will give him a more satisfactory idea as to the actual effect of the tariff on import trade."[9]

On one hand, his hesitation in giving his opinion makes sense. By now the company had business contacts in Europe who supplied some of the finer dry goods, and it would take a while to see how the tariff would affect that part of the business. But Levi was also hedging. He knew that his comments would be printed and read by his colleagues and customers, and he did not want to make a bald statement about the issue until he knew exactly how it would affect his own business. Given his loyalties as a staunch and sturdy Republican, it's surprising that he would not go on record supporting a Republican economic measure. But there were many who did not think the tariff bill was good for America, so it was a divisive issue, even within the party.

In April 1891, Levi was joined by his fellow merchants at a meeting convened by San Francisco's mayor and Board of Supervisors, in order to plan another presidential visit. This time it was Benjamin Harrison, who had defeated Democratic incumbent Grover Cleveland in 1888. Levi served on the Finance Committee, along with William Crocker, son of the railroad magnate, and James Phelan, who would one day be San Francisco's mayor. The Executive Committee included former mayor Edward Pond and a young but already influential William Randolph Hearst, now owner of the *San Francisco Examiner.*

As he had done before, Levi was responsible for collecting money from the district surrounding the corporate headquarters, and within two weeks he had gathered together $2,000. After a few days of worry that not enough money would be raised, and some squabbling over tickets to the banquet, the presidential visit was organized and went off according to plan, on the evening of April 27, at the sumptuous Palace Hotel. Levi was among those who did get a ticket and the opportunity to shake the president's hand.

Although Jacob Davis was the superintendent at the factory and advised Levi on all things to do with product construction, Levi kept a close eye on sales and distribution of the riveted clothing. Republican politics were aligned with his philosophies about business and free trade, and Levi put his time and money where those interests did the most good. He was on the board of the new Gas Light Company, gas being a product that was now a necessity for daily life, and was also lucrative for those invested in it. But he still believed in doing good for others, and his reach began to exceed his grasp, especially when it came to the welfare of San Francisco.

In March 1887 Francis Newlands, a prominent banker, and son-in-law of Comstock backer and Bank of California founder William Sharon, went on a tour of southern California. When he came back, he gave an interview to the *Daily Alta California* and could barely control his outrage. With a sense of indignity that still divides California today, he ranted about how Los Angeles was outpacing San Francisco in progress, real estate development, and even personality. "The enthusiastic people are the new people," he said. "We have been asleep in San Francisco." He went on to list the advantages that the northern city had over its southern neighbor. "You can hardly take a step in any direction, particularly on the hills of the city, without being delighted by a beautiful view of the ocean, the bay and the mountains." There was no doubt, he concluded, that San Francisco "ought to be the Paris of America."[10]

A number of prominent local men—called the "heaviest taxpayers" by the *Alta*—went on record agreeing with Newlands, and wrote up a petition asking Mayor Pond to inaugurate a program of municipal improvements through an additional tax levy. On March 30 a few of these heavy hitters were interviewed by the newspaper, including Levi Strauss, who had also signed the petition. He was happy to express his enthusiasm about the petition: "Yes sir; I want to have the city improved, and have not the slightest objection to having my taxes increased for that purpose. . . . I am in favor of everything that can benefit San Francisco. Fix up the streets, overhaul the sewers, overhaul the Park as fast as possible, and in every way make the city attractive. . . . I am entirely in sympathy with any movement to give San Francisco a vigorous and healthy boom."[11]

A public meeting to discuss municipal improvements took place in late June, but it was not successful. Most of the speakers were politicians, who did not convince the city's business community, or even regular citizens, that paying for the improvements was a good idea. A writer for the *Daily Alta California* thought that the men who signed the original petition would have been better speakers, and included Levi on the list, saying that they could have really whipped up the crowd.

The Board of Supervisors took up the question of a special tax levy in September but filed it away, and although some portion of city taxes did go toward municipal improvements, the bigger picture was not realized. Three years later, the need for city improvements met a new need to find work for the unemployed, and the Citizens' Relief Committee of Two Hundred was born.

Mayor Pond called together many of the men who had signed the 1887 petition, and on March 7, 1890, he asked them to meet at the Chamber of Commerce to talk about how to find jobs for men who were out of work. After presentations by businessmen and members of the clergy, the mayor appointed an Executive Committee of ten men, including Levi Strauss. They met the following day, talked about how money would be raised, and decided that they would first put men to work in Golden Gate Park.

The city had acquired the parklands in 1868 and turned its sand dunes into a popular gathering place by the late 1880s. When John McLaren became superintendent in 1887, he spearheaded the park's transformation into the lush landscape and recreational destination it is today. But maintenance was a constant problem. The committee decided that any man who signed up and worked at the park would be paid $1.50 per day, and began to solicit money for the special fund. By the end of March there was money in the bank, and nearly one thousand men had signed up for work. Even the heavy rains of that month did not deter Superintendent McLaren and his new crew. The work continued through March of the following year, after which time the committee no longer had any funds, but some men had found full time work, and others skirted destitution because of the committee's efforts.

Levi's charity work paralleled the time he spent on the committee. One of the organizations that meant the most to him was the Society for the Prevention of Cruelty to Children. It was incorporated in 1876, just a year after New York organized its own Society for the Prevention of Cruelty to Children, the first of its kind in the world. In San Francisco, the society was endorsed and supported by the San Francisco Board of Supervisors, which had passed a stringent ordinance a few months earlier to protect the city's children. The specific protections in this ordinance demonstrate just how easy it would be for an adult to exploit a vulnerable child in any American city. No one could use a child for the "vocation, occupation, practice, service or purpose of singing, playing on musical instruments, rope or wire walking, dancing, begging or peddling, or as a gymnast, contortionist, rider or acrobat, in any place whatsoever."[12] The society's officers held meetings in which other officers and members reported on instances of abuse they observed while patrolling the city. It had the authority to intervene in cases, call in the police, and impose fines. Levi was elected a member of the society in 1879, became one of its vice presidents in 1887, and remained on the board until his death.

Throughout the 1880s Levi also directed the company to send relief funds for disasters in Charleston, South Carolina, and Liguria, Italy (earthquakes); Nanaimo, British Columbia (mine disaster); and León, Mexico, and Johnstown, Pennsylvania (floods).

If you stopped anyone on the street in San Francisco and asked him or her if Levi Strauss was a familiar name, and if his generosity was well known, the answer would have generally been yes. But if you asked the same questions of a journalist named Isidor Choynski, he would have given you a different response, and one that occasionally made it into the Jewish newspaper *The American Israelite,* where he wrote a column under the name "Maftir." Born in Poland, Choynski made his way to San Francisco in 1854, where he was a journalist, publisher, and antiquarian book dealer. He delighted in skewering his fellow Jews, especially those who were much wealthier than he was, and who were more assimilated into secular or Christian society.

Levi Strauss was an occasional victim of Choynski's pen, even when the writer was forced to praise him. When the company won a medal for its riveted clothing at one of San Francisco's many Mechanics' Institute fairs—held to showcase the city's progress and products—Choynski wrote, "The next prize was awarded to Levi Strauss, another charitable Jew, and also a bachelor; but he does things handsomely, when he does them at all."[13] Yet when Levi Strauss & Co. gave a large amount of bedding to San Mateo's Armitage Orphanage, Choynski withheld any backhanded compliments and simply reprinted an article from the *Pacific Churchman,* which included Levi on a list of local Jews who "give systematic support to this most worthy and wisely administered charity."[14]

In 1889 Levi turned sixty years old, and he was the picture of a well-fed, prosperous businessman. He was about five feet, six inches tall, and his formerly luxurious, but still-dark hair was slowly receding from a prominent forehead. He began to pose for more photographs, the serious portraits often made of prominent American men at the end of the century. He had traded his full, under-chin beard for an outcropping that descended from his chin and within a few years would be completely white. His deep-set, dark eyes looked confidently at the camera, and though he is very serious in these shots, contemporary descriptions of the man paint for us a different picture.

In 1888 Levi allowed embroidery and lace merchant Henry Lash to use his books to check the credit ratings of mutual customers. Lash sometimes sent his eighteen-year-old son Samuel in his stead, and the young man was always awed at seeing Levi in the flesh. Years later he told his own son Henry how these visits stayed with him, and what impressed him the most was that everyone in the office called the esteemed businessman Levi, and not Mr. Strauss. Levi was kind to the star-struck youth, and would always tell him to send his regards to his father. "I was just a kid, an office boy," Samuel told his son Henry, "but I still remember Levi Strauss as one of the finest, kindest, and friendliest gentlemen I've ever met."[15]

CHAPTER 15

FOR OVER TWENTY YEARS

The year 1890 was a busy one for Levi. Nearly every month or turn of the season saw him working on or participating in all the activities that now defined his life.

January: Levi attended the annual meeting of the Society for the Prevention of Cruelty to Children and continued to serve as a vice president.

February: Levi, Louis Sloss, Isaias Hellman, and the firm of Scholle Bros. purchased the stock of San Francisco's Nevada Bank. The Comstock Silver Kings had been the ruling partners, but after the death of James C. Flood, the bank's position—and finances—had been wobbly. Isaias Hellman was also Bavarian-born, from Reckendorf, a few villages away from Levi's Buttenheim birthplace. By 1890 he was a major banker, landowner, and investor in southern California, and with his involvement in the bank, more investors and stockholders lined up. He and Levi corresponded early on in the process, with Levi making recommendations about appointing directors.

March: Levi served on the Citizens' Relief Committee of Two Hundred.

Spring: The company introduced a less expensive version of the original heavy denim overalls. The Amoskeag Manufacturing Company called its highest-quality denim "XX," and, because the XX brand was so well known, the company used that same term as the name for its copper-riveted overalls. The new denim trousers were simply called "No. 2," to differentiate them from the original. These were also made of nine-ounce denim, but the material was woven in such a way that it was not as sturdy—and certainly not given the name "XX." The pants featured a linen patch instead of a leather one, and were sewn with cotton thread, instead of the linen thread used on the XX. The price difference could be as much as fifty cents, depending on where the pants were sold, and over the long haul, the cheaper option made economic sense for many customers.

June: Levi Strauss & Co. was awarded both the dry goods contract for San Quentin State Prison and the contract for "striped flannel" at Folsom.

August: Levi attended a performance of the play *Seven Ages* at the Baldwin Theatre. The production included orchestral music, light opera, burlesque, comedy, and a Greek chorus, and it received rave reviews.

At the end of the month Levi became one of the founding members of the Pacific Coast Auxiliary of the Jewish Publication Society of America. Its purpose was to publish and raise awareness of Jewish authors throughout the country. Both Levi and nephew Jacob Stern became life members. Another was fellow merchant Ferdinand Toklas, whose daughter Alice B. Toklas would become famous for her partnership with Oakland-born Gertrude Stein and for her influence on the Parisian avant-garde in the early twentieth century.

September: Levi Strauss & Co. won a silver medal for its overalls at the California State Fair. And on September 12, Levi attended a reception for California Republican gubernatorial candidate Colonel Henry H. Markham, who was elected the following year and served one term in Sacramento.

December: Levi Strauss and his nephews Jacob, Sigmund, Louis, and Abraham Stern officially incorporated the family firm in the state of California. On December 16 they held their first board meeting, assigned stock, and wrote up the meeting minutes in a ledger that was faithfully kept and was one of the few items to survive the 1906 earthquake and fire. Levi was the president and chairman, with Jacob Stern—the oldest nephew— serving as the corporation's first vice president.

The day before the first board meeting, the women at the Fremont Street factory had walked off the job. Because the XX overalls cost more than the No. 2 overalls, the workers thought they should get more money for making the more expensive pants. Aghast, Jacob Davis went to the headquarters on Battery Street and conferred with Levi and other managers. The 350 women on the sewing line had trooped down to Music Hall, about seven blocks away on Mission between Fifth and Sixth, to await the company's response. At two o'clock that afternoon Jacob went to the hall and told the women the company had acceded to their demands, and the machines were back on again by three o'clock. Local union leaders had tried to get the women to organize, but once they had achieved their aim, they decided not to rock the boat any further.

A few oddball things happened this year as well, including an attempted burglary at Levi Strauss's home on the night of August 11. A man named C. Schwartz was caught in the act and placed on trial in October. And someone named Louis Pillsbury, claiming he was making the rounds of downtown businesses in order to collect money for an old blind woman named Mrs. Cleveland, turned out to be another scam artist, who conned $20 out of the Levi Strauss & Co. employees. Mrs. Cleveland, it turned out, "existed only in his mind."[1]

As the 1890s progressed, so did each of these categories of Levi's business and personal life: the dry goods and riveted clothing business, Republican politics, Jewish life and faith, San Francisco business and finance, family, and philanthropy.

There were a lot of changes on the riveted end of things. In the spring of 1892 the reissued patent expired and the look of the XX overalls was altered, both subtly and more overtly. Since about 1890 the right front pocket bag on the inside of the pants had featured a stamped statement about the origin and quality of the riveted clothing, complete with the Two Horse design at the top. The bag also included some text:

> For Over 17 Years
> Our celebrated XX Blue Denim Copper Riveted Overalls have been before the public
> THIS IS A PAIR OF THEM!
> They are positively superior to any in the United States, are made by white labor, and enjoy a national reputation.
> They are made of selected nine ounce Amoskeag Denim, and sewed with the strongest linen thread.

We shall thank you to carefully examine the sewing, finish and fit.

See that this pair bears the quality number which is XX, and also our Trade Mark, as above.

LEVI STRAUSS & CO.

San Francisco, Cal.

Two years later most of this information, along with a more sophisticated design, was printed on a piece of linen-backed oilcloth, which was cotton fabric treated with heavy coats of linseed oil (sort of an early version of vinyl). The printed cloth was sewn onto the right back pocket of the overalls. This item, now called the Guarantee Ticket, served many purposes.

The most important was marketing and brand recognition. Competition was on its way, and if a store owner folded the pants just right on his shelves, with the ticket showing, then customers could pick out those Two Horse overalls quickly among other brands. The ticket included a representation of one of the medals the company had won, along with the Two Horse logo, and illustrations of the medals framed either side of the ticket, with a repeat of most of the language from the pocket print filling out the center. At the top was a repeat of the "For Over ... Years" statement, now given as "For Over 20 Years." The date at the top was changed again in 1899, to "For Over 26 Years," and was refreshed occasionally as the twentieth century wore on.

The copper rivets, which had been stamped with "L.S. & Co. SF May 1873," no longer featured the patent date. From 1892 until today, the language on the rivets has been "L. S. & Co. S. F. Cal."

Something else came along in the wake of the patent expiration, too. Both the XX and the No. 2 overalls received new names. Or, rather, numbers. For reasons lost to the flames of 1906, Levi Strauss & Co. started assigning "lot" or ordering numbers to its products. The original XX riveted overall was now Lot 501. No. 2 became Lot 201, although "No. 2" was still printed in the background of the linen patch. The patches—leather or linen—had both the lot number and size printed along the bottom. This innovation could have been another reaction to competition, or perhaps because the company was making so many products, it was easier for store owners to order by number rather than by a description.

The customers who shopped at these small general stores and men's haberdasheries were laborers, of course, and in the 1880s and 1890s they worked in a number of industries where riveted overalls were very welcome.

Miners could find them at H. B. Stevens in Calico, California, near Death Valley, and in Douglas City, Alaska, at the store of S. O. Wheelock. When gold was found in Canada's Yukon region and Alaska in the late 1890s, more stores opened up, giving men more opportunities to buy Levi Strauss & Co. clothing.

Men working in agriculture in Sebastopol, California, famous for the Gravenstein apple, could buy Levi Strauss & Co. overalls at J. C. Good-fellow's. And the men working the irrigation ditches in Phoenix, Arizona, built on the ghostly remains of ancient Hohokam Indian canals, could get their pants from J. S. Todd, among many other retailers.

Cattlemen and cowboys everywhere wore the overalls. Cowtowns like Sheridan, Wyoming, offered many places to buy the pants, including Harris & Barnett. H. W. Yeager & Co. served the men of Flatonia, Texas.

Any town with a railroad station—hundreds, thanks to the web of railroad lines throughout the West—always had at least one store where engineers, stokers, and other workers could stock up.

By the mid-1890s the company's salesmen had more ammunition in their traveling sample cases to help sell the riveted clothing, especially once the patent had expired. They would roll into their territory with handfuls of brightly colored, beautifully designed flyers, which they gave away to all their retail accounts. These flyers had interesting, informative, or comical imagery of the clothing on the front, with language on the back about the products and their superiority to the competition, along with simple line drawings for easy identification. Like the Two Horse patch, the flyers served a dual purpose. An eye-catching image appealed to those who had limited reading skills, while the text on the flip side provided concrete information for making an informed buying decision.

A lot of thought went into the design of these advertising pieces. One item from around 1899 features seven drawings of working men wearing the vast array of Levi Strauss & Co. clothing: a miner, a railroad worker, a longshoreman (moving a box with both the company name and what looks like a Star of David on the side, a nice piece of subliminal advertising), a cowboy, a carpenter, a teamster, and a man driving a wagon, possibly the salesman himself. A final image depicts a boy and a girl playing outdoors. The clothing ranges from the basic overalls, to standard bib overalls (part of the line since the early 1890s), oiled coats (to repel water), suit coats, and aprons, all garments in either denim or cotton duck. In the center of this collection of consumers is the Two Horse design, and on the back, with "For 26 Years The Standard" prominently printed, is the raw information about each garment. It's a very effective way to get a lot of information across very quickly.

The best of these is from 1897. A man in a red shirt and denim overalls is hanging by his knees and hands on a fence. A large spotted dog with brown ears has the waistband of the man's overalls clamped firmly in his jaws, and its paws are off the ground as it grips the pants tightly. On the fence is a billboard-sized Levi Strauss & Co. advertisement, listing all the products they made, and invoking the copper rivets, with the statement "Every Pair Guaranteed." There is a tree behind the fence, and the man's hat is on the ground, a level of detail that adds to the flyer's appeal. At the bottom are the words "Never Rip, Never Tear, I Wish They Did Now." But the best part is the man's face.

It's the very likeness of Levi Strauss himself.

Or close enough to at least invoke the company's founder. And here is a clue to his character. Aware of his own notoriety, even outside of San Francisco, Levi was willing to be caricatured in the name of sales.

Levi Strauss & Co. even created an early version of the "gift with purchase." As stores still do today, if a customer bought a Levi Strauss & Co. item, he or she received a souvenir that could be taken away and used at home in some form. One item was a small calendar. The front shows a large pair of riveted overalls with a blonde girl in one leg and a brunette girl in the other. On the bottom are the words "The Owner's Favorite Pair." The back has the actual calendar, and the name and location of the retailer, which was printed for free.

Another gift with purchase was the trade card. In the nineteenth century, just about any company with a product or service to sell created these

small colorful cards. Like flyers, the cards featured images that quickly conveyed a marketing message and that also had a purpose once the consumer
took them home. Trade cards were collectible, much like baseball cards,
and people regularly pasted them into scrapbooks or swapped them with
friends.

Levi Strauss & Co. printed up quite a few cards in the 1890s. Some of
them came in a set, and were simple depictions of a garment or of a man
wearing a garment: overalls, engineer overalls, Spring Bottom Pants, a
blouse, a jumper, or a coat. Rounding out this set was a beautifully colored
rendering of the Two Horse design. The cards were also featured on the
front of a flyer, and on the back of the flyer was a highly stylized illustration
of women at work in the large, well-lit sewing factory, one of whom wears
a flower in her hair. "Home Industry" is printed at the top, and at the bottom, "Section of Levi Strauss & Co.'s Overall Factory. This Factory Gives
Employment To Over 500 Girls." However exaggerated, both the design
and the language were meant to show that the company was progressive,
prosperous, and a supporter of hiring American workers.

Other cards came out as singles. One showed a man head-to-toe in
denim plowing a field, along with the phrase "The Best In Use for Farmers, Mechanics and Miners." Another depicted a man in a brown cotton
duck outfit on a horse, framed by "The Horseman's Favorite Garments."
Variations on the Two Horse design also showed up, one of which has a
man inside the overalls but which are not being torn apart by the harnessed
horses. "It's No Use They Can't Be Ripped" floats above his head.

The variety of flyers and cards shows that the company understood it
needed to have a diversity of images and approaches for its ever-increasing
list of retail customers. And it always seemed to have a few accounts that
were a little on the off-kilter side. In 1897, Mark E. Frank, who sold men's
clothing and accessories, went out of business. In a newspaper article written about his debts and the men he owed money to (including Levi), Frank
was described as a "well-known hypnotist and haberdasher."[2]

Another colorful character was Elias Jackson "Lucky" Baldwin. He had
arrived in San Francisco the same year as Levi and made a quick fortune
in hotels, bricks, and real estate. He got the "Lucky" nickname when he

snatched up some holdings in the Comstock and then sold them at their peak, making him even richer. He built the Baldwin Hotel and the Baldwin Theatre as a joint structure, which took up the entire block at the corner of Market and Powell. He also developed the Santa Anita rancho in southern California with the largest stable of race horses in the country. But by the 1890s his money had begun to drain away, due partly to lawsuits filed on account of some of his extramarital activities.

In May 1898 Levi filed suit against Baldwin for money owed, in the amount of $1,040, likely for supplies for the hotel. It's not known if Levi ever recovered his money, but it could have been difficult. In November of that year, the hotel and theater burned down to the foundation, and Baldwin did not rebuild.

And, as predicted, once the patent expired, companies in San Francisco and Los Angeles began to make their own riveted clothing. Neustadter Brothers of San Francisco already had a brand of overalls called Boss of the Road, for which David Neustadter had patented a continuous fly in 1877. The new brand was also called an "Improvement in Overalls," and through fabric construction rather than rivets, it was meant to go head-to-head with Levi Strauss & Co.'s products. Around the turn of the century, brands such as Can't Bust 'Em, Non-Pareil, and Stronghold entered the market. Both Boss of the Road and Non-Pareil were manufactured by dry goods competitors and, very likely, social acquaintances, the latter being the house brand of Murphy, Grant & Co.

We don't know how often Levi attended services at Temple Emanu-El, which had been in its stunning Sutter Street location since 1866; that is, we don't know how observant he was as a worshipper. But we do know that he cared about how his faith was practiced in the city. He was a founding member and first vice president of the Concordia Club when it was organized back in 1865, and he kept up with its activities. Many of the club's members were also members of Temple Emanu-El. In the 1880s the club was located at Stockton and O'Farrell streets, but in the fall of 1891 a splendid new headquarters opened at the corner of Post and Van Ness. Levi Strauss, J. H. Neustadter, and Moses Hyman held a mortgage on the building, and although there was some grumbling that member dues would be increased to help cover its cost, most Concordians understood that the increase was necessary.

In 1894 a women's charitable auxiliary was formed at temple. Called the "Emanu-El Sisterhood for Personal Service," the women in this organization were agents of both charity and assimilation. Their original headquarters were south of Market on Ninth Street, and the group had committees that offered everything from employment assistance to sewing classes. The overarching aim of the Sisterhood was to pull Jews out of poverty, give them training, and turn them into good Americans. The women went into the saddest places in San Francisco and interacted personally with families in need, giving more than just lip service to charity.

Levi Strauss was on the Sisterhood's advisory board from the year it was incorporated until his death. He and his fellow (male) advisors were sounding boards for the women and their plans for expanding their influence as the new century approached. In February 1900, for example, the Sisterhood held a huge amateur vaudeville performance at the Columbia Theatre to raise additional money. It was described as a "monster benefit," and it raised over $6,000.

Levi was outspoken about his faith, how it was perceived, and how the public perception of his faith affected business. In 1891 the *San Francisco Chronicle* ran an article about the participation of Jews in the upcoming Columbian Exposition in Chicago, stating that Jews would be taking part "not simply in their capacity as Americans, but also in their relation to the national Government as Hebrews."[3] In other words, they were going to emphasize their special love of liberty and adherence to the Constitution as Jews, rather than as Americans. It was "Our Superiority" all over again, as far as Levi was concerned. He made his opinion very clear: "We should not under any condition thrust into the Columbian exposition a religious element. It would be impertinent. It would provoke a state of affairs disastrous to the success of the exhibition which is to display the resources and genius of the country, not its religious sentiments. I am emphatically opposed to any such scheme."[4]

He had reason to worry. Although anti-Semitism only lurked under the surface of San Francisco's life and business, it still was simmering, waiting to strike. Jews sometimes had to justify their rare freedom from cultural tyranny. In the April 1895 issue of *Overland Monthly,* a prominent magazine of western life and literature, Gustav Adolf Danziger, Jewish himself, published a long article titled "The Jew in San Francisco: The Last Half Century." In his introduction, he explained that "prompted by a spirit of fairness and a liberal mind, the editor of this magazine has asked me to write an article that should contain 'a fair, square, honest discussion of what they (the Jews) have done for the City and State; how they have achieved their great fortunes, and who among them has become prominent in letters, in politics, etc.' "[5]

It is telling that amassing fortunes was first on the list.

Danziger was explicit about the contributions of Jews to the city's "Finance, Commerce, Politics, Charity, Art, Literature, Journalism, Law, Medicine, Education, Stage and Music," and he interviewed a number of prominent men on these topics. He mentioned Jacob and Rosa Stern's charity work, and he included Levi in a short list of "merchant princes." In his discussion of the city's commercial men, he said that most of them were public-spirited and encouraged local enterprise. "Daniel Meyer, Levi Strauss, and other wealthy Jews, never stand back where the welfare of the city is concerned," he asserted.[6] It's a remarkable article, giving San Francisco's Jews well-earned praise while not setting them up above their Gentile counterparts.

The issue of Jewishness came up again in 1899.

In 1894 a Jewish artillery officer in France named Alfred Dreyfus was falsely convicted of passing military secrets to Germany, his religion having been more damning than the spurious evidence against him. He was court-martialed and shipped off to Devil's Island, a penal colony in French Guiana. Two years later evidence pointed to another officer as the real traitor, and though this was originally covered up, the officer was eventually court-martialed but found not guilty of the crime. Dreyfus endured another trial in 1899, when he was again found guilty. The issue divided France in everything from politics to religion, leading citizens to openly face and talk about Jewish identity and anti-Semitism.

In September 1899, as Dreyfus was enduring his second ordeal, Paris was preparing for a splendid exposition that would open in April of the following year. Jews all over the world began to talk about boycotting the event, and a number of America's leading Jews went on the record with their opinions. Men in New York, Baltimore, Chicago, New Orleans, Louisville, and Pittsburgh were solicited on the topic, and Levi Strauss was the representative voice for San Francisco. The men were divided in their opinions, which were published in the *Los Angeles Herald,* but the majority were against a boycott, and for many of the same reasons that Levi himself gave: "The Jews should do nothing at all, whether Dreyfus is convicted or not. But, if he is convicted, it certainly ought to affect the Paris exposition, and I believe it will. It is not Jews only, but the people of the whole world, who are waiting to see if France can do her duty to Dreyfus. If she is unable to do it, the enlightened nations will show her what they think."[7]

Throughout his life, Levi's most emotional public statements were always about his faith, and about how he hoped he and his fellow Jews would be perceived. Here, as he said back in 1891, Jews should not make a stand as a group, despite the obvious anti-Semitism underlying the Dreyfus affair. However, he believed that the world would stand *with* Jews, if the injustice against Dreyfus continued. It was an optimistic belief in the face of a lot of evidence to the contrary. But, as it happened, the worm turned. The president of France pardoned Dreyfus on September 19, just a week after Levi and the other men spoke out in American newspapers.

Levi was outliving many of the other pioneering Jewish merchants of San Francisco. He served as a pallbearer for Martin Sachs in 1894, Mendel Esberg in 1896, and Moses Dinkelspiel in 1897. This was a great honor, and Levi no doubt took comfort in his faith as he grieved the loss of old friends.

In 1893, he needed that comfort more than ever.

On the morning of October 25, Levi's nephew Nathan Strauss left his Manhattan home at Broadway and West 57th Street and rode downtown to the office of J. Strauss Brother & Co. at 88 West Broadway. He arrived at nine o'clock, said good morning to the workers he ran into on the way to his private office, and issued a few orders about business. He stayed in his office for about a half hour, then walked out again and went into the nearby lavatory. A few minutes later a porter heard what sounded like a pistol being fired. He ran into the bathroom and found Nathan slumped against the wall, with a bullet wound in his right temple. On the floor next to him was a pearl-handled .32 caliber revolver with one empty chamber.

Within seconds clerks and managers surrounded Nathan's still form. One man ran out to fetch a policeman and someone at the station called an ambulance. A doctor arrived along with it, and Nathan was taken to the Chambers Street Hospital. There, although doctors tried to remove the bullet, they knew the wound was mortal, and someone was dispatched to give the bad news to Nathan's wife, Minnie, and bring her to the hospital. She arrived with her daughter, also named Minnie, but they were too late; he died twenty minutes before they got there.

Speculation about the reasons for Nathan's suicide began to bubble around the city and in newspaper headlines before his body was even cold. He was nervous. He had run the business into the ground. He was a well-known fan of race horses, so he must have lost money gambling. He and his wife were not getting along. He was a drinker.

None of this was ever proved, and the rumors only added to his family's pain, both in New York and San Francisco. Abraham Stern had come out from California to visit his cousin only a few weeks earlier and told a reporter that Nathan had been in good spirits and happy at home. He also said the family questioned whether it was even suicide at all.

But when lawyers went over Nathan's accounts a month later, they were stunned to report that his fortune was a lot smaller than they had expected. And they were never able to figure out why or how this happened. Although everyone eventually accepted the fact that Nathan killed himself, his reasons were never fully discovered to anyone's satisfaction.

Levi had plenty of activities on hand to keep him busy, and these must have helped him deal with the grief over Nathan's suicide. He was a generous supporter of the planned Midwinter Fair, which was the San Francisco version of Chicago's Columbian Exposition and which would take place in Golden Gate Park in 1894. He traveled outside of California once more in April 1893 to attend a gathering of western businessmen called the Trans-Mississippi Commercial Congress. This group, which met at regular intervals throughout the late nineteenth century to talk about issues that affected the expansion of western commerce, gathered in Ogden the year that Levi came along with the California contingent. He also continued to serve on the boards of other firms, ranging from the city's gas company to Liverpool, London and Globe Insurance.

When San Francisco's police force needed more men in 1895, some people in town felt that the supervisors should no longer have the final say on who would be appointed. Police Commissioner Moses Gunst, who was one of the critics of the old policy, stated that "of course . . . if a United States Senator, a Superior Judge, or Levi Strauss, Lloyd Tevis or Mr. Crocker should recommend a man the recommendation would carry weight, as they are big taxpayers and leading citizens."[8]

The reason Levi's name came up in these many contexts was revealed by a reporter for the *San Francisco Morning Call* in 1892. The paper profiled city businessmen in their offices, with the offices themselves serving to reveal the character of the men who presided within them. The profile began with a description of Levi himself: "The chief of one of the largest wholesale importing and manufacturing firms on the coast is Levi Strauss, an old-timer and well known man in the downtown district. Mr. Strauss wields an immense influence, not only by his wealth and immense business connections, but also because he is a very popular man."

The reporter went on to write a glowing description of Levi's private office, which anyone could walk into "without ceremony." There, everything was plain, undecorated, fitted for "strictly business" only. The two desks in the room (one for Levi and one for his "confidential man") were littered with packages of samples, price lists, letters, papers, and books. But visitors would rarely find Levi in his office. Instead, "Levi Strauss prefers to do his talking while leaning against a pile of blankets out in the storerooms to conversation at the desk. When he talks, however, he is a very accommodating man, and you will find him quite an agreeable conversationalist, although he has to entertain a great many callers every day of his life, owing to his business."[9] He also conversed with and gave welcome advice to his employees. In doing so he sometimes revealed himself more deeply than he would ever have done directly with a reporter.

There is little existing information about the company's early employees. But we do know about Joe Frank. Born in Oregon in 1876, Joe was hired as an order clerk at Levi Strauss & Co. in July 1896. He was in the dry goods end of the business and was in charge of orders for collars, cuffs, armbands, and so forth. He worked from seven o'clock in the morning until six o'clock at night. In 1898 he was promoted to salesman and had most of California and part of Oregon as his territory. Another early employee, Henry Richman, wrote up some informal reminiscences late in his life about Joe and about Levi:

> Mr. Strauss was very quiet, affable, always immaculately dressed. Joe was really an admirer of him. In 1898, Joe was at S.F. Headquarters, charging around to various department heads, intensely discussing and arguing. Mr. Strauss walked up to Joe and asked if he could see him in his office. When Joe was seated, he was asked, "Joe did you have a good year?" Joe proceeded to inform his Boss what a fantastic year he had had. Mr. Strauss listened quietly and patiently until Joe finished and then he said "Remember, Joe the more business you do, the more problems and trouble you will have." End of conversation, Xmas greetings exchanged and Joe left. Joe never forgot that talk. He spoke of Mr. Strauss with great admiration, every chance he could.[10]

Jacob Davis continued to flourish as the man in charge of the riveted clothing end of the business. He, Annie, and their six living children (at least one child died in infancy) were still at 1635 Sacramento Street in the late 1890s. In the city directory he was alternately listed as a factory foreman or overall manufacturer, but whatever the terminology, it always reflected his status as a manager, something that can only have been gratifying.

CHAPTER 16

ALL WILL BE SUNSHINE FOR
SAN FRANCISCO AND CALIFORNIA

Levi was admired by his many nieces and nephews, and family weddings abounded throughout the 1890s. In June 1892 Henry Sahlein married Carrie Fisher, the daughter of company employee Philip Fisher. Born in New York in 1839, Philip was living in San Francisco by 1862, where he worked as a bookkeeper at Levi Strauss & Co. He married and raised a large family, and by the 1890s he was the company secretary and cashier, and very likely the "confidential man" mentioned in the 1892 *Call* article. He organized many of the company's philanthropic ventures, and was an avid bike racer. Of all the employees whose activities made the local papers, the most hilarious was an event involving the Fisher family in 1893.

In the wee hours of November 27 the Fisher household awoke with a start at the sound of their doorbell ringing. A couple of the children looked out their window and, seeing no one at the front door, went back to bed. The bell rang again, this time over and over, and then it stopped. It was so loud that lights started to go on in the adjacent houses on Washington Street near Larkin. Philip's eighty-six-year-old father stormed down the stairs and threw open the door, and even as he saw that there was no one on the stoop, the bell began to ring yet again. The newspaper did not report how the family solved the problem but had a lot of fun with it. "Had some unkind friend projected his astral form at 2 o'clock in the morning, or was the electric bell out of order."[1]

On October 3, 1892, Sigmund Stern married Rosalie Meyer, whose family made its fortune in dry goods and banking in Los Angeles. The Meyers had moved to San Francisco in 1883, where Rosalie's father, Eugene, began working for the firm of Lazard Frères. She was originally engaged to Sig Greenbaum, from one of San Francisco's oldest merchant families, but the engagement was called off. Within a short span of time, Rosalie accepted Sigmund Stern's proposal of marriage, which came as somewhat of a shock to her older relatives. But in the end everyone was happy about the union. The wedding took place at the Meyers' home at Pine and Gough Streets, and Levi's Nevada Bank business partner Isaias Hellman, a good friend of the family, was also in attendance.

Four years later Sigmund's brother Abraham married Rosalie's sister Elise in New York, in January 1896. Louis Stern, the final nephew to marry, wed Lucie Cahen in January 1899. Hattie Stern was the last of the unmarried girls. She and merchant Samuel Heller were married around 1883, and they also moved into the family home on Leavenworth.

However, one important member of the family did not get married: Levi himself.

It was rare for a Jewish man, especially a wealthy one, to remain a bachelor. Culturally, marriage was something that was expected and, generally, looked forward to. But singlehood was less unusual in San Francisco than in other locations. The first generation of Jews who came to the city in the 1850s came as bachelors, but there were few Jewish women on hand to choose as wives. Once the men were on the road to prosperity they were also older, and if more women were now living in San Francisco, they were younger and frequently chose partners their own age. Some men married outside their faith, and that opened up the pool of eligible partners. Others, though single, were not celibate and found willing sexual partners outside the obligations of marriage.

There is no way to know for sure why Levi didn't marry, though. Perhaps he was observant enough that he did not want to marry a Gentile woman. Perhaps being an uncle fulfilled enough of a need for family. But he was frequently consulted about the quality of other marriageable men. Harriet Lane Levy, in her book *920 O'Farrell Street: A Jewish Girlhood in*

Old San Francisco, said that men like Levi were sought out when the daughters of fellow merchants got engaged. Potential husbands were dissected by a cadre of the father's friends and colleagues. When Harriet Levy's sister Addie wanted to marry Oakland merchant August Friedlander, her father Benjamin consulted Levi Strauss about his eligibility. According to Levi, August was "the brains of the business."[2]

Another explanation for Levi's single state comes across in an interview he gave to the *San Francisco Bulletin* in October 1895. "I've been in the harness now for forty-three years, and I could not live without my daily duties. I am a bachelor and I fancy on that account I need to work more, for my entire life is my business. I don't believe that a man who once forms the habit of being busy can retire and be contented. . . . My happiness lies in my routine work."[3] If he ever aspired to another kind of happiness, he didn't leave any surviving clues.

For all his dedication to his work, Levi found time for relaxation, beyond attending the occasional theater performance. In June 1895 he spent some time at Paso Robles Springs, in southern California. Known for its natural hot springs even today, the region was a draw for people from all over the state who wanted to take the waters for their health and enjoy the amenities of a fine hotel. It would have been an easy train journey for Levi from San Francisco.

Levi occasionally took another journey, also southward but closer to home, throughout the 1890s. He went to the Hotel Del Monte, on the Monterey Peninsula. Built in 1880 by the Big Four of the Southern Pacific Railroad in order to boost passenger service, the Del Monte was an opulent, modern, slightly gaudy, and beautifully landscaped hotel perfectly suited to the kind of clientele who could afford high railroad ticket prices. It burned down in April 1887 but was rebuilt and reopened a scant eight months later, and was no less a destination than its predecessor.

During one visit to the Hotel Del Monte, probably in 1898, Levi enjoyed the company of his niece-in-law Rosa, wife of Jacob Stern. In a letter to her sister-in-law Rosalie, Sigmund's wife, about their visit, she exclaimed, "What do you think of Uncle Levi remaining here so long—and he is enjoying it immensely—he had lots of company until yesterday . . . enough to make a "little game" in the evening."[4] Levi wrote a personal note at the bottom of Rosa's letter before she mailed it. He said he was glad to hear that Sigmund was feeling better after a recent illness, though he thought his nephew still needed more rest: "I think if you and him would come down here for about 2 or 3 weeks it would do you & Sig a world of good—how is little Elize give her a kiss for me."[5]

You can feel Levi's contentment, both in the words of his niece, and in his own expression of concern for his family. His nephew's health was on his mind, as was the welfare of one of the latest additions to the clan. "Elize" was Elise Stern, Sigmund and Rosalie's daughter, born in 1893.

Both the Del Monte and Paso Robles Springs were appealing to a man like Levi because they were not restricted. That is, they did not forbid Jews from staying there, which was often the case in other cities, even in the Gilded Age, which got that way in no small part due to the contributions of Jewish businessmen. By this time Levi was used to not having doors slammed in his face because of his faith, and he no doubt enjoyed the time he spent in both places.

In the mid-1890s Levi was in his mid-sixties, of an age to think about retirement, indeed, well past it for a man of his generation. But remember what he said back in 1895 about still being in "the harness." It was a harness that he chose to put on every day, and even as his friends were passing their businesses along to their sons, or passing away, Levi embarked on a period of incredible productivity that would last until his death.

Throughout his life, Levi gave time and money, and lent his name, to commercial and charitable causes ranging from a new Board of Trade, to the Emanu-El Sisterhood, to defending white labor, to honoring Civil War veterans. As the century came to a close, Levi knew his life had more past than future in it. Looking at where he put that time and money in his last few years tells us what was truly important to him.

Merchants like Levi had quite a few worries: Were they were carrying the right merchandise? Could they could find suppliers for the merchandise they wanted? Could they continue to find new customers? Was the competition running them into the ground? But the fundamental issue that affected all merchants, no matter what their line, was transportation.

In a place like San Francisco which, even in the 1890s, still imported some goods from outside California, the ability to receive and ship out your products was a core concern. And if you were a farmer in the astonishingly rich Central Valley, you had to be able to send your fruits and vegetables efficiently to waiting markets.

Levi was concerned with transportation very early in his career, starting with conditions within San Francisco itself. In July 1866 he and more than thirty other business and property owners on Sacramento Street placed a notice in the *Daily Alta California*: "We, the undersigned, owners and agents of property on Sacramento street, do hereby pledge ourselves one to the other to oppose the construction of a railway on said street, as contemplated by Legislative enactment."[6] The men felt that building and maintaining railroad lines in front of their Sacramento Street real estate would be injurious to their property, despite the obvious benefits of greater mobility for passengers around the city. Whether it was due to their agitation or some other reason, the street railroad was never built.

Levi joined with others that same month to approve the laying down of "Nicolson pavement" throughout the city, and approached the Board of Supervisors to approve the cost. Nicolson pavement was a process of laying out wooden blocks much like cobblestones. The Nicolson process was less expensive, and the pavement absorbed sound a bit better. However, being wood, the blocks had a tendency to rot, not to mention being slippery in icy weather. But the pavement was a vast improvement over the mud and warped wooden planks that still filled some streets, and it soon appeared throughout downtown San Francisco. Another change took place by 1897, when asphalt began appearing in place of wooden pavement throughout the country. In that year Levi went on record again with his fellow merchants, urging the supervisors to begin tearing out the old streets and replacing them with the modern and more efficient asphalt.

Then there was the issue of getting products into and out of the city. Until the completion of the transcontinental railroad in 1869, men moved their goods around with horses, wagons, and steamships. Merchants, especially, hailed the railroad as the shining savior of their business, but by the early 1880s, they realized that they were actually the new technology's prisoner.

The Central Pacific was the western portion of the transcontinental rail-road, financed by the men known as the Big Four: Charles Crocker, Mark Hopkins, Collis P. Huntington, and Leland Stanford. In 1868, even before the last spike was driven in Utah, the men had already begun to take over rail transport in California by purchasing the Southern Pacific. Founded in 1865 as a line from San Francisco to Yuma, the SP was attractive to the Big Four for its proximity to the Colorado River and Los Angeles, and the men built new lines to these regions by the late 1870s. The SP became trans-continental on its own by linking to lines belonging to the Santa Fe Rail-road farther east. By 1884 the Southern Pacific had controlling interest in the Central Pacific, though this was moot as both were owned by the Big Four. Levi began using the Central Pacific railroad for shipping goods to his warehouse from New York in 1878.

The Southern Pacific now had a monopoly on freight lines and therefore freight rates throughout California and its important nearby hubs. With its California Steam Navigation Company and its oceanic line called the Occi-dental and Oriental line, the SP also ruled the water. It squeezed out small shippers while giving preferential rates to large corporations like Standard Oil. Since the SP was the only game in town, merchants and farmers were forced to pay its rates with no recourse.

In the late 1870s the company cheated San Joaquin Valley farmers out of their land and offered the real estate at higher rates to purchasers of its choosing, who would then allow the railroad to build more lines on their property. In May 1880 an armed confrontation between the farmers and potential buyers turned bloody at a place called Mussel Slough, near Han-ford in today's Kings County. The railroad won in the end, with some farm-ers going to prison and others giving up and selling out. For this the SP was soon labeled "the Octopus," and Frank Norris's famous 1901 novel by that name kept the memory of the hated railroad alive.

Businessmen and organizations had tried to counter the railroad's monopoly on freight rates since 1879, when the new California state con-stitution was drawn up. It provided for a Board of Railway Commissioners, elected from all regions within the state. The commissioners had the power to regulate freight rates and could impose penalties against the railroad for noncompliance. This was hailed as a giant leap forward in commerce and common decency, but the euphoria was short-lived. It soon became obvious that the commissioners were in the pay of the railroad and interested only in looking after their benefactors. New boards threw out corrupt members but could never make any headway in reducing the cost of shipping for California's myriad industries.

While the railroad was showing its true colors, men like Levi were looking south for a solution to their transportation and distribution problems.

When Levi was making plans to leave New York for San Francisco, he chose the Panama route across the isthmus. But he had another option: Cornelius Vanderbilt's Nicaraguan line. Vanderbilt, the millionaire who built his shipping fortune from one little ferry in New York Harbor, saw the potential for a Central American canal and even proposed one for Nicaragua during the Gold Rush. It didn't take off, but his system of steamers and overland stage coaches across that country was a stiff competitor for the men who managed the transit across Panama. That route was shorter, but since Nicaragua was closer to the United States by about five hundred miles, traveling via Nicaragua meant people arrived in California a couple of days sooner.

As transport improved across both land barriers, merchants in San Francisco and politicians in Washington began to think that Vanderbilt's idea for a canal just might work. In 1880 Levi served on a special Board of Trade committee called the Special Committee on the Interoceanic Canal, along with merchants Louis Sachs and William Merry, and commission shipping agent William Dodge. The men studied all the available documentation on the canal's cost, engineering challenges, and potential benefits.

For men like Levi and his committee, the Nicaragua canal would not only become a vital link in the commercial chain between Europe, New York, and San Francisco, it could also be a vital transit route for the military, if ever necessary. While this was less important to merchants, they knew it was important to Washington politicians. The line would also help open up nearby markets in the American South, as it would run closer to ports such as Mobile, New Orleans, and Galveston than New York and Boston. From an engineering standpoint, Nicaragua was perfect, as it already had a navigable lake and river. Levi and his committee wrote up a long memorandum, which they presented to the Board of Trade on April 8, 1880. With a typical nineteenth-century flourish they ended their document this way: "Our coast, our country and the world are ready for this great and beneficent enterprise."

The canal idea stayed alive for many years. In 1892, Levi was a delegate to the Nicaragua Canal Convention held in San Francisco in March of that year. The goal of the gathered members was again to speak with one voice to Washington, hoping to support efforts there. It seems to have worked: both political parties included the Nicaragua canal in their platforms during the presidential race of 1896 between William McKinley (Republican) and William Jennings Bryan (Democrat).

In the meantime, the conflict between San Francisco's merchants and the railroad reached a breaking point in October 1891. A British ship pulled into port in San Francisco with a cargo of American goods. The shippers were from New York: they had loaded their merchandise onto a ship bound for Antwerp, which then sailed back across the Atlantic and around Cape Horn to San Francisco. This actually proved cheaper than paying for cross-continental rail service. The absurdity of the situation caused a number of San Francisco businessmen to take the matter into their own hands.

On October 11, 1891, the group held a public meeting at the Chamber of Commerce to organize into an association to protect the city's mercantile interests. The men adopted the name "Traffic Association of California" and formed committees to look at the problem and devise solutions. After many meetings and opinions, the consensus was that California needed a competing railroad.

Throughout 1893 and 1894 the association tried to drum up interest in a railroad to link San Francisco and the San Joaquin Valley, which would secure an unimpeded and less expensive flow of goods into and out of the city. Raising the money was a problem and nothing came of the attempts. Then, in January 1895, sugar millionaire Claus Spreckels got involved and everything changed.

Spreckels emigrated to the United States in 1848 from his native Germany, arriving in San Francisco in 1856. He opened a grocery but soon became interested in sugar refining, already underway throughout the Bay Area. With amazing speed he acquired control of local refineries and established the state's sugar beet industry to fuel them. He then spread his influence to the sugarcane fields of Hawaii and was, by the 1890s, a powerful capitalist.

Despite its failure to organize a new railroad, the Traffic Association was still alive, and decided to try once more to achieve its goal. The group called together a meeting of property owners and merchants on January 22, 1895. Included in the gathering were Claus Spreckels and Levi Strauss. Spreckels, who had not been part of the earlier fight against the Southern Pacific, had come to see how the railroad's monopoly was hurting California's prosperity and, by extension, his own. As the group assembled and speeches began, one attendee voiced a light-hearted but no less pointed opinion about the topic under discussion: men in the San Joaquin Valley said that of every three drops of rain that fell there, two were owned by railroad magnate Collis P. Huntington. Taking the podium, Spreckels pledged $50,000 toward the project and suggested that the association appoint a committee of twelve men to come up with ways to raise the rest of the money needed and whip up support. Spreckels himself chose the committee members, including Levi Strauss.

They had to do more than just meet and talk. Many of the committee members and those who attended the meeting subscribed enough money to get the project started. Levi Strauss personally gave $25,000, a $700,000 value today. The men chose the name "San Francisco and San Joaquin Valley Railroad" for the new venture, though it was generally known as "The Valley Railway" (sometimes "Railroad") or "The Valley Road," the word "road" often used as a synonym for "railroad."

Even average citizens in San Francisco could see the benefit of breaking the back of the Southern Pacific. Higher freight rates meant higher prices at the stores. Anyone who wanted to could also buy shares in the new railroad, and by April 1895 everyone from individual citizens to major bankers held stock. Levi Strauss owned 250 shares, in addition to his original subscription.

Articles about the association and its new committee soon plastered the pages of local newspapers, with the committee's members hailed as the right men for the job. A few members were interviewed in local papers about the railroad throughout the spring, Levi among them, and his passion for the project is very clear. "With a competing railroad and the Nicaragua canal, all be sunshine for San Francisco and California," he exclaimed, and then went on to say, "I am heartily in accord with this movement or any other movement that will lift us from our present lethargic state. . . . The valley road will not only be an immense benefit to this city, but will also open up the great, and in many respects, undeveloped resources of the productive San Joaquin valley . . . the new railroad is by no means a money-making scheme; it is a necessity."[7]

Like the other big thinkers in San Francisco, Levi understood the importance of the San Joaquin Valley in making California prosper, and keeping it that way. And he also knew that it wasn't enough to just give money to the promoters and hope the railroad did what it was supposed to. The city's merchants had to use the service themselves, to show its usefulness and value to others. Levi told the *San Francisco Call,* "Of course I shall give preference to the valley road. It is a line in which I am personally interested. I shall do all in my power to throw business in its way." The paper identified him as "one of the most active promoters of the new road."[8]

Ground was broken in Stockton on July 22, 1895, and the China Basin area of San Francisco, where the San Francisco Giants play baseball today, was chosen as the site for the northern terminus of the railroad. The trains were running to Merced by June 1896 and, as promised, the rates were far below those of the Southern Pacific. In response, the SP lowered its rates, and for the first time shippers had an actual choice. By October 1896 the new railroad had reached Fresno, and a celebration complete with speeches, a parade, and a free barbeque recognized the achievement. Continued rate wars were lucrative for commerce and personally satisfying for those who loathed the Big Four. Construction continued throughout 1897, and in July 1898 the line was completed between Stockton and Bakersfield, with a spur into Visalia.

During the building of the Valley Road, and even as it proved to be a force against the Octopus, rumors had swirled that the Santa Fe Railroad wanted to extend its service into San Francisco. The Santa Fe had evolved from the Atchison, Topeka, & Santa Fe Railroad, founded in 1860 in Kansas. It had expanded westerly through Colorado, New Mexico and Arizona through the 1870s and 1880s, and the railroad's owners now wanted a piece of the Pacific. Through the end of the 1880s, Santa Fe extended lines to Needles and the Mojave, Los Angeles, and San Diego. San Francisco was the next target.

Santa Fe officials visited San Francisco, even when the Valley Road was just a dream, and at their annual meeting in December 1898, directors voted to buy the capital stock of the San Francisco and San Joaquin Valley Railway. The deal was quickly done, with stockholders receiving the par value of their stock and the Santa Fe acquiring rail lines that merged easily with their own.

Some men accused Spreckels of selling out, but in reality the Valley Road (as Levi had predicted) was not a moneymaker and might not have survived on its own. The San Joaquin Valley was rich and being farmed, but was (Levi again) undeveloped. To the small farmer or store owner, the name on the side of the engine didn't mean much. Competition for the best rates was the important thing. In Levi's words, "If the deal is an honest one and competing line is to be brought into the state then the Valley Road was not built in vain. Its purpose will be accomplished no matter who may be the owners so long as it is not the Southern Pacific."[9]

Levi's involvement with the Valley Road is one of the best examples of his career-long desire to advance San Francisco business. He constantly worked toward this goal and was quoted on it over and over again. He knew that making San Francisco an attractive place to live had a domino effect aimed right at commercial prosperity. Good streets and beautiful parks made for happy and contented citizens who, in turn, were confident enough to invest in that city's future, whether through bonds, buildings, or buying overalls. Whenever the opportunity arose, whether it was bringing fairs, fraternal organizations, or mining conventions to San Francisco, Levi did what he could to make them happen. And although the Nicaragua canal project eventually died, as supporters of Panama won over Teddy Roosevelt after the turn of the century, Levi did not live to see that personal disappointment.

As he aged, as he saw San Francisco grow the way he had hoped it would, Levi knew that he needed to keep up his efforts and not become complacent. Business success was never a given. As long as San Francisco was good for business, Levi Strauss & Co. would also thrive. This meant that his nephews would have jobs in the family business, and their families would be comfortable and cared for. Levi's employees, their families, his fellow merchants, his fellow Jews: everyone had a stake in the city's continued dominance on the coast.

Life could be good in San Francisco and the surrounding Bay Area, but its advantages weren't a given. San Francisco might be the Queen of the Pacific, but it still had raw and dangerous edges. Levi had supported Jewish and Christian orphanages since his first days in the city, when his help was especially needed, but in the early 1880s he turned his attention to something that was necessary for children to be able to thrive: education. And he started with the youngest children first, by supporting kindergartens.

The first kindergarten was established in San Francisco in 1863. The concept was fairly new, based on the principles of a German educator named Frederick Froebel. As they still do today, kindergartens used music, games, objects, and pictures to gently prepare children for learning. San Francisco's kindergartens were among the country's first, as well as being among the most successful and enduring.

Some kindergartens were managed by the city's School Department, such as the Union Street kindergarten, at 512 Union in today's North Beach district. In 1887 the department decided to close the school for a period so that its principal, Anna Stovall, could get specialized training for kindergarten teaching. This left a lot of children without a place to play and learn, so Levi and merchants Henry Miller and Louis Sloss donated money to allow the kindergarten to reopen, and in record time. The school was closed on March 16 and the children filed back in the doors on March 28. The kindergarten was now under the auspices of the Golden Gate Primary School, with the newly trained Miss Stovall firmly in charge.

A few of the city's kindergartens were privately managed and were in constant need of funds. Newspapers were full of articles about upcoming and successful fund-raisers for a variety of these little schools. On March 22, 1887, as the drama of the Union Street kindergarten was under way, the First Presbyterian Church held a benefit at Irving Hall, in the financial district, to benefit the Buford Free Kindergarten, located south of Market on Harrison Street. Levi, his nephew Jacob Stern and his wife Rosa, were in the audience for the musical event called "The Dairymaids Convention."

By 1890 Levi was a regular supporter of the Pioneer Kindergarten Society, which managed three schools, in three very different San Francisco neighborhoods: Silver Star, at Pacific and Sansome, downtown; Adler, at Second and Folsom, near Jacob Davis's first home; and Heydenfeldt Mail Dock, at 218 Brannan Street near the waterfront. What these kindergartens had in common was their differences. That is, these schools didn't service just one segment of the city's population. Children from the upper-middle class to the deepest of blue-collar families could go to a kindergarten, and go there for free, whether run by the Board of Education or a board of ladies, thanks to the support of private citizens like Levi.

Ever the committee man, Levi was tapped by the Merchants' Association in May 1897 to join a group of twenty men to assist the Board of Regents of the University of California, across the bay in Berkeley. New York native Jillis Clute Wilmerding, who had made a fortune in business after moving to San Francisco in 1849, died in 1894 and left $400,000 to the Regents to open an industrial, or trade school. Wilmerding wanted the school to be run by the university but wanted it located in San Francisco. Its purpose was to train working-class boys in trades such as carpentry, bricklaying, plumbing, blacksmithing, and mechanical drawing, among others, supplemented by basics such as English, math, and geography. With a diploma in hand, young men could get a leg up in the world.

With this kind of money available, many Bay Area cities wanted the school for themselves, and the Regents would have been happy for it to open in Berkeley as well, but Mr. Wilmerding's wishes were clear. The committee, therefore, composed of the cream of the city's business elite—Mayor James Phelan, former mayor Edward Pond, Adolph Sutro, Charles and Henry Crocker, and Levi Strauss, among them—knew they had to find a site in San Francisco. It was fitting that merchants were chosen for this job. The students coming out of the new school would enter the world of commerce, perhaps even work for some of the committee members themselves someday. The school would also be good for the city because boys would not end up idle because they didn't have the opportunity for an education. That was bad for business. And merchants were the engine of San Francisco. They got things done, even if what needed to be done wasn't directly related to commerce. It made sense to put Wilmerding's donation in their hands.

Months of meetings, visits, and arguments took place, and in December 1897, the committee picked a site in the Potrero district, an industrial area south of the city center. Another industrial school called the California School of Mechanical Arts had been in the same area since 1874, also founded by a rich San Franciscan, James Lick, who made his money in real estate and investments. Although the committee members hoped to get land donated for Wilmerding, in the end funds were raised to buy the property right next to the California School. Levi donated $500 toward the purchase price, and in January 1900 the Wilmerding School opened with seventy-five pupils. The two schools eventually merged and moved to a new location, and today serve as Lick-Wilmerding High School.

Being on the school site committee was not Levi's first interaction with the University of California Regents. His association with the university began in 1896 and soon led to the creation of his most generous and most enduring charitable legacy.

CHAPTER 17

A CITY MAN

The University of California was chartered in 1868, opening its doors to students for the first time in Oakland in 1869, on the campus of a school called the College of California. It moved to Berkeley in 1873, graduating its first twelve students that same year. The university struggled financially and administratively but by 1895 had one thousand students on campus. Agriculture, mining, geology, and engineering were its first and strongest curricula, followed by medicine, and the university attracted important instructors. Local financiers and philanthropists soon realized the school's enormous potential and began to provide support in myriad ways. Phoebe Hearst, for example, widow of mining millionaire George Hearst and mother of newspaper magnate William Randolph Hearst, set up a scholarship for female students.

On January 13, 1896, Levi Strauss, along with merchant Louis Sloss, Silver King James L. Flood, and Oakland-based commission and grain merchant George W. McNear, wrote a letter to the Regents, the university's administrators:

> We have been informed by Regent Reinstein that the library of the University of California has always been closed, at night, because of a lack of funds for the lighting of the building.

> Desiring to increase the advantages offered by the library through having it open during the evening we beg to subscribe for that

purpose, each, the sum of Two hundred and fifty dollars making one thousand dollars which we are told is sufficient to have the building lit by electric light.[1]

The donation was accepted at the Board of Regents' meeting the following day, and the secretary was instructed to send a letter of thanks to the four men. In addition, librarian J. C. Rowell, his assistants, and the janitor all agreed to devote their time free of charge for a year to take care of the students who used the library at night. On February 29, with electricity supplied by the engines in the Mechanics' Building, the library was lit for the first time, during a celebration called the "Student Workmen's Promenade Concert." Students had spent nearly three days cleaning up the campus and making graveled walkways, and decided they deserved a party to honor the occasion. There were speeches, of course, and university president Martin Kellogg acknowledged the men who made the illuminated library possible.

The university was open to anyone, male or female, and received some funding from the State Legislature. The Regents knew that less fortunate students would benefit greatly from the opportunity to obtain a diploma, and in March 1897 decided to set aside some of the state funding for a scholarship, to be called the State of California Scholarship. Four students from each of the seven congressional districts would receive a scholarship each year, twenty-eight in total, each in the amount of $125. The meant $3,500 per year out of the university's coffers, nearly $100,000 today.

On March 6, 1897, Levi wrote another letter, this time under his own signature and care of Regent Jacob B. Reinstein, who read it to the board at the March 7 meeting:

> Dear Sir:
> I have noted in the newspapers that while the Legislature was considering the Bill to increase the income of the University of California a suggestion was made to set apart $3500 per annum to aid worthy and poor students from each of the Congressional Districts of the State to obtain an education at the University. I should be pleased to be permitted to duplicate the generosity of the State in the matter of said scholarships and request you to kindly communicate the terms of this letter to the Honorable the Board of Regents of the University.

The University of California has already risen to a plane that challenges the admiration of the entire country and I deem it a privilege
to aid those connected therewith.

The proper officers are hereby authorized to draw on me each year
until further notice for the sum of $3500.

I am dear sir
Yours very truly
Levi Strauss[2]

According to the newspapers that reported on the meeting, loud
applause rang out after the letter was read. The board immediately voted
to write a resolution of thanks, and also voted unanimously to name the
scholarship for its benefactor: the Levi Strauss Scholarship. As a writer for
the *San Francisco Chronicle* noted, many present commented that "a city
man has thus recognized the fact that the University is for the whole State."[3]
And it is also worth noting that Levi gave this money personally, not as a
corporate donation.

Levi's benevolence may not have been a surprise to Regent Reinstein. A
well-known San Francisco lawyer, Reinstein was a friend and likely fellow
worshipper at Temple Emanu-El. The topic probably may well have come
up before Levi sent his letter.

Students applying for the scholarship had to live in California. They also
had to demonstrate character, ability, and need, and be enrolled in under-
graduate programs (there were other programs for graduate students). The
funding was for one academic year, and students could reapply in succes-
sive years.

The first Levi Strauss Scholarships were awarded in July 1897 for the
1897–98 academic year. The students represented the entire geography of
the Golden State, from Jessie Bohall of Arcata, to Willard Giles Parsons
of Los Angeles. Among the twenty-eight winners were eleven women, a
testament not only to the university's open mind and liberal admission policy, but also to the progressive thinking of the students' hometowns and
districts. In March 1898 the first crop of scholarship winners formed the
Levi Strauss Scholarship Club, and Covina native Carl Warner was named

president. He distinguished himself again as a member of the debate team
that beat perpetual rival Stanford University for the Carnot Medal, awarded
annually for debates between the two schools on topics relating to contemporary French politics. The student who displayed the greatest skills as a
speaker received the medal, and Carl Warner was the recipient that spring.

On the evening of March 23, 1898, Levi Strauss was entertaining a few
friends at his home: Phoebe Hearst, University of California law professor
William Carey Jones, and Regent Jacob Reinstein. There was a knock at
the door, and in trooped all twenty-eight Levi Strauss Scholarship winners
carrying a large album. They formed a phalanx around Levi and his guests,
and opened the album, displaying a frontispiece with the words "Mr. Levi
Strauss, from the Holders of the Levi Strauss Scholarship, University of
California." Inside the album was a resolution of thanks to their benefactor,
which included a short history of the scholarship and a heartfelt expression
of what the scholarship meant to them:

> In offering this slight token of words, that would tell our hearts'
> esteem and affection for our benefactor, we express our trust that
> the true and real appreciation of his generous thoughtfulness will be
> shown by the right use we make of the opportunities he has placed
> within our reach and by lives worthily and usefully spent, and that
> all Levi Strauss scholars now and in after years will strive to be noble
> exemplars of that modest demeanor, generous action, broad sympa-
> thy and spotless honor typified by the name of Levi Strauss.[4]

The fact that three of the most significant people associated with the
university were at Levi's home on this particular night means that they, at
least, knew what was up. And even though the newspapers reported that
the students surprised Levi with their appearance and presentation, he may
have been told to expect it. Even so, this can hardly have diminished his
pleasure at the recognition, as well as the novelty of hosting a classroom-
size collection of students.

Levi obviously enjoyed the company of young people. He had lived with
his Stern family relatives since he was thirty-four years old, surrounded by
nieces and nephews who called him Uncle Levi. Now, at the end of the

1890s, the house at 621 Leavenworth was still a multifamily household. Levi shared it with Jacob and Rosa Stern and their daughter Fannie, as well as Hattie Stern Heller, her husband Samuel, and their son Walter. Perhaps seeing how the children thrived in this atmosphere of privilege allowed him to better see how education, at least, could make life better for those who had to struggle.[5]

As 1896 began to head toward 1897, Levi felt a sense of personal and professional optimism, which he expressed to a reporter for the *San Francisco Chronicle,* who asked him about how the city was faring as it came out of a financial slump that had begun in 1893. Levi responded, "The feeling is better and there is a much more encouraging outlook. I find the feeling general among my business associates. There is no doubt that the coming season will be a very prosperous one. Our correspondents inform us that at all points of the State and Coast the people are jubilant over the election of McKinley, which they regard as an assurance of better times."[6]

Levi didn't just pay lip service to McKinley. His Republican loyalties ran deep, and for weeks before the 1896 election, he literally paraded his support for the party and its platform. Levi was a staunch proponent of something called "sound money," which in essence meant he believed that only gold should be used to back the country's money supply. "Silverites," or those who backed "bimetallism," thought that silver should be traded in the same value as gold, even though the real market value of silver was much lower. Silver-backed currency led to greater and more frequent inflation, which was a benefit to small farmers and others who could take advantage of fluctuating prices to help pay off their debts.

Republicans were horrified by the silver lobby. They felt that gold was the strongest system, not only for the United States but for the country's international trade. Bimetallism would lead to unemployment and rising prices, and the domino effects these could bring. To further their cause, and to ensure McKinley's election, Republicans across the country formed "Sound Money Leagues." The California league was founded in October 1896 and met regularly at the Chamber of Commerce headquarters in San Francisco, with Levi a member of its executive committee. They had one aim: "to disseminate the doctrine of sound money and to educate the

voters of California to the end that the State will join with the great majority in sending an electoral vote that will assure us of sound-money legislation for at least the next four years."[7]

The league decided to make a splash to get its point across. On October 31, 35,000 San Franciscans marched down Market Street in support
of sound money, the gold standard, and William McKinley. Merchants
marched together, and Levi Strauss & Co.'s own Philip Fisher managed the
500-strong "textile" group. Levi joined the marchers for the entire route,
all of whom carried and operated noisy wooden rattles. McKinley barely
earned California's important electoral votes on Election Day, November
3, but they were enough to get him into the White House. Bimetallism continued to be a contentious topic across the country, but it faded after the
turn of the century, especially when gold from the Yukon began to fill up
America's bank vaults.

McKinley supporters also backed his international policies. In 1895 the men
and women of Cuba, who had labored under the yoke of a Spanish colonial
government, turned to violence and the swift revenge of guerilla warfare.
Spain retaliated by rounding up and imprisoning the rebels. Americans
watched what was happening, though many were reluctant to get involved,
William McKinley among them. Intervention could lead to war, and Civil
War veterans like the new president were not anxious to see another one.
Republicans a generation younger, such as Theodore Roosevelt, could
not understand this attitude. As assistant secretary of the Navy before he
became vice president during McKinley's second term, he advocated for a
strong seagoing force as a way to assert American authority overseas.

In 1896 Republicans had promised potential voters that their policies
would not only counter economic downturns but also act as a force for
good worldwide. Roosevelt felt strongly that the United States had a political and moral obligation to go to war against Spain to protect Cuba for its
own sake and for America's interests. When the U.S.S. *Maine* blew apart in
Havana harbor on February 15, 1898, Roosevelt got his war.

San Francisco's merchants felt the same about Cuba and about the righteousness of what became known as the Spanish-American War. On March

20, 1897, a mass meeting was planned as a rally for "Love of Liberty and Cuba's Cause." Held in Metropolitan Temple near Fifth and Market streets, it showed the world that San Francisco believed Cuba to be "cut off from the rest of the world, struggling, outraged, yet persistently and loyally fighting for freedom."[8] Mayor James Phelan led the meeting, and Levi's name was on the published list of prominent citizens who attended.

In January 1898 San Francisco held a Mining Fair, to commemorate the fiftieth anniversary of the discovery of gold. Displays and entertainments went on for over a month, and on February 28 the day's proceeds (the admission price was twenty-five cents) were collected and given to a fund to assist those who lost loved ones on the *Maine*. Levi was named by the fair's promoters to a supervising committee, to make sure the money got to the right place.

The war was also being fought in the Philippines, another Spanish stronghold of interest to the United States. The islands were an important refueling station in the Pacific, and if Spain lost its hold on them, their beachheads could be overtaken by another country, which would be disastrous for the United States. McKinley's war was on a number of fronts, and supporters like Levi put their money and merchandise where their politics were.

When a number of Kansas volunteers were stranded in San Francisco on their way to Manila without pay or supplies, the women of San Francisco pulled themselves together to collect what the young men needed, and enlisted local merchants to help. Levi Strauss & Co. donated sixty sets of underwear, and company employees also expressed their support for the men fighting abroad. In May 1898 they collectively donated $36 to the Red Cross, over $1,000 today.

The United States signed a treaty with Spain in December 1898, but that did not end Levi's involvement with the war and its soldiers. San Francisco threw a massive reception in August 1899 for returning veterans of the Spanish-American War, and Levi Strauss & Co. donated $100 toward defraying the costs. Levi also made sure that employee Charles J. McDonald did not lose his job after volunteering, and he took up his duties again in October 1899.

That May, after a number of San Francisco citizens had put the idea into his head, Mayor James Phelan formed a committee to raise the funds to build a monument to Admiral George Dewey. The commander had led the force that defeated the Spanish in the Battle of Manila Bay on May 1, 1898, the first, and tide-turning naval engagement of the Spanish-American War. Ordinary people, merchants, educators, and philanthropists showed their support with letters to the editor and with donations. Levi Strauss personally gave $500 to the fund. He was also in the audience when President McKinley attended the groundbreaking on May 23, 1901. McKinley did not live to see the monument's completion; he was shot by an assassin in Buffalo, New York, on September 6, 1901, and died eight days later. His successor, Theodore Roosevelt, presided over the unveiling in May 1903, just eight months after Levi's death.

The twentieth century opened in much the same way that the twenty-first century did: with heated debates about whether it began in 1900 or 1901, and hilarious newspaper articles about resolutions that got broken as soon as they were made, especially by politicians. Pastors at local churches stressed the need for looking back as well as forward, and asked congregants to engrave resolutions on the soul instead of in sand. Merchants used the turning of the year to predict prosperity and also to stress the value of saving money and being a smart shopper. Watch your nickels, they said, and the dollars will take care of themselves. "Start the new century right" ran many big display ads in local papers.

Levi may have stayed in touch with relatives who remained in Buttenheim, or at least kept up with the life of his home village. Sometime during 1900 he heard that officials needed money to renovate the crumbling cemetery, and he sent 1,028 Reichsmark to Buttenheim, about half the sum needed. His father, uncle, and many other relatives were buried there, and even the passing of fifty years since he had seen his village did not mean he had forgotten it. It was one of the most meaningful personal donations of his life, deeply symbolic of how far he had come.

The headquarters building got a new look in 1900. When the company moved into the space at Pine and Battery Streets in 1867, the address was 14–16, part of a larger structure that also housed Bachman Bros., the same family into which Levi's niece Caroline married. By 1894 the company had expanded further into the building, and the official address was 10–12 Battery Street. Bachman Bros. was no longer in business, though Leopold, Caroline's husband, was still a merchant.

In January 1900 Levi made plans to expand even further and hired contractor James A. McMahon and famed local architect Albert Pissis to build a new extension to the building. Like many of San Francisco's architects who would become nationally famous, Pissis studied at the École de Beaux Arts in Paris, and was the first in the city to do so. Born in Mexico in 1852, his father was French and his mother Mexican, and the family moved to San Francisco in 1858. Pissis moved back to the city after finishing his studies abroad, and with his partner William P. Moore began to design homes in San Francisco. His firm won the contract to design a new Hibernia Bank in 1889, and when that building was under construction, Pissis was approached by Levi Strauss & Co.

It was a good choice. Pissis blended the new with the old to create an elegant building. He went on to design some of San Francisco's most iconic structures: the Flood Building at Powell and Market, and Temple Sherith Israel on California Street, among them. He was also responsible for many of the post-1906 designs in the city, which included the new Levi Strauss & Co. factory at 250 Valencia Street, built to replace the factory at 32½ Fremont Street, which was lost to the fires.

By the end of 1901, the company dominated lower Battery Street along numbers 10 to 24. Levi had also decided that he needed additional factory space. In August 1900 newspapers reported that the firm was opening a factory at Fifth and Broadway in Oakland. The sewing machines there began to run in September, and both shirts and overalls rolled off the loading dock.

Business was beyond booming, and in addition to printing up colorful flyers and simple price lists, Levi Strauss & Co. printed up its first full catalog in 1900. The inside covers sported ads for company products, and the riveted clothing was always featured on the first few pages with simple but effective line drawings. The dry goods inventory rounded out the back matter, illustrated with drawings and photographs of the handkerchiefs, purses, bolts of cloth, and clothing brands that the company wholesaled, such as BVD underwear. Piles of the catalogs were thrown into salesmen's sample cases for distribution to their customers across the West.

Levi made his regular visits to the meetings of the Society for the Prevention of Cruelty to Children in 1900, and gave $50 to assist the widow and children of fireman John E. Sweeney, who had died pulling a man from a burning building. The company donated $200 to San Francisco's Admission Day festival fund, planned for September, commemorating fifty years of statehood. At the end of the year Levi also went to a big party celebrating the fiftieth anniversary of Eureka Benevolent Society. And he remained a fixture on the advisory board of the Emanu-El Sisterhood for Personal Service.

But in June 1900, Levi made a business decision that was not his finest hour.

On January 2 of that year the steamship *Australia* came through the Golden Gate, bringing a hold of cargo from Hawaii. Like New York, San Francisco had a quarantine station to check ships and crews for disease: Angel Island, close to the shores of Marin County across the bay. Officers there knew that bubonic plague was stalking the residents of Honolulu's Chinatown, so they went over the ship from stem to stern but did not find any rats, known to be carriers of the plague. They were there, though. And once the *Australia* was docked on the waterfront, the rats found their way off the ship and into the city, many of them ending up in Chinatown, where cramped quarters provided the perfect breeding grounds.

On March 6 a man named Wong Chut King, who was living in a run-down hotel at Jackson and Dupont (now Grant Avenue), was discovered unconscious in his room. He had been sick for days and, fearing that he would die, hotel employees moved him to a nearby coffin shop, where death soon arrived. A police physician was needed to write up the certificate, and when F. P. Wilson arrived and began to examine the body, he was shocked at what he saw. Wong's lymph nodes were badly swollen and there was a large sore on his leg that looked like a festering insect bite. Wilson drew some fluid from the nodes and, along with a health officer, went to the office of Wilfred Kellogg, the city bacteriologist. They examined the fluid under a microscope, and it didn't take long for them to realize what had killed Wong: bubonic plague.

Police and city officials acted quickly, blocking off Chinatown with ropes, telling all Caucasians to leave the area, and telling the Chinese they had to stay. Decades of conflict and fear allowed even the most intelligent physicians and scientists to buy into the assumption that the Chinese were foul disease carriers in general, and now their homes were also seen as potential spreaders of plague.

It was near impossible to keep the news a secret, and to keep residents within Chinatown's borders. Tests on lab animals injected with plague bacteria did not die, and when the press found out, health officials were ridiculed. They were forced to end the quarantine, but they hadn't kept it going long enough. The animals did eventually die, and more people did the same. Three men died just a few days after Wong, at a speed that startled local doctors. Fearing another quarantine, the Chinese told no one about the people who died from the plague, hiding their bodies and then smuggling the remains out of the area. But the barriers went up again in May, and this time they were of barbed wire, an action that caused riots.

Politicians and merchants were terrified of what would happen if news of a plague epidemic reached other centers of commerce, or even just local customers. Joseph Kinyoun, the public health officer, was firm in his efforts to keep the epidemic within Chinatown, but he also thought that disclosure was good medicine. He publicized the problem and warned officials in other states that anything or anybody coming from California could be plague-infested.

Merchants and California governor Henry T. Gage exploded. And things got even worse when they heard that Dr. George F. Shrady, the medical correspondent for the *New York Herald,* was on his way to San Francisco to see the situation for himself. He met with Kinyoun, toured Chinatown, and saw actual bacterial samples taken from infected residents. He spoke publicly about what he saw, and health officials thought his influence could turn the tide and help them at least get city officials to admit what they knew was the truth.

But Shrady surprised and shocked them. On June 2, 1900, the *San Francisco Call* ran a headline in large type saying "San Francisco Free from

Danger of Contagion." The entire first page was dedicated to a discussion of Shrady's visit and his conclusion that there was no plague in the city. It is no coincidence that this came after Mayor James Phelan hosted a banquet in the physician's honor at the swank Pacific Union Club. Shrady was also given a tour through Golden Gate Park and the Cliff house, and installed in a sumptuous room at the Palace Hotel. One evening, while enjoying its comforts, Shrady was visited by none other than the governor himself.

On June 14, city papers printed up a copy of Gage's fourteen-point letter to Secretary of State John Hay in Washington. The governor took pains to reassure Hay that San Francisco was, and always had been, free of plague. The final point was the most telling. The question of plague touched "the commercial and other interests of San Francisco." To bolster his argument, fifteen prominent local men put their names at the bottom of the letter, which were also reprinted in the paper. Levi's name was at the top of the list of "Bankers, Merchants, Etc."

It was San Francisco at its schizophrenic best. Kinyoun was transferred out of the city in disgrace, replaced by Rupert Blue, who found a way to work with city officials to privately admit that there was danger but in a way that did not strangle commerce. Calls for the complete destruction of Chinatown were quelled, and a strenuous program of rat-killing, fumi- gation, and demolition of the worst garbage-strewn buildings brought the problem under control by 1905.

It is hard to believe that Levi and the other merchants were not aware that plague did indeed exist in the city. Their businesses had been under attack before: by fire, economic turmoil, politics, and shipwreck. But noth- ing could have done more damage than the specter of disease, especially when linked to the Chinese, a people still misunderstood and reviled more than twenty years after Denis Kearney's public invective. Levi was con- nected to important politicians in many ways. He attended that banquet for George Shrady, and when Governor Gage gave an address at a Repub- lican rally a few months later in September, Levi was one of the meeting's vice presidents.

Levi's stature in the city, and the respect shown him by everyone from politicians, to competitors, to family members, was itself linked to the stature of the business that bore his name. Having shown that he could support vigilante justice in the 1850s, it is no surprise that he could support political denial forty years later. The man who could sue a friend for infringing his patent could turn a blind eye to medical truths when necessary.

In 1901 the Oakland factory was humming, the work force was increased on Fremont Street, and the riveted overalls got a second back pocket, on the left side, mirroring the original one on the right. This could have been a response to design changes on competitors' garments or to market changes across all types of clothing. It was the first major alteration to the design of the pants since their introduction in 1873. The company now knew that the pants were indispensable, which indicates that the company knew they were indispensable to the working man. The continued production of riveted clothing by competitors was also a clue.

Then, in July, Levi's complacency about the smoothness of his business operations was jolted and the company was thrown into the teeth of a major labor strike. San Francisco's workforce had waxed and waned as the nineteenth century came to a close. The 1893 financial downtown had been hard, but between the Spanish-American War and the gold discoveries in Canada and Alaska, the economy managed to right itself. However, manufacturing was still at the mercy of workers, who were moving to other West Coast cities, which were building up their industrial sectors and offering wages that sometimes surpassed those of San Francisco. This gave labor an advantage over management, and by 1900 there were ninety labor unions in San Francisco, which enrolled twenty thousand workers.[9]

Agitation provoked an equally strong response from employers and merchants. They also formed associations to protect their interests. The Employers' Association, organized in April, was the latest, and its tactics were as fierce as the toughest labor union. Its members, which included Levi Strauss & Co., held sway even over businesses that supported the aims of working men. No member could settle with a union on its own, for example; permission had to come first from the executive committee. It had real power, even in influencing the mayor to use the police against laborers when necessary. Although membership was supposed to be secret, everyone knew who the members were: the most prosperous and powerful businesses in the city.

By the spring of 1901, organized labor had managed to increase its power, and in April its members called for a series of strikes among teamsters, machinists, and other groups. Associated industries such as lumber, fruit, and hay, normally hauled by drayers and teamsters, supported the strikers, and a work stoppage began quickly along the waterfront at the end of July. This caused a ripple effect well outside of San Francisco, and officials on both sides of the labor question took some extreme actions, occasionally leading to violence.

The City Front Federation, founded in February 1901, blended sailors, longshoremen, and teamsters unions into one force. In August, as the strike gained momentum, the federation called for a boycott on products manufactured by businesses that were members of the Employers' Association, secrecy notwithstanding. Levi Strauss & Co. and merchants Neustadter Bros. and Murphy, Grant & Co. were on the hit list.

Rival newspaper editors entered this fray early on. The *San Francisco Call* was owned by John Spreckels, son of sugar magnate Claus Spreckels, and it was the voice of city commerce. Its opposite number was William Randolph Hearst's *Examiner,* which gleefully took the side of labor. The two men and their papers went after each other during the strike, with Levi finding himself in the middle.

On September 4, 1901, the *Examiner* ran an article claiming that half of the Levi Strauss & Co. labor force was sitting idle because the company had laid off four hundred of the eight hundred "girls" employed there. The reason was the City Front Federation boycott. Not only that, the paper claimed that truckloads of overalls were being returned to the Battery Street headquarters by the firm's customers, presumably because of their support for the strike.

The very day this article appeared, Levi and possibly Jacob Stern penned a long response to the article and sent it to the offices of the *Examiner,* asking Hearst to correct his errors. The "idle" work force, they said, was a temporary stoppage due to problems with the steam power at the factory, which made the sewing machines sputter off and on, leaving operators unable to get their work done. Some employees stuck around to wait for repairs, while others left either to do other activities or to go home for a while. By early afternoon everything was fixed and all operators were at their machines again.

As for the returned overalls, no one had sent any pants back to Battery Street.

The *Examiner* refused to print a retraction. So, on September 4, Levi sent a copy of his letter to John Spreckels, along with this short note: "The accompanying letter, which is self-explanatory, was sent by us yesterday to the editor of the Examiner, who has made no attempt to correct in his paper the erroneous statements therein pointed out. In the interest of justice and fair dealing we would ask that you give such publication of the inclosed letter as you may deem advisable."[10]

Spreckels lost no time in using this opportunity to his advantage. On September 6 he printed Levi's letter in full, under the headline "Truth Is Suppressed and Error Published." Articles about the strike, the workers, and what were now potential settlement talks were sprinkled throughout every issue of his *Call*. Hearst's refusal to print Levi's letter gave Spreckels a chance to write his most invective-filled editorial about his rival, which he printed in his September 24 edition, titled "Stroke of the Rattlesnake." Among the "lies" he attributed to Hearst were the ones his rival editor had told about Levi Strauss: "Were you not lying when you said: 'Levi Strauss & Co. are feeling the effect of the boycott levied against it by the organized labor of San Francisco. Workingmen are refusing to buy overalls manufactured by a firm pledged to stifle unionism. Four hundred of the 800 girls employed by the big Fremont-street factory were yesterday laid off'? Was not the lie published maliciously, and for the purpose of inciting further boycotts and causing further harm to California's industries?"[11]

What's ironic is that one of these "lies" was very much the truth: Levi no doubt wished for trade unions to go away. The strike was settled in October, with labor coming out ahead in strength, which it would use to good advantage in the future.

CHAPTER 18

IMPERISHABLE

Levi's name came up in the rotation for Grand Jury selection again in January 1902, and he kept up his usual schedule as the year progressed. He was re-elected as a vice president of the Society for the Prevention of Cruelty to Children, and also remained on the advisory board of the Emanu-El Sisterhood. He sold some personal property in Riverside and bought more in San Diego. He had purchased a house in the Sonoma County town of Petaluma, north of San Francisco, which Jewish chicken farmers were about to make famous as "The Egg Capital of the World." The company also owned a few more buildings throughout San Francisco. In addition to the headquarters on Battery and the factory on Fremont, there were six warehouses scattered throughout the South of Market district, from Howard, to Front, to Beale, to First Streets.

When a volcano eruption in Martinique took lives and property in May, Levi arranged for the company to donate $500 to the relief fund. He buried another friend and colleague, Louis Sloss, in June, and saw his own name appear on another list of the richest "Hebrews" in the United States.[1] A fire at the Oakland factory caused $1,000 in damage in August, but production was soon up and running again. In September Levi attended the dedication ceremonies for the new headquarters of the Emanu-El Sisterhood, on Folsom between Eighth and Ninth Streets. He also spent some time at the Hotel Del Monte.

Levi had made one final stand for San Francisco commerce earlier that spring. In April he signed a telegram alongside the names of over thirty-five other prominent San Franciscans, and it was sent to Senate President Pro Tempore William P. Frye in Washington. Theodore Roosevelt did not have a vice president after he took over the White House in the wake of William McKinley's assassination the previous year. Frye, a senator from Maine, served as the temporary head of the Senate, which was considering important legislation about Chinese immigration to America that spring.

In 1882, Congress passed the Chinese Exclusion Act, which imposed a ten-year moratorium on the immigration of Chinese laborers. Men who wanted to come to America had to prove they were not laborers; that is, they were not there to take American jobs. This effectively closed the door to California, as the terms of the act made it near to impossible for them to prove they were anything but a laborer.

The act expired in 1892, but with the passage of the Geary Act, which reinforced the Chinese Exclusion Act, it was extended for another ten years. The Senate was about to make its provisions permanent. In their telegram, Levi, Isaias Hellman, Claus Spreckels, William Crocker, and others said that continued exclusion of what they termed "legitimate Chinese merchants" was an act of "gross injustice." It was also bad for business. Although Levi and the other commercial men of San Francisco still owned their prejudices against Chinese who threatened American workers, they had no issue with those who wanted to sell their products. Despite the merchants' plea, the extension was passed without debate, and the telegram was passed to the clerk. However self-serving, it took guts for Levi and his colleagues to go on record against the wishes of the United States Senate, and on such an emotionally charged issue.

During the week of September 22, Levi began to feel unwell, though he had been fine after his recent visit to the Hotel Del Monte. On Wednesday the 24th he felt bad enough that doctors and a nurse were called to the house. "Liver congestion" was the diagnosis, and Levi was ordered to bed. By Friday the 26th he felt well enough to have dinner with Jacob, Rosa, and the rest of the family that evening. A nurse had been in attendance earlier in the week and was still on hand as Levi went to bed around eight o'clock. A little while later the nurse heard him groaning. She went to his bedside and asked how he felt, and he replied, "Oh, about as comfortable as I can under the circumstances." He then turned his head on his pillow and peacefully died.[2]

The obituaries began to appear on Sunday. The San Francisco *Call*, always a friend of Levi and his company, printed a huge photograph on the front page topped with a prominent headline and subhead:

LEVI STRAUSS, MERCHANT AND PHILANTHROPIST,
DIES PEACEFULLY AT HIS HOME.

His Life Devoted Not Only to Fostering the Highest Commercial Conditions, But to the Moral, Social and Educational Welfare and Development of the Young Men and Women of the State[3]

The *San Francisco Chronicle*'s headline read "Unexpected Call for Levi Strauss."

The *Oakland Tribune* went right to the point. "Levi Strauss Dead."

Newspapers from Utah to New York ran Levi's obituary in their pages, and though the articles were much shorter than the California versions, Levi's name was prominent enough by 1902 to at least rate a mention. The *Call* and the *Chronicle* summarized his life from his birth in Bavaria, to the founding of his company, to his good works around the city and across the state. His bachelorhood was mentioned only in the context of his happy life with his nephews and their families at the "splendid home" on Leavenworth.

The Board of Trade issued a resolution on September 27, honoring Levi's service to the board, as well as his "good deeds and unblemished reputation." All members were requested to close their businesses so that they could either attend the funeral or simply show respect for his passing.

Levi's funeral was held at 10:30 a.m. on Monday, September 29. Like other family funerals, it took place at the house, with friends, colleagues, and two hundred Levi Strauss & Co. employees filling the parlor where his mauve-colored coffin rested. The crowd, by necessity, spread out to the staircase, down the hall, and all the way into the street. Although the family asked that people refrain from sending flowers, many could not resist, and the room was made even more crowded by enormous floral tributes.

Rabbi Jacob Voorsanger of Temple Emanu-El gave the eulogy to the assembled, and though his praise of Levi and his life was typical, it was also heartfelt and personal:

> His whole life was a pledge of his honor. His name in the mercan-
> tile community may, as it will, pass away, but his character is imper-
> ishable. The community is better for his having lived in our midst.
> It is better not because he established a large mercantile establish-
> ment, but because he was a pure man who loved God and kept His
> commandments. In public as well as in private life he was without
> reproach. The estimate of his honorable life cannot be computed in
> dollars and cents. . . . Good he was, endowed with native goodness.
> Prominent though he was, he was most unpretentious, and came
> down to the level of every-day life and loved his fellow man. To his
> family he was the beloved patriarch, who rejoiced in their joys, and
> sorrowed with them when trouble came into their hearts.[4]

Following the eulogy, the casket was taken out of the house, escorted by twenty pallbearers, among whom were Adam Grant, Isaias Hellman, Philip Fisher, Henry Sahlein, and Leopold Bachman. The coffin was then loaded into a horse-drawn hearse, and company employees followed the vehicle as it moved slowly to Post Street, Mason Street, and then down below Market to Third and Townsend. The 11:45 Southern Pacific train—the railroad Levi fought so hard against—was waiting to take him and his family to Home of Peace Cemetery in Colma, south of San Francisco. There, a graveside service was attended by members of the Eureka Benevolent Association and the First Hebrew Benevolent Association. Rabbi Voorsanger said a few more words, Levi's casket was placed into a handsome mausoleum, and the ceremony was over.

The final ritual was the reading of Levi's will. Between the business, his charitable donations, and the legacies he left to relatives, his estate was worth $1,667,500: nearly $50 million today.

Not surprisingly, he left the business to his four nephews. His nieces received bequests in the hundreds of thousands of dollars, and the money went to them directly, not to their husbands to manage for them. Nathan's children were also provided for. Caroline Bachman had died sometime before her uncle, and her children also received personal bequests. Philip Fisher received $10,000, "as a token of my regard for his faithful services as our confidential bookkeeper for many years."[5]

Levi didn't forget his favorite charities. The Pacific Hebrew Orphan Asylum received $20,000; the Home for Aged Israelites on Silver Avenue $10,000; the Eureka Benevolent Association $5,000; the Protestant and Catholic orphanages $5,000 each; and the Emanu-El Sisterhood $2,500.

He also honored the police and fire departments, which had both been of service to him throughout his life and career. Five hundred dollars went to the widows' and orphans' fund of the Police Department, and Sigmund Stern presented the check to Chief of Detectives John Martin on October 4. That same day a check in the amount of $500 was sent to Fire Chief Dennis T. Sullivan, to benefit the Firemen's Mutual Aid Society. Sullivan told the *San Francisco Call* that the check "came in the nature of a pleasant surprise to the members of the department."[6] Less than four years later, Sullivan would lose his life in the first moments of the earthquake and fire of April 18.

Within a few months of Levi's death, Hattie Heller took $1,000 of her inheritance and gave a donation to Mount Zion Hospital in her uncle's name. This institution was the creation of a group of Jewish citizens who had met in late 1887 to plan a hospital for the "indigent sick," regardless of their race or religion, and supported by San Francisco's Jewish leaders. Ten years later, in January 1897, it opened its doors on Sutter Street near Divisadero in Lower Pacific Heights, managed by the Mount Zion Association and the rabbis of the three most important temples in the city. Today, it is part of the University of California Medical Center, still in its original neighborhood.

Jacob Davis continued to work for the company until sometime around 1906, when he sold his interest in the patent back to Levi Strauss & Co. He died on January 20, 1908, and was buried at Hills of Eternity in Colma, the cemetery managed by congregation Sherith Israel.

Jacob's son Simon, who had started working for the firm around 1894 as a clerk, moved up the ladder to factory superintendent by the time of the quake, and stayed with Levi Strauss & Co. into the 1920s. In 1935 he founded his own clothing company, which he named for his own son and which is still in business today: Ben Davis Clothing.

The four Stern boys honored their uncle in two meaningful ways.

Jacob Stern called a board meeting a few weeks after Levi's death. He, Sigmund, and Abraham met at the Battery Street headquarters on October 20, and the minutes of the meeting began with a list of the attendees: "The Board of Directors of this Corporation met in the office of the Corporation this day at the hour of 10 and at the Call of the Board Vice President. All the members of the Board of Directors were present excepting Louis Stern, who was absent attending to the business of the company in New York City and Levi Strauss, who died since the last meeting of this Board and whose place as Director has not yet been filled."[7]

No sentiment, no tribute, just a simple statement of how the company had changed and why, and then they got down to business.

And they kept the business going. They were all well versed in the day-to-day running of both the dry goods and overalls business, and the transition from founder to successors was smooth. And when all was lost in 1906, the men rebuilt the firm again.

Starting over, they could have started with a new name, perhaps something like "Stern Bros." But that never entered their heads. The firm, its reputation, and its riveted denim pants, all owed their existence to one man, and it was his name that went on the new permanent headquarters building at Pine and Battery, when it opened two years later. The company was, and would always be, Levi Strauss & Co.

People write and read biographies because their subjects stood out for doing something, for being something out of the realm of the everyday. They created something new, solved a problem, sparked a movement, altered established courses, methods, and thinking. Or they were a catalyst for these things to happen.

That's what Levi was. He didn't invent blue jeans. But without him the most iconic garment in fashion history might never have been more than just duck cloth pants on the rear ends of Nevada miners and teamsters. Without Levi's business sense and vision, which allowed him to see the potential of those little metal rivets, the overalls might have seen the light of day but would not have thrived.

Levi didn't run orphanages and kindergartens, but he saw to it that their doors were kept open for those who ran them and for those who desperately needed the safety of their walls.

He wasn't a teacher, but he gave enough money to a growing university so that its teachers could steer new generations of students toward the future.

He didn't hold any political office, but his good advice, solid bank account, and respected voice were sought out by politicians and policy makers.

His vast dry goods business allowed families in remote locations to have a few comforts in the midst of hardship.

San Francisco is famed for firsts and for icons of all kinds: the cable car, the Golden Gate Bridge, the Beat Generation, the Summer of Love, and the rise of the hippie, gay liberation, the tech revolution. These inventions, designs, and cultural revolutions blossomed because San Francisco had a solid core for them to spring from; granted, that core was commerce, the antithesis of the city's reputation today, but without it, without the gold that the city's past rested on, its future residents would have had no place to come to. And Levi Strauss was one of the men who set that firm foundation.

The jeans were a first, too, and in their own way, also changed the world.

Western working men now had sturdy pants that stood up to the harshest mine, lumber camp, or cattle drive. They were made to last, letting miners and cowpunchers keep a little more of their hard-won money. And by the early twentieth century, so many people were calling the pants *Levi's*, the company had to register the name as a trademark.

The list goes on. In silent movies, real cowboys hired as extras wore their personal pairs of Levi's overalls, and early cowboy stars like William S. Hart wore them at their homes high in the hills above Los Angeles.

The dude ranch arrived in the 1920s, and easterners eager for a taste of the storied West headed that direction. They donned the riveted pants and jackets, along with the more Saturday-night dance-themed shirts and gabardine trousers the company added to its new Western Wear lines. Adding the first jeans for women in 1934, Levi Strauss & Co. helped women look good even as they ate beans around a campfire.

When Hollywood needed a bad boy for the postwar generation, it chose the denim-wearing motorcycle rider, the pants as dangerous as Marlon Brando's Johnny in *The Wild One*. Asked what he was rebelling against, he swiveled in his tight Levi's jeans, and said, "Whadda you got?"

College students whose eyes were opened, or lives permanently radicalized, began to wear the pants as they fought to end war and champion civil rights. Now called "jeans," these pants were a far cry from those nineteenth-century blues of Huckleberry Finn's day. Wearing jeans meant solidarity with the oppressed, and making a statement as personal as a raised fist.

In the 1970s young women began to wear jeans as a way to assert their personal and professional freedom, wearing them for everyday instead of just weekends, and not just in the West.

Jeans began to spread beyond the States as early as the 1950s, with their authentic American message of freedom especially prized in a Berlin Walled world, where they were so feared they could only be obtained in secret, and could also be used as currency.

From the 1980s to today, the blue jean has become a staple of high fashion, even as it is still worn by cowboys, ranchers, and working men across the globe. Today's jeans are the descendant of a simple invention and a well-informed business decision, made by two immigrants who knew their lives would be better in America. In reinventing themselves as Americans, they created the most American of garments.

Levi Strauss's name today means blue jeans, but in his own day, jeans didn't even enter the equation. The "Merchant and Philanthropist" headline on his obituary, and the order in which those words appeared, would have pleased him as an accurate summation of his life.

There were many other such honorable and successful businessmen in nineteenth-century San Francisco whose names are known only to historians. And it is here that jeans do fit into the equation. Levi Strauss & Co. sold quality products at a fair price. People bought the riveted clothing, used it, loved it, and so adopted it into their lives that all jeans were one day called *Levi's*. Each succeeding generation has formed its own bond with this iconic clothing. And the bond is also with the man they are named for.

Levi Strauss: the man who made the world a little better, and a lot bluer.

NOTES

Chapter 1. Enlightened Nationalities

Excellent primary source material about the history of Jews in Bavaria can be found in the Bavarian State Archives in Bamberg, Germany. The archives contain all the documentation the Strauss family filed in order to emigrate. I am indebted to Tanja Roppelt, director of the Levi Strauss Museum in Buttenheim, and consultant Gabriele Gonder Carey for translating these materials. Amos Elon's *The Pity of It All: A Portrait of the German-Jewish Epoch, 1743–1933*, and James F. Harris's *The People Speak! Anti-Semitism and Emancipation in Nineteenth-Century Bavaria* are stellar works on Jewish life in Bavaria and the conditions that propelled the midcentury migration to America.

Chapter 2. The Fate That Has Been Assigned to Me

Hasia R. Diner has published excellent books on Jews in both Bavaria and New York, and on the links between these homelands. These include *A Time for Gathering: The Second Migration, 1820–1880*, and *The Jews of the United States*. Elon's *The Pity of It All* and Harris's *The People Speak* were also critical sources for this chapter.

1. *Auswanderungsantrag von Rebecca Strauss under ihren Kinden ach Amerika an die Regierung von Oberfranken aus dem Johre 1847*, Bavarian State Archives.
2. Ibid.
3. Ibid.
4. Kohn, "A Jewish Peddler's Diary, 91.
5. Ibid., 93.
6. *New-York Daily Tribune*, June 4, 1847.
7. Kohn, "A Jewish Peddler's Diary," 95–96.
8. Ibid., 99.
9. *New-York Tribune*, May 14, June 8, 1841.
10. Wise, *Reminiscences*, 38.

Chapter 3. Store-Princes

Jewish migration and life in New York are topics that have engaged authors for decades, and a few works were particularly important for this book. These include Naomi Cohen's *Encounter with Emancipation: The German Jews in the United States, 1830–1914;* Eric E. Hirschler's *Jews from Germany in the United States;* and Jacob Rader Marcus's *Memoirs of American Jews, 1775–1865.* The aforementioned works by Hasia R. Diner were also useful here. Stanley Nadel's *Little Germany: Ethnicity, Religion, and Class in New York City, 1845–1880,* was especially useful for understanding the Strauss family's neighborhood.

For the topic of work life in New York, I relied most heavily on Robert Ernst's *Immigrant Life in New York City, 1825–1863;* Goldstein and Greenberg's *A Perfect Fit: The Garment Industry and American Jewry,* based on an exhibit at the Yeshiva University Museum; and Sean Wilentz's *Chants Democratic: New York City and the Rise of the American Working Class, 1788–1850.*

1. Foster, *New York in Slices by an Experienced Carver,* 4.
2. Lazarus Isaacs Estate Papers, 1859, call no. P-239.
3. *New-York Daily Tribune,* May 15, 1847.
4. Foster, *New York by Gas-Light,* 59.

Chapter 4. A Limitless Opening for Industry and Talent

There is an abundance of primary source material concerning travel across the Isthmus of Panama in the nineteenth century, including accounts written by Sarah Merriam Brooks, Joseph W. Fabens, Jessie Benton Frémont, and Jonathan Dean Long. Excellent secondary sources include Lynn A. Bonfield's "When Money Was Necessary to Make Dreams Come True: The Cost of the Trip from Vermont to California via Panama"; and Herbert Howe Bancroft's histories of California. The best of the secondary sources remains John Haskell Kemble's *The Panama Route, 1848–1869.*

Ava F. Kahn's books on the history of Jewish life in California and the West, whether written alone or in collaboration with other authors such as Ellen Eisenberg, Marc Dollinger, Robert E. Levinson, and William Toll, is the bedrock of any study on this topic. Her book *Jewish Voices of the California Gold Rush: A Documentary History, 1849–1880,* was especially helpful. Harriet and Fred Rochlin have also contributed to this field, as has Robert Levinson, with his own book *The Jews in the California Gold Rush.*

1. *Asmonean,* July 26, 1850.
2. Ibid., December 10, 1852.
3. Bancroft, *California Inter Pocula,* 158–59.
4. Ibid., 181.

Chapter 5. Hard Labor and Wild Delights

Ava F. Kahn's work is also relevant for this chapter, as it straddles both the New York and San Francisco portions of the story. Peter R. Decker's *Fortunes and Failures: White-Collar Mobility in Nineteenth-Century San Francisco* is an excellent source for information about commerce and consumers in San Francisco history, and was used for a number of chapters in this book.

A number of works about the formation of cities, San Francisco in particular, were especially helpful. Gunther Barth's insights into the development of western cities can be found in *Instant Cities: Urbanization and the Rise of San Francisco and Denver*. Philip J. Ethington's *The Public City: The Political Construction of Urban Life in San Francisco, 1850–1900*, and Roger Lotchin's *San Francisco 1846–1856: From Hamlet to City* provided excellent grounding into what prepared San Francisco for its merchants.

1. Kahn, ed., *Jewish Voices of the California Gold Rush*, 52.
2. *Daily Alta California*, October 30, 1853.
3. Soule, Gihon, and Nisbet, *Annals of San Francisco*, 492–93.
4. Ibid., 638.
5. Decker, *Fortunes and Failures*, 17.
6. Kahn, ed., *Jewish Voices of the California Gold Rush*, 252.
7. *Daily Alta California*, June 18, 1853.
8. Soule, Gihon, and Nisbet, *Annals of San Francisco*, 500.
9. Levy, *920 O'Farrell Street*, 161
10. *Daily Alta California*, June 15, 1853.

Chapter 6. Steamer Day

Peter R. Decker's *Fortunes and Failures* was especially useful here in understanding the daily activities of early San Francisco merchants. Soule, Gihon, and Nisbet's *The Annals of San Francisco*, helpfully reprinted in 1966, provides delightful color commentary on life in nineteenth-century San Francisco.

Ava F. Kahn's work on the Jewish Gold Rush experience continued to be a prime source for this chapter. Through his published works and our personal communications, Robert J. Chandler provided context and reading materials for the sections on Gold Rush finance, and the Baker Library at the Harvard Business School holds the R. G. Dun & Company collection of credit reports.

The source for Levi's donation to the Orphan Asylum Society is the archives of the society's successor organization: Edgewood Center for Children and Families.

1. Soule, Gihon, and Nisbet, *Annals of San Francisco*, 505.
2. Ibid., 627.
3. *Daily Alta California*, September 18, 1858. Quoted in Kahn, *Jewish Voices of the California Gold Rush*, 392–94.
4. Henry J. Labatt, "The Commercial Position of the Jews in California," *Voice of Israel*, 1856. Quoted in Kahn, *Jewish Voices of the California Gold Rush*, 255.
5. Decker, *Fortunes and Failures*, 100.

Chapter 7. Treasonable Combinations

Robert J. Chandler's work on California in the Civil War helped provide the background for this chapter, and his suggestions for the best places to find newspaper articles were especially helpful. Oscar Lewis's *San Francisco: Mission to Metropolis* has an excellent section on Civil War San Francisco.

Passages through the Fire: Jews and the Civil War, from the American Jewish Historical Society, was a tremendous source for understanding the Jewish community's response to the conflict. Jewish activity during the war was also frequently covered in the local papers.

1. *Daily Alta California*, April 25, 1861.
2. Ibid., May 12, 1861.
3. *Evening Bulletin* (San Francisco), May 13, 1861.
4. Stephens and Bolton, eds., *Pacific Ocean in History*, 367.
5. *Daily Alta California*, September 2, 1861.
6. *Quincy (IL) Daily Whig*, Jan 17, 1872.
7. Lewis, *San Francisco*, 129.
8. *Daily Alta California*, November 6, 1864.
9. Lewis, *San Francisco*, 134.
10. *Daily Alta California*, October 21, 1868.
11. Twain, *Roughing It*, 374.
12. Daily Alta California, October 29, 1863.
13. *Hebrew* (San Francisco), January 22, 1864, quoted in Sharlach, *House of Harmony*, 17.
14. *Daily Alta California*, January 11, 1865.
15. Ibid., December 27, 1867.

Chapter 8. Our Solid Merchants

Barbara Berglund's *Making San Francisco American: Cultural Frontiers in the Urban West, 1846–1906,* was a very useful source for the information on early San Francisco trials. Robert J. Chandler's article "Some Political and Cultural Pressures on the Jewish Image in Civil War San Francisco" gave additional context for Jewish life in the postwar period. Ava F. Kahn has done excellent work on the history of the Sunday laws. And William Issel and Robert W. Cherny's *San Francisco 1865–1932: Politics, Power, and Urban Development* was an important source for this entire chapter.

1. *San Francisco Bulletin*, February 24, 1859.
2. *Daily Alta California*, February 27, 1859.
3. Berglund, *Making San Francisco American*, 39.
4. *Mariposa (CA) Gazette*, September 2, 1865.
5. Helper, *The Land of Gold*, 58.
6. *Daily Alta California*, May 27, 1866.
7. Quoted in Chandler, "Some Political and Cultural Pressures," 148.
8. *Daily Alta California*, October 6, 1862.
9. Quoted in Chandler, "Some Political and Cultural Pressures," 161.

10. *Daily Alta California,* June 17, 1864.

11. Ibid., October 12, 1866.

12. Credit report, R & G Dun, August 1871, R. G. Dun & Co. Collections.

13. *San Francisco Chronicle,* February 11, 1872.

14. Ibid.

15. Ibid.

Chapter 9. "The secratt of them Pants is the Rivits"

Because all of the Levi Strauss & Co. records were lost in 1906, the best source for information about the invention of jeans is the patent infringement court cases that came directly afterward. The best of these sources is the case against H. W. King, filed in 1876 and settled in 1880. For this case Levi Strauss and Jacob Davis gave depositions about the first use of rivets, how the men obtained a patent, and early sales of the riveted products. The case against H. B. Elfelt of 1874 was also useful here. Early information about the life of Jacob Davis comes from John Marschall's *Jews in Nevada: A History* and from the work of Guy Rocha, former Nevada State Archivist.

1. *Levi Strauss, Louis Strauss, Jonas Strauss, William Sahlein, and Jacob W. Davis, v. Henry W. King, E. W. Dewey, and William C. Browning, Complainants' Record* (hereafter cited as *Levi Strauss et al. v. Henry W. King et al.*), 168.

2. Ibid., 169.

3. Jacob Davis affidavit, *Levi Strauss v. H. B. Elfelt, et al.,* District of California Circuit Court of the United States, Ninth Judicial Circuit, June 17, 1874.

4. Ibid.

5. *Levi Strauss et al. v. Henry W. King et al.,* 173.

6. Ibid., 2044–45.

7. Ibid., 2046.

8. Ibid., 2048.

9. A. H. and R. K. Evans to the Examiner of Patents, October 11, 1872, copy of letter in Levi Strauss & Co. Archives.

10. *Levi Strauss et al. v. Henry W. King et al.,* 2049.

11. Ibid.

12. Ibid., 2050.

13. Ibid., 2051.

14. Jacob Davis to United States Commissioner of Patents, May 7, 1873, Levi Strauss & Co. Archives.

15. Ibid.

16. "Jacob W. Davis of Reno, Nevada, Assignor to Himself and Levi Strauss & Company, of San Francisco, California. Improvement in Fastening Pocket-Openings," Patent Number 139,121, May 20, 1873.

17. *Pacific Rural Press,* June 7, 1873.

18. Ibid., June 28, 1873.

Chapter 10. Patent Riveted Clothing

As with the previous chapter, information on the early years of the blue jean comes from nineteenth-century patent infringement cases. The history of Manchester and the Amoskeag Manufacturing Company can be found in *Amoskeag: Life and Work in an American Factory-City*, by Tamara Hareven and Randolph Langenbach, and in *Manchester: The Mills and the Immigrant Experience*, by Gary Samson. Information on denim and indigo came chiefly from Stephen Yafa's *Big Cotton: How a Humble Fiber Created Fortunes, Wrecked Civilization, and Put America on the Map*, and Jenny Balfour-Paul's *Indigo*.

Jules Tygiel's *Workingmen in San Francisco, 1880–1901*, is a premier source for San Francisco labor history, as are Peter R. Decker's *Fortunes and Failures*, and Jeffrey Haydu's *Citizen Employers: Business Communities and Labor in Cincinnati and San Francisco, 1870–1916*. History of the early clothing industry comes from Claudia Kidwell and Margaret C. Christman's *Suiting Everyone: The Democratization of Clothing in America*, Michael Zakim's article "A Ready-Made Business: The Birth of the Clothing Industry in America," as well as the Harvard Business School case study "Samuel Slater, Francis Cabot Lowell, and the Beginnings of the Factory System in the United States."

1. *Daily Alta California*, April 4, 1867.
2. Ibid.
3. Ibid.
4. *San Francisco Chronicle*, April 14, 1878.
5. Hargrove, *The Weaver's Draft Book and Clothiers Assistant*.
6. Stephen Yafa, *Big Cotton*, 86.
7. Little, *Early American Textiles*, 74.
8. Dagg, "Eliza Lucas Pinckney," 71.
9. Samson, *Manchester*, 39.

Chapter 11. Towers of Strength

Tygel and Decker's books were both useful for this chapter, and I further relied heavily on newspaper reporting from the period. I am also indebted to Sara Gilbert, whose research uncovered Levi Strauss's real estate holdings in Emory City, British Columbia.

1. *San Francisco Chronicle*, July 19, 1873.
2. Tygiel, *Workingmen in San Francisco*, 23.
3. Ibid.
4. *Sacramento Union*, July 23, 1873.
5. *New York Times*, October 11, 1874.
6. *Daily Alta California*, April 2, 1875.
7. *San Francisco Bulletin*, April 14, 1879.

8. An excellent summary of this process can be found in Clare B. Crane, "The Pueblo Lands: San Diego's Hispanic Heritage," *The Journal of San Diego History* 37, no. 2 (Spring 1991): 104–27.

9. *San Diego Union*, March 28, 1883; *San Diego Evening Tribune*, July 2, 1901.

10. *San Francisco Chronicle*, February 25, 1878.

11. Ibid., February 26, 1878.

12. *Daily Alta California*, February 5, 1874.

Chapter 12. Home Industry

Many scholars have taken up the topic of the history of Chinese immigration and work in California. The sources on which I relied the most were *Chinese San Francisco, 1850–1943: A Trans-Pacific Community*, by Yong Chen; *Picturing Chinatown: Art and Orientalism in San Francisco*, by Anthony W. Lee; *Driven Out: The Forgotten War against Chinese Americans*, by Jean Pfaelzer; *Chinese Labor in California, 1850–1880: An Economic Study*, by Ping Chiu; and *The Indispensable Enemy: Labor and the Anti-Chinese Movement in California*, by Alexander Saxton. Newspaper articles were also useful here.

Information on the business comes from the R. G. Dun & Company credit reports in the Baker Library at the Harvard Business School.

1. *Pacific Rural Press*, August 8, 1874.

2. Ibid.

3. *Levi Strauss et al. v. Henry W. King et al.*, 2055.

4. Ibid., 2020.

5. *Independent*, April 4, 1874.

6. *Los Angeles Herald*, January 9, 1874.

7. Credit report, R & G Dun, January 3, May 1, 1874, R. G. Dun & Co. Collections.

8. *Levi Strauss et al. v. Henry W. King et al.*, 2038.

9. *Pacific Coast Law Journal*, February 28–August 14, 1880 (San Francisco: W. T. Baggett, 1880), 486.

10. *San Francisco Bulletin*, May 1, 1880.

11. *Chicago Daily Inter Ocean*, May 1, 1880.

12. Saxton, *Indispensable Enemy*, 4.

13. *San Francisco Daily Morning Call*, April 8, 1876.

14. *San Francisco Chronicle*, April 9, 1876.

15. Kahn, ed., *Jewish Voices of the California Gold Rush*, 457.

16. Diary of Annie Bosworth, November 26, 1877, San Francisco History Center, San Francisco Public Library.

17. *Daily Alta California*, May 13, 1878.

Chapter 13. Very Strong Opinions

The *Official Gazette* of the U.S. Patent and Trademark Office, whose issues are all online, was an excellent source for finding information about the company's trademarks and Jacob Davis's additional patents. Newspaper articles from the period provided the context, especially for the company's prison and Indian service contracts. The best works about these topics are Shelley Bookspan's *A Germ of Goodness: The California State Prison System, 1851–1944*; and Cathleen D. Cahill's *Federal Fathers and Mothers: A Social History of the United States Indian Service, 1869–1933*.

1. United States Patent and Trademark Office, *Official Gazette* 13 (January 1–June 25, 1878): 1130.

2. State of California, City and County of San Francisco, trademark affidavit, California State Archives, series TM1–TM3552, 1861–1899, F3631:20–24, July 9, 1881.

3. United States Patent and Trademark Office, *Official Gazette* 13, no. 3 (January 15 1878): 105.

4. *The Citizen*, February 6, 1881.

5. *Sacramento Daily Record-Union*, March 7, 1881.

6. *Daily Alta California*, December 4, 1884.

7. Ibid., March 12, 1885.

8. Ibid., April 2, 1885.

9. San Francisco Bulletin, February 14, 1881.

10. Bancroft, *History of California*, vol. 7, 706.

11. *Daily Alta California*, September 25, 1877.

12. Ibid., November 8, 1877.

13. *San Francisco Evening Bulletin*, January 20, 1881.

Chapter 14. The Best Interests of the People of This State

Information about Jonas Strauss and his family, in this chapter as well as elsewhere, comes from Dr. John Michael. Newspaper articles, genealogical research in census records, and city directories were sources for the information about the Stern and Sahlein families throughout the book. And in this, as well as in many other chapters, the garments and archival materials in the Levi Strauss & Co. Archives were the most useful artifacts for understanding the changes made to the jeans over the years.

Robert J. Chandler's work on the history of early printing in San Francisco was invaluable for this chapter, as well.

1. *Daily Alta California*, January 9, 1884.

2. Credit report, R & G Dun, June 11, 1875, R. G. Dun & Co. Collections.

3. *Daily Alta California*, November 8, 1885.

4. Quoted in ibid., March 2, 1880.

5. Ibid., June 4, 1888.

6. Ibid., May 30, 1885.

7. Ibid., May 6, 1891.

8. Ibid., March 1, 1887.

9. Ibid., October 7, 1890.

10. Ibid., March 12, 1887.

11. Ibid., March 30, 1887.

12. Ibid., May 30, 1876.

13. *American Israelite,* September 10, 1886.

14. Ibid., January 7, 1892.

15. Henry Lash to Levi Strauss & Co., June 1, 1960, Levi Strauss & Co. Archives.

Chapter 15. For Over Twenty Years

Information about Isaias Hellmann can be found in the collections of the California Historical Society and in Frances Dinkelspiel's, *Towers of Gold: How One Jewish Immigrant Named Isaias Hellman Created California.* The historical advertising collections in the Levi Strauss & Co. Archives contain the best examples of early advertising, and even more ads can be found in the pages of historical newspapers.

Paula Freedman provided me with the context for the history of Temple Emanu-El and the Sisterhood for Personal Service, and Fred Rosenbaum's *Visions of Reform: Congregation Emanu-El and the Jews of San Francisco, 1849–1999* is also an excellent reference for the temple's history.

1. *Daily Alta California,* December 11, 1890.

2. *San Francisco Call,* March 31, 1897.

3. *San Francisco Chronicle,* July 7, 1891.

4. Ibid.

5. Danziger, "The Jew in San Francisco," 381.

6. Ibid., 398.

7. *Los Angeles Herald,* September 11, 1899.

8. *San Francisco Call,* September 8, 1895.

9. *San Francisco Morning Call,* November 25, 1892.

10. Henry Richman manuscript, undated, Levi Strauss & Co. Archives.

Chapter 16. All Will Be Sunshine for San Francisco and California

Because Levi Strauss was such a well-known and active San Francisco businessman, he appeared frequently in the local press, which was a main source for much in this chapter. Fred Rosenbaum's *Cosmopolitans: A Social and Cultural History of the Jews of the San Francisco Bay Area* provided context for Jewish life in turn-of-the-century San Francisco.

The history of the Valley Road was covered extensively in San Francisco newspapers, and was brilliantly summarized in Hans Christian Palmer's unpublished 1955 University of California Berkeley thesis, "The Valley Road: The San Francisco and San Joaquin Valley Railway, 1895–1900." Arthur Wheeler's *The Valley Road,* from 1896, is an excellent contemporary account.

1. *San Francisco Morning Call,* November 28, 1893.

2. Levy, *920 O'Farrell Street,* 221.

3. *San Francisco Bulletin,* October 12, 1895.

4. Rosa Stern to Rosalie Stern, undated, Levi Strauss & Co. Archives.

5. Ibid.

6. *Daily Alta California,* July 20, 1866.

7. *San Francisco Chronicle,* January 28, 1895.

8. *San Francisco Call,* March 29, 1895.

9. *Mariposa (CA) Gazette,* December 17, 1898.

Chapter 17. A City Man

The archival material about the Levi Strauss Scholarship is held at the Bancroft Library, University of California, Berkeley. Tanja Roppelt gave me the information about Levi's 1900 donation to his home town in Germany.

My main source for Republican politics in this book was Heather Cox Richardson's *To Make Men Free: A History of the Republican Party.* Marilyn Chase's *The Barbary Plague: The Black Death in Victorian San Francisco* was useful not only as a history of the Chinese in San Francisco, but also for the controversy surrounding the cover-up of the bubonic plague in the city in 1900. And Jules Tygiel's *Workingmen in San Francisco* helped me understand the strikes of the late nineteenth and early twentieth centuries.

1. Levi Strauss et al. to Jacob B. Reinstein, January 13, 1896, Levi Strauss & Co. Archives.

2. Levi Strauss to Jacob B. Reinstein, March 6, 1897, Levi Strauss & Co. Archives.

3. *San Francisco Chronicle,* March 10, 1897.

4. *San Francisco Call,* March 25, 1898.

5. The Levi Strauss Scholarship is still awarded today (as of 2016), at the University of California, Berkeley.

6. *San Francisco Chronicle,* November 10, 1896.

7. "Sound Money," *Overland Monthly and Out West Magazine* 28, no. 166 (October 1896): 482.

8. *San Francisco Call,* March 19, 1897.

9. Tygiel, *Workingmen in San Francisco,* 298.

10. *San Francisco Call,* September 6, 1901.

11. Ibid., September 24, 1901.

Chapter 18. Imperishable

Sources about the history of the Chinese in San Francisco used for earlier chapters were also helpful here for understanding the Geary Act. Levi's activities at the end of his life, as well as his death, funeral, will, and legacies, were covered extensively in San Francisco newspapers. Information about Jacob and Simon Davis in this chapter comes from their descendant, Frank Davis, of Ben Davis Clothing.

1. *Richmond (VA) Dispatch,* July 29, 1902.

2. San Francisco Call, September 28, 1902.

3. Ibid.

4. *San Francisco Chronicle,* September 29, 1902.

5. *San Francisco Call,* October 10, 1902.

6. Ibid., October 5, 1902.

7. Levi Strauss & Co. Minute Book, October 20, 1902, Levi Strauss & Co. Archives.

BIBLIOGRAPHY

Archives and Manuscript Collections

Amoskeag Manufacturing Company Records. Manchester Historic Association, New Hampshire

Bancroft Library, University of California, Berkeley

Bavarian State Archives, Bamberg, Germany

Calaveras County Archives, San Andreas, California

California Historical Society, San Francisco

California State Archives, Sacramento

California State Library, Sacramento

California State Railroad Museum, Sacramento

Edgewood Center for Children and Families, San Francisco

Isaacs, Lazarus. Papers. American Jewish Historical Society, Center for Jewish History, New York.

Levi Strauss & Co. Archives, San Francisco

Levi Strauss Museum, Buttenheim, Germany

National Library of Panama, Panama City

Nevada State Archives, Carson City, Nevada

New York Public Library, New York

R. G. Dun & Co. Collections. Baker Library, Harvard University

San Francisco History Center, San Francisco Public Library

Society of California Pioneers, San Francisco

Wells Fargo Bank Archives, San Francisco

Government Documents

Naturalization records, U.S. National Archives and Records Administration, Northeast Region, RG 21

Patent infringement cases, U.S. National Archives, Pacific Sierra Region, RG 21

U.S. Federal Census for 1850, 1870, 1880, 1890, 1900

Newspapers and Other Periodicals

Amador (CA) Ledger
American Israelite (Cincinnati)
Asmonean (New York)
Chicago Daily Inter Ocean
Daily Alta California (San Francisco)
Daily Nevada State Journal (Reno)
Dry Goods Reporter (San Francisco)
Fresno (CA) Weekly Republican
Independent (Helena, MT)
Koniglich Bayerisches Intelligenzblatt fur Oberfranken (Bayreuth, Germany)
Los Angeles Herald
Mariposa (CA) Gazette
Merchants' Association Review (San Francisco)
Morning Call (San Francisco)
Morning Oregonian (Portland)
New York Times
Ogden (UT) Standard
Pacicic Coast Law Journal (San Francisco)
Pacific Rural Press (San Francisco)
Panama Herald (Panama City)
Panama Star (Panama City)
Quincy (IL) Daily Whig
Reno Evening Gazette
Sacramento Daily Record-Union
Salt Lake (UT) Herald
San Francisco Bulletin
San Francisco Call
San Francisco Chronicle
San Francisco Examiner
San Francisco Herald
Weekly Gazette and Stockman (Reno)
Weekly Reno Gazette

Books and Articles

Albion, Robert Greenhalgh. *The Rise of New York Port, 1815–1860.* New York: Charles Scribner's Sons, 1939.

American Jewish Historical Society. *Passages through the Fire: Jews and the Civil War.* New York: Yeshiva University Museum, 2013.

Arndt, Karl J. R. *German-American Newspapers and Periodicals, 1732–1955*. New York: Johnson Reprint Corporation, 1965.

Asbury, Herbert. *The Barbary Coast*. Garden City, NY: Garden City Publishing, 1933.

Balfour-Paul, Jenny. *Indigo*. London: British Museum Press, 1998.

Bancroft, Hubert Howe. *California Inter Pocula*. San Francisco: The History Company, 1888.

———. *History of California*. Vol. 7, 1860–1890. San Francisco: The History Company, 1890.

Barker, Malcolm E. *More San Francisco Memoirs, 1852–1899: The Ripening Years*. San Francisco: Londonborn Publications, 1995.

Barth, Gunther. *Instant Cities: Urbanization and the Rise of San Francisco and Denver*. Albuquerque: University of New Mexico Press, 1975.

Berglund, Barbara. *Making San Francisco American: Cultural Frontiers in the Urban West, 1846–1906*. Lawrence: University Press of Kansas, 2007.

Bergquist, James M. "German Communities in American Cities: An Interpretation of the Nineteenth-Century Experience." *Journal of American Ethnic History* 4, no. 1 (Fall 1984): 9–30.

Betts, W. Colgrove. "The Philadelphia Commercial Museum." *The Journal of Political Economy* 8, no. 2 (March 1900): 222–33.

Board of Trade of San Francisco. *Sixtieth Anniversary Report*. San Francisco: Board of Trade, 1937.

Bonfield, Lynn A. "When Money Was Necessary to Make Dreams Come True: The Cost of the Trip from Vermont to California via Panama." *Vermont History* 76, no. 2 (Summer/Fall 2008): 130–48.

Bookspan, Shelley. *A Germ of Goodness: The California State Prison System, 1851–1944*. Lincoln: University of Nebraska Press, 1991.

Brechin, Gray. *Imperial San Francisco: Urban Power, Earthly Ruin*. Berkeley: University of California Press, 1999.

Bremner, Robert H. *Giving: Charity and Philanthropy in History*. New Brunswick, NJ: Transaction Publishers, 1996.

Brooks, Sarah Merriam. *Across the Isthmus to California in '52*. San Francisco: C. A. Murdock, 1894.

Burrows, Edwin G., and Mike Wallace. *Gotham: A History of New York City to 1898*. Oxford: Oxford University Press, 1999.

Burton, Jean. *Katharine Felton and Her Social Work in San Francisco*. Stanford: James Ladd Delkin, 1947.

Cahill, Cathleen D. *Federal Fathers and Mothers: A Social History of the United States Indian Service, 1869–1933*. Chapel Hill: University of North Carolina Press, 2013.

Cahn, Frances, and Valeska Bary. *Welfare Activities of Federal, State, and Local Governments in California, 1850–1934*. Berkeley: University of California Press, 1936.

Cain, Julie. *Monterey's Hotel Del Monte*. Charleston, SC: Arcadia Publishing, 2005.

Chandler, Robert J. "Jews, Honor, and James H. Hardy." *Western States Jewish History* 23, no. 4 (July 1991): 304–13.

———. *San Francisco Lithographer: African American Artist Grafton Tyler Brown.* Norman: University of Oklahoma Press, 2014.

———. *Servant of the People: Wells Fargo in Old Town San Diego, 1852–1870.* Fernley, NV: Douglas McDonald, 2006.

———. "Some Political and Cultural Pressures on the Jewish Image in Civil War San Francisco." *Western States Jewish History* 20, no. 2 (January 1988): 145–70.

———. "A Stereotype Emerges." *Western States Jewish History* 21, no. 4 (July 1989): 310–12.

———. "That Lurking Prejudice: San Francisco, 1869–1870." *Western States Jewish History* 27, no. 4 (July 1995): 205–14.

Chase, Marilyn. *The Barbary Plague: The Black Death in Victorian San Francisco.* New York: Random House, 2003.

Chen, Yong. *Chinese San Francisco, 1850–1943: A Trans-Pacific Community.* Stanford: Stanford University Press, 2000.

Cherny, Robert W. "Patterns of Toleration and Discrimination in San Francisco: The Civil War to World War I." *California History* 73, no. 2 (Summer 1994):131–40.

Chiu, Ping. *Chinese Labor in California, 1850–1880: An Economic Study.* Madison: The State Historical Society of Wisconsin, 1963.

Coblentz, Stanton A. *Villains and Vigilantes.* New York: Thomas Yoseloff, 1936.

Cobrin, Harry A. *The Men's Clothing Industry: Colonial through Modern Times.* New York: Fairchild Publications, 1970.

Cohen, Naomi. *Encounter with Emancipation: The German Jews in the United States, 1830–1914.* Philadelphia: The Jewish Publication Society of America, 1984.

Crane, Clare B. "The Pueblo Lands: San Diego's Hispanic Heritage." *The Journal of San Diego History* 37, no. 2 (Spring 1991): 104–27.

Cross, Ira B. *A History of the Labor Movement in California.* Berkeley: University of California Press, 1935.

Dagg, Carole. "Eliza Lucas Pinckney and the Fortunes of Colonial Indigo." *Handwoven,* May/June 1966, 71.

Danziger, Gustav Adolf. "The Jew in San Francisco: The Last Half Century." *Overland Monthly and Out West Magazine* 25, no. 148 (April 1895): 381–410.

Decker, Peter R. *Fortunes and Failures: White-Collar Mobility in Nineteenth-Century San Francisco.* Cambridge: Harvard University Press, 1978.

Dillon, Richard H. *Iron Men: Peter, James, and Michael Donahue.* Point Richmond, CA: Candela Press, 1984.

Diner, Hasia R. *The Jews of the United States.* Berkeley: University of California Press, 2004.

———. *A Time for Gathering: The Second Migration, 1820–1880.* Baltimore: The Johns Hopkins University Press, 1992.

Dinkelspiel, Frances. *Towers of Gold: How One Jewish Immigrant Named Isaias Hellman Created California.* New York: St. Martin's Press, 2008.

Directory of Manufactures and Products of the State of California and Alphabetical and Classified List of Members of the Manufacturers and Producers Association of California. San Francisco: H. S. Crocker Company, 1898.

Dolkart, Andrew S. *Biography of a Tenement House: An Architectural History of 97 Orchard Street in New York City*. Santa Fe: The Center for American Places, 2006.

Eisenberg, Ellen, Ava F. Kahn, and William Toll. *Jews of the Pacific Coast: Reinventing Community on America's Edge*. Seattle: University of Washington Press, 2009.

Elon, Amos. *The Pity of It All: A Portrait of the German-Jewish Epoch, 1743–1933*. New York: Picador, 2002.

Ernst, Robert. *Immigrant Life in New York City, 1825–1863*. Port Washington, NY: Ira J. Friedman, 1965.

Ethington, Philip J. *The Public City: The Political Construction of Urban Life in San Francisco, 1850–1900*. Berkeley: University of California Press, 2001.

Fabens, Joseph W. *A Story of Life on the Isthmus*. 1853. Facsimile of the first edition. Whitefish, MT: Kessinger Publishing, 2010.

Folsom, Burton W., Jr. *The Myth of the Robber Barons: A New Look at the Rise of Big Business in America*. Herndon, VA: Young America's Foundation, 2007.

Foster, George G. *New York by Gas-Light: With Here and There a Streak of Sunshine*. New York: Dewitt & Davenport, 1850.

———. *New York in Slices by an Experienced Carver*. New York: W. F. Burgess, 1849.

Fraser, Steven. "Combined and Uneven Development in the Men's Clothing Industry." *Business History Review* 57 (Winter 1983): 522–47

Fremont, Jessie Benton. *A Year of American Travel*. New York: Harper & Brothers, 1878.

Friedman, Lawrence J., ed. *Charity, Philanthropy, and Civility in American History*. Cambridge: Cambridge University Press, 2003.

Glanz, Rudolf. *Studies in Judaica Americana*. New York: KTAV Publishing House, 1970.

Goldstein, Gabriel, and Elizabeth Greenberg, eds. *A Perfect Fit: The Garment Industry and American Jewry*. Lubbock: Texas Tech University Press, 2012.

Gregory, Joseph W. *Gregory's Guide for California Travellers via the Isthmus of Panama*. San Francisco: Book Club of California, 1949.

Grinstein, Hyman B. *The Rise of the Jewish Community of New York, 1654–1860*. Philadelphia: The Jewish Publication Society of New York, 1945.

Hall, Lee. *Common Threads: A Parade of American Clothing*. Boston: Little, Brown, 1992.

Hareven, Tamara K., and Randolph Langenbach. *Amoskeag: Life and Work in an American Factory-City*. Hanover, NH: University Press of New England, 1978.

Hargrove, John. *The Weaver's Draft Book and Clothiers Assistant*. Baltimore: I. Hagerty, 1792.

Harris, James F. *The People Speak! Anti-Semitism and Emancipation in Nineteenth-Century Bavaria*. Ann Arbor: University of Michigan Press, 1994.

Harte, Bret, and Mark Twain. *Sketches of the Sixties*. San Francisco: John Howell, 1927.

Haydu, Jeffrey. *Citizen Employers: Business Communities and Labor in Cincinnati and San Francisco, 1870–1916*. Ithaca, NY: Cornell University Press, 2008.

Helper, Hinton Rowan. *The Land of Gold: Reality versus Fiction*. 1855. Facsimile of the first edition. Carlisle, MA: Applewood Books, 2014.

Higham, John. *Send These to Me: Jews and Other Immigrants in Urban America*. New York: Atheneum, 1975.

Hirschler, Eric E., ed. *Jews from Germany in the United States*. New York: Farrar, Straus and Cudahy, 1955.

Issel, William, and Robert W. Cherny. *San Francisco 1865–1932: Politics, Power, and Urban Development*. Berkeley: University of California Press, 1986.

Kahn, Ava F., ed. *Jewish Life in the American West*. Berkeley: Heyday Books, 2002.

———, ed. *Jewish Voices of the California Gold Rush: A Documentary History, 1849–1880*. Detroit: Wayne State University Press, 2002.

Kahn, Ava F., and Marc Dollinger, eds. *California Jews*. Lebanon, NH: University Press of New England, 2003.

Kaplan, Marion A., ed. *Jewish Daily Life in Germany, 1618–1945*. Oxford: Oxford University Press, 2005.

Kemble, John Haskell. *The Panama Route, 1848–1869*. Columbia: University of South Carolina Press, 1990.

Kidwell, Claudia, and Margaret C. Christman. *Suiting Everyone: The Democratization of Clothing in America*. Washington, D.C.: Smithsonian Institution Press, 1974.

Kinder, Gary. *Ship of Gold in the Deep Blue Sea*. New York: Vintage, 1999.

Kohn, Abraham. "A Jewish Peddler's Diary, 1842–1843." Translated by Abram Vossen Goodman. *American Jewish Archives* 3, no. 3 (June 1951): 91.

Lee, Anthony W. *Picturing Chinatown: Art and Orientalism in San Francisco*. Berkeley: University of California Press, 2001.

Leighton, Caroline C. *West Coast Journeys, 1865–1879*. Seattle: Sasquatch Books, 1995.

Leishman, Nora. "The Mechanics' Institute Fairs, 1857 to 1899." *The Argonaut: Journal of the San Francisco Historical Society* 10, no. 2 (Fall 1999), 40–57.

Lennon, Nigey. *The Sagebrush Bohemian: Mark Twain in California*. New York: Paragon House, 1993.

Levinson, Robert E. *The Jews in the California Gold Rush*. Berkeley: Commission for the Preservation of Pioneer Jewish Cemeteries and Landmarks of the Judah L. Magnes Museum, 1994.

Levi Strauss, Louis Strauss, Jonas Strauss, William Sahlein, and Jacob W. Davis, v. Henry W. King, E. W. Dewey, and William C. Browning Complainants' Record. New York: Industrial School of the Hebrew Orphan Asylum, 1878.

Levy, Harriet Lane. *920 O'Farrell Street: A Jewish Girlhood in Old San Francisco*. Garden City, NY: Doubleday, 1947.

Lewis, Oscar. *San Francisco: Mission to Metropolis*. Berkeley: Howell-North Books, 1966.

Lipsky, William. *San Francisco's Midwinter Exposition*. Charleston, SC: Arcadia Publishing, 2002.

Little, Frances. *Early American Textiles*. New York: Century, 1931.

Lloyd, B. E. *Lights and Shades in San Francisco*. Berkeley: Berkeley Hills Books, 1999.

Long, Jonathan Dean. "A Journey from New York to San Francisco in 1853 via the Isthmus of Panama." In *New England Historical & Genealogical Register* 91 (1937), 312–19.

Lotchin, Roger. *San Francisco 1846–1856: From Hamlet to City*. Lincoln: University of Nebraska Press, 1974.

Marcus, Jacob Rader. *Memoirs of American Jews, 1775–1865.* 3 vols. Philadelphia: The Jewish Publication Society of America, 1955

Marryat, Frank. *Mountains and Molehills.* London: Longman, Brown, Green, and Longmans, 1855.

Marschall, John P. *Jews in Nevada: A History.* Reno: University of Nevada Press, 2008.

McCullough, David. *The Path between the Seas: The Creation of the Panama Canal, 1870–1914.* New York: Touchstone, 1977.

Minter, John Easter. *The Chagres: River of Westward Passage.* New York: Rinehart & Company, 1948.

Morris, Charles R. *The Tycoons: How Andrew Carnegie, John D. Rockefeller, Jay Gould, and J. P. Morgan Invented the American Supereconomy.* New York: Times Books, 2005.

Nadel, Stanley. *Little Germany: Ethnicity, Religion, and Class in New York City, 1845–1880.* Urbana and Chicago: University of Illinois Press, 1990.

Nickliss, Alexandra M. "Phoebe Apperson Hearst's 'Gospel of Wealth,' 1883–1901." *Pacific Historical Review* 71, no. 4 (November 2002), 575–605.

Nuno, Gregory J. "A History of Union Square." *The Argonaut,* Summer 1993, 22–30.

Orsi, Richard J. *Sunset Limited: The Southern Pacific Railroad and the Development of the American West, 1850–1930.* Berkeley: University of California Press, 2005.

Palmer, Hans Christian. "The Valley Road: The San Francisco and San Joaquin Valley Railway, 1895–1900." Master's thesis, University of California, Berkeley, 1955.

Pfaelzer, Jean. *Driven Out: The Forgotten War against Chinese Americans.* New York: Random House, 2007.

Pope, Jesse Eliphalet. *The Clothing Industry in New York.* New York: Burt Franklin, 1970.

Reinhardt, Richard. *Four Books, 300 Dollars and a Dream: An Illustrated History of the First 150 Years of the Mechanics' Institute of San Francisco.* San Francisco: Mechanics' Institute, 2005.

Richards, Leonard L. *The California Gold Rush and the Coming of the Civil War.* New York: Alfred A. Knopf, 2007.

Richards, Rand. *Mud, Blood, and Gold: San Francisco in 1849.* San Francisco: Heritage House, 2009.

Richardson, Heather Cox. *To Make Men Free: A History of the Republican Party.* New York: Basic Books, 2014.

Rochlin, Harriet, and Fred Rochlin. *Pioneer Jews: A New Life in the Far West.* Boston: Houghton Mifflin, 1984.

Roppelt, Tanja. *Abenteuer Jeans: Eine Reise zu den Ursprungen der blauen Hose.* Bamberg: Verlag Frankischer Tag, 2008.

Rosenbaum, Fred. *Cosmopolitans: A Social and Cultural History of the Jews of the San Francisco Bay Area.* Berkeley: University of California Press, 2009.

———. *Visions of Reform: Congregation Emanu-El and the Jews of San Francisco, 1849–1999.* Berkeley: Judah L. Magnes Museum, 2000.

Samson, Gary. *Manchester: The Mills and the Immigrant Experience.* Charleston, SC: Arcadia Publishing, 2000.

"Samuel Slater, Francis Cabot Lowell, and the Beginnings of the Factory System in the United States." Harvard Business School Case Study. Cambridge: Harvard Business School, 1995.

Saxton, Alexander. *The Indispensable Enemy: Labor and the Anti-Chinese Movement in California*. Berkeley: University of California Press, 1971.

Schorman, Rob. *Selling Style: Clothing and Social Change at the Turn of the Century*. Philadelphia: University of Pennsylvania Press, 2003.

Schott, Joseph L. *Rails across Panama: The Story of the Building of the Panama Railroad, 1849–1855*. Indianapolis: The Bobbs-Merrill Company, 1967.

Sharlach, Bernice. *House of Harmony: Concordia-Argonaut's First 130 Years*. Berkeley: Western Jewish History Center, 1983.

Shevitz, Amy Hill. *Jewish Communities on the Ohio River: A History*. Lexington: University Press of Kentucky, 2007.

Soule, Frank, John H. Gihon, and Jim Nesbit. *The Annals of San Francisco*. 1855. Facsimile of the first edition. Palo Alto: Lewis Osborne, 1966.

"Sound Money." *Overland Monthly and Out West Magazine* 28, no. 166 (October 1896): 482.

Spann, Edward K. *The New Metropolis: New York City, 1840–1857*. New York: Columbia University Press, 1981.

Stephens, H. Morse, and Herbert E. Bolton, eds. *The Pacific Ocean in History*. New York: Macmillan, 1917.

Taggart, Harold F. "The Party Realignment of 1896 in California." *The Pacific Historical Review* 8, no. 4 (December 1939), 435–52.

Tannenbaum, William Zvi. *From Community to Citizenship: The Jews of Rural Franconia, 1801–1862*. Vol. 1. Stanford: Stanford University Press, 1989.

Taper, Bernard. *Mark Twain's San Francisco*. New York: McGraw Hill, 1963.

Tomes, Robert. *Panama in 1855. An Account of the Panama Rail-Road, of the Cities of Panama and Aspinwall, with Sketches of Life and Character on the Isthmus*. 1855. Reprint, Ann Arbor: University of Michigan, 2010.

Twain, Mark. *Roughing It*. Berkeley: University of California Press, 1972. First published 1872 by American Publishing Company.

Tygiel, Jules. *Workingmen in San Francisco, 1880–1901*. New York: Garland Publishing, 1992.

Walker, David H. *Pioneers of Prosperity*. San Francisco: David H. Walker, 1895.

Wells, Henry, and Edwin B. Morgan. *Truly Yours, Henry Wells: A Group of Letters Written by Henry Wells to Edwin B. Morgan*. Aurora, NY: Wells College Press, 1945.

"What the Railroad Will Bring Us." *The Overland Monthly* 1, no. 4 (October 1868), 297–306.

Wheeler, Arthur. *The Valley Road: A History of the Traffic Association of California, the League of Progress, the North American Navigation Company, the Merchants' Shipping Association, and the San Francisco and San Joaquin Valley Railway*. San Francisco: Wheeler Publishing, 1896.

Wilentz, Sean. *Chants Democratic: New York City and the Rise of the American Working Class, 1788–1850*. Oxford: Oxford University Press, 2004.

Wise, Isaac Mayer. *Reminiscences*. Translated and edited by David Philipson. Cincinnati: Leo Wise and Company, 1901.

Yafa, Stephen. *Big Cotton: How a Humble Fiber Created Fortunes, Wrecked Civilizations, and Put America on the Map*. New York: Viking, 2005.

Zakim, Michael. "A Ready-Made Business: The Birth of the Clothing Industry in America." *Business History Review* 73 (Spring 1999), 61–90.

Zarchin, Michael M. *Glimpses of Jewish Life in San Francisco*. Oakland: The Judah L. Magnes Memorial Museum, 1964.

Zerin, Edward. *Jewish San Francisco*. Charleston, SC: Arcadia Publishing, 2006.

INDEX

LYNN DOWNEY, whose family has lived in the West for more than a century, is a native of the San Francisco Bay Area. She holds degrees in history and library science from San Francisco State and the University of California, Berkeley, and is a widely published historian of the West. Downey is a recipient of the Society of California Archivists Sustained Service Award and received a Charles Donald O'Malley Short-Term Research Fellowship at the Louise M. Darling Biomedical Library of the David Geffen School of Medicine, UCLA. She served as the Levi Strauss & Co. Historian for twenty-five years and is now a consulting archivist, historian, and writer. Her website is www.lynndowney.com.